FIFTH EDITION

GOOD REASONING MATTERS!

A Constructive Approach to Critical Thinking

Leo A. Groarke
Christopher W. Tindale

OXFORD

UNIVERSITY PRESS

OXFORD
UNIVERSITY PRESS

Oxford University Press is a department of the University of Oxford.
It furthers the University's objective of excellence in research, scholarship,
and education by publishing worldwide. Oxford is a registered trade mark of
Oxford University Press in the UK and in certain other countries.

Published in Canada by
Oxford University Press
8 Sampson Mews, Suite 204,
Don Mills, Ontario M3C 0H5 Canada

www.oupcanada.com

Library and Archives Canada Cataloguing in Publication

Groarke, Leo
Good reasoning matters! : a constructive approach to critical
thinking / Leo A. Groarke, Christopher W. Tindale. — 5th ed.,
University of British Columbia ed.

Includes index.

First ed. by J. Frederick Little, Leo Groarke and Christopher Tindale.

ISBN 978–0–19–901000–4

1. Reasoning—Textbooks. 2. Critical thinking—Textbooks.
I. Tindale, Christopher W. (Christopher William) II. Title.

BC177.L58 2013   168   C2013-902044-6

Cover image: Tim Ridley/Dorling Kindersley/Getty Images

This book is printed on permanent (acid-free) paper ∞.

Printed and bound in Canada

2   3   4 — 20   19   18

MAKING ROOM
FOR ARGUMENT

The basic unit of reasoning is the **argument**. In this chapter we introduce its elements and situate them within the contexts in which arguments occur. You should emerge with an understanding of the following key concepts:

- ▶ arguments
- ▶ premises and conclusions
- ▶ arguers
- ▶ systems of belief
- ▶ specific and universal audiences
- ▶ proponents and opponents.

Forty years after it produced the work that made it famous, the British comedy troupe Monty Python is a hit on YouTube. One of its classic skits is *The Argument Clinic*. It begins with an eager man telling a receptionist that he'd "like to have an argument." She directs him to "room 12" where, after a misadventure in a "room for abuse," he opens the door, smiles at the man behind the desk, and asks: "Is this the right room for an argument?"

If you think this odd, you're right. Usually, the expression "room for argument" is a way of saying that something is open to debate. But not in Monty Python, where a "room for argument" is an office you go to when you want to have an argument. If this sounds like your own office, then you may be a lawyer, a graduate student, or a professor. In real life, there are many offices, and many other rooms, for argument. The latter include debating halls, court rooms, legislative assemblies, seminar rooms, and our own homes. One finds other important places for argument in the physical and virtual spaces that make up books, scientific journals, newspapers, magazines, television shows, advertisements, websites, Facebook pages, and the condensed messages contained in Twitter tweets.

This is a book about arguments that inhabit these and other spaces. To make room for the discussion that will follow—and to show you why you should take it seriously (to provide you with an argument to this effect)—we need to begin by examining the meaning of "argument" and its role in our lives.

Why Make Room for Argument?

EAGER YOUNG MAN: Is this the right room for an argument?
MAN AT THE DESK: I've told you once.
EAGER YOUNG MAN: No you haven't.
MAN AT THE DESK: Yes I have.
EAGER YOUNG MAN: When?
MAN AT THE DESK: Just now.
EAGER YOUNG MAN: No you didn't.
MAN AT THE DESK: Yes I did.
EAGER YOUNG MAN: Didn't.
MAN AT THE DESK: Did.

What follows is a series of the same denials and insistences from each man, until the one looking for an argument gives up in exasperation and observes that what they are doing is not arguing but just contradicting each other.

In ordinary language the word "argument" can mean contradiction or, more generally, "disagreement." In these cases, the paradigm example of an argument is a *vehement* disagreement: a harangue, a quarrel, a yelling match. In this sense, the two men in Monty Python's argument clinic *are* arguing. Arguments like this are a significant, sometimes painful reality. But they are not the kinds of argument that are the subject of this book.

Those who study "argumentation" (philosophers, psychologists, logicians, rhetoricians, dialecticians, communication theorists, and others) typically understand an "argument" as an attempt to provide evidence or *reasons* for some point of view. Disagreement often leads to argument in this sense, for it raises the question whether there are reasons to favour our point of view, or the views of those with whom we disagree. So conceived, arguments help us judge the evidence for and against different points of view. This is why they play such an important role in helping us decide what views we should accept and reject.

The subjects of our arguments are many and varied. They include metaphysical questions about the world and our place within it. The recent discovery of many Earth-like planets has sparked much debate and argument. Are the scientific calculations that this discovery depends on reliable? Do they make plausible the claim that we are not alone in the universe? What implications are there for our religious beliefs and our place in the cosmos? What moral and political obligations do we have if we do find a planet inhabited by other forms of life? An argument about the latter underlies the story narrated in the Hollywood film *Avatar*, the most financially successful movie of all time.

Other arguments are rooted in moral, political, and social issues. Does freedom of religion include the right to polygamous marriage? Are gay, lesbian, and other kinds of couples (sisters, brothers) who live together entitled to the benefits the government grants to traditionally married couples? Is the website WikiLeaks justly criticized for releasing thousands of secret government documents? Does it threaten our security, or does it champion the cause of open, honest and transparent government? Are those who have tried to halt its operations—and take its founder, Julian Assange, to court—guilty of censorship? More generally, is it true, as some have suggested, that our new world of email, cell phone technology, instant video, Skype and the World Wide Web undermine censorship in a way that will usher in new democracies and grass roots political engagement?

Another important source of argument is the economy. Much has been made of the failure of economists to predict the global financial crisis instigated by the collapse of the American housing market. Some argue that this is evidence that shows that the assumptions embedded in classical economics are flawed. Others attempt to extrapolate from recent problems, using them as evidence for predictions about the global economy, as the effects of the financial crisis reverberate around the world. Politicians of different stripes offer arguments in support of and against the proposition that policies of economic stimulus are the way to deal with crises of this sort. Proponents of radically different kinds of reform debate what should be done for the provinces, states, cities and individuals who have been saddled with debts they cannot manage. Governments ponder the question whether a new economic reality requires a new approach to pensions, wages, and poverty.

Other arguments play a central role in our private and professional lives, providing the evidence we rely on when we decide what university or college is right for us, what car we should buy, and where we should live. We consider the arguments of our friends, bloggers, and book and movie reviewers when we decide what to read and what to see. We engage with the books and movies we consume actively, arguing about them and the perspectives they suggest. You should not be shy in demanding reasons for our own claim that a book like the present one can help you decide what beliefs to accept and reject.

We might easily expand our list of topics for argument. The important point is that it demonstrates the pervasive role that arguments play in our lives. This is one reason for taking a book about arguments seriously. But the prevalence of argument does not, by itself, show that you should buy this book or study argument. If argumentation was easily understood, constructed, and assessed, you might not need a book or a course on argument. Studying argument is a good idea because argument is a difficult and complex subject. This is reflected in the fact that errors in judgement and reasoning, and the faulty arguments that result, are commonplace.

We think that you will see this for yourself as you work through the many real life examples we have included in this book. In the meantime, it is worth noting that psychological research has uncovered many biases that interfere with ordinary reasoning. Among other things, it suggests that we tend to be overconfident in our judgements and our reasoning, a bias that is called the "overconfidence effect."

Consider the results of a set of studies by Dunning, Griffin, Milojkovic, and Ross (*Journal of Personality and Social Psychology*, Vol. 58, No. 4, 1990, pp. 610–621) that examined the impact of overconfidence on social prediction: "We compared people's expectations of success in predicting the actions of their peers with their actual performance, and our findings seem unambiguous and consistent. People proved to be markedly overconfident in general. Moreover, they proved to be most overconfident precisely when they were most confident. . . ." In one of their studies, the researchers found that students significantly overestimated the accuracy of their predictions about the behaviour of roommates with whom they had extensive day-to-day contact.

The overconfidence effect suggests that we think too highly of our understanding of the situations in which we find ourselves. Confirmation bias suggests that we favour arguments that confirm the biases and beliefs we already have, ignoring or dismissing evidence that contradicts them. Lord, Ross, and Lepper (*Journal of Personality and Social Psychology*, Vol. 37, No. 11, 1979, pp. 2098–2109) presented students with opinions on capital punishment with two studies, one confirming and one disconfirming their existing beliefs about the deterrent effect of capital punishment. Though there was no reason to favour one study over the other, they found that the students clearly favoured the study that supported their pre-existing views. In discussing the study that provided evidence against the deterrent effect of the death penalty, an opponent of capital punishment wrote that "No strong evidence to contradict the researchers has been presented." In response to the same study, a proponent of capital punishment dismissed the findings, writing that "The research didn't cover a long enough period of time."

The over confidence effect and confirmation bias suggest that we are too confident of our beliefs, and tend to dismiss the evidence that might change them. A host of other biases that have been studied raise questions about most people's ability to objectively assess the evidence for and against particular points of view. Among other things, there is evidence that we accept or reject some perspectives, not because of the reasons for accepting (or rejecting) them, but because of the way they are "framed" (in a way that emphasizes losses rather than gains, for example).

A bias called "the halo effect" occurs when people assume, as they often do, that people with good looks (or other positive attributes) are intelligent, pleasant, moral, and so on. More generally, the evidence suggests that people have a natural tendency to depend on simplistic stereotypes (about Americans, Canadians, the Chinese, the French, "foreigners," men with beards, professional women, welfare recipients, and so on) when making decisions and forming opinions.

In many cases, we are not even aware of biases that interfere with our assessment of the evidence at our disposal. In a famous set of experiments by Nisbett and Wilson (*Psychological Review*, Vol. 84, No. 3, 1977, pp. 231–259), an experimenter conducted a "consumer study" in which he laid out four pairs of pantyhose and asked consumers to pick the pair that they preferred. All four pairs were identical, but consumers were significantly more likely to select whatever pair was placed furthest to the right. For some reason, it seems that people (in our culture), seem to have a strong preference for the right-most object in a series.

It would be interesting to speculate on the reason for this (Is it because most people are right-handed? Is it because we read from left to right?) but the important point is that the people considering the pantyhose did not know that this was why they favoured it. When asked, they explained their preference by saying something about the strength or the sheerness or some other quality of the pantyhose. When the experimenter explicitly suggested that the position might have been a contributing factor, the subjects rejected this as peculiar.

There is a great deal that might be said about such biases and the reasons we incline toward them. For that kind of theorizing we recommend a course in cognitive psychology. In this book, it is enough to say that there are all sorts of ways in which these biases influence, and sometimes undermine, attempts to argue, even in scientific and theoretical contexts. In the course of our lives, the issues that this raises are exacerbated by many conscious and unconscious attempts to exploit these biases in argument. In marketing, politics and law courts, they often inform successful advertisements, political campaigns, and appeals to a judge or jury. In many cases, poor arguments successfully convince an audience of a particular point of view, not because they present compelling evidence for the perspective they propound, but because they illegitimately play upon our biases.

Consider the vodka advertisement we have recreated on the next page. It is an attempt to encourage us to drink a particular brand of vodka. We will discuss the mechanics of visual messages in Chapter 6. For the moment, it is enough to note that the crux of the image's meaning is the transformation that occurs when the content of a huge bottle of vodka splashes from the sky and transforms the slow and sleepy life of the village below into the activity and excitement in the urban metropolis it becomes. It is not easy to capture exactly the content of the image in a sentence, but we might roughly summarize it as the claim that "You should drink our vodka because it will transform your sleepy life into one of bustling activity and excitement."

When we summarize the message of the advertisement in this way, we can see it as an attempt at argument: as an attempt to provide a *reason* for drinking the brand of vodka highlighted in the advertisement. What is the reason? It is the claim that doing so will turn your sleepy life into one of bustling excitement. When the message is conveyed in this way, the lameness of the argument becomes apparent. Why should we accept that the consumption of vodka of any brand will transform one's life—literally or figuratively—from the life one experiences in a sleepy village to what one expects in an exciting urban centre like Toronto or New York? And yet the advertisement may still be effective. It may convince people to buy the vodka in question, not because it provides a compelling reason to do so, but because it is fun, playful, vivid, eye-catching, imaginative, and creative (some would point to its sexual overtones). It is a creative tour de force, especially when viewed in colour.

The study of argument is one way to minimize the influences that may interfere with the careful weighing of evidence for and against particular claims that are put to us. In the case of the vodka advertisement, assessing its strength as an argument can show us that it fails to provide convincing evidence for the proposal that we should buy the vodka in question. Thus, skill at assessing argument is one way to counter the many influences that conspire against our ability to reason well. More generally, the biases we must contend with underscore the importance of learning to reason well. Coupled with the prevalence of argument in all facets of our lives, this makes argument an important topic that you will do well to take seriously.

Image created by Dana Scott, © Leo Groarke

Illustration 1.1   "Transform your sleepy life"

EXERCISE 1A*

1. List four potential topics for argument.

2. Name an argumentative topic you have heard discussed, read about or seen on television or the World Wide Web in the last two days. Summarize an argument on the topic: i.e. explain what reasons might be provided in favour of, or in opposition to, a

*In this and other exercise sets, answers to starred questions are provided in the "Selected Answers" section of the course website.

relevant point of view. What is the claim the proposed argument tries to establish? What reasons does it provide in support of it?

3.* Summarize the argument we have provided in claiming that this is a book you should take seriously.

2 Defining Argument

We can illustrate the elements of argument with an example of the kind of argument adduced in a Sherlock Holmes detective story. It begins with a claim, usually unexpected. Suppose the claim is:

> The crime was committed by someone in the house.

In answer to protests from his partner, Doctor Watson, Holmes inevitably backs his claim with reasons that support it. Reasons like:

(1) The living room window is open, but there are no footprints outside, even though the ground is soft after yesterday's rain.
(2) The clasp on the box was not broken but opened with the key that was hidden behind the clock.
(3) The dog did not bark.

These three reasons make up Holmes's argument. They provide evidence for the claim that the crime was an "inside job."

In keeping with this example, we define an *argument* as *a set of reasons offered in support of a claim*. The reasons may be presented orally, in a written text, or by means of photographs, symbols, and other non-verbal means (we discuss the latter in Chapter 3). They provide the evidence that is supposed to back the claim in question. The claim for which the reasons are given in support is called the argument's *conclusion*. The reasons are called its *premises*.

The simplest arguments have only one premise. In *The Argument Clinic* Monty Python's man looking for an argument presents one when he denies that an argument can be the same as a contradiction, retorting, "No it can't. An argument is a connected series of statements intended to establish a definite proposition."

Monty Python's man looking for an argument presents one himself when he denies that an argument can be the same as a contradiction, In support of this claim he defines "argument" as a series of connected statements that are intended to establish a further statement.

This one-premise argument can be summarized as follows:

> **Premise:** An argument is a connected series of statements intended to establish a definite proposition.
> **Conclusion**: It can't be the same as a contradiction.

In the Holmes example, the conclusion is supported by three premises—the three statements we have labelled (1), (2), and (3). Other arguments may have any number of premises. A complex extended argument, which might be the subject of a book or speech or film, might contain hundreds of premises arranged in sub-arguments that establish different parts of the case made for the principal conclusion.

Some Real-Life Examples

We take our first examples of real arguments from two Easter articles in a southern Ontario newspaper (*The Record*, 7 April 2007, p. A15). In "Quest for the Real Jesus Continues," the author describes the early followers of Jesus as people who "stood up to be counted among those who had witnessed that God returned Jesus from the dead." He continues:

> Could this just be an opinion, a hallucination, or a legend? Unlikely. There were too many eye-witnesses. The resurrection didn't happen in a dark corner, it didn't happen in a private place. It was a public event.

This is a paradigm example of an argument. The conclusion is the claim that "It is unlikely that the resurrection of Jesus was just an opinion, a hallucination, or a legend." The premise is that "There were too many eye-witnesses—the resurrection didn't happen in a dark corner or a private place, it was a public event." The argument offers the premise as evidence for the conclusion.

In a second article, "Christianity endures scrutiny and questioning" (*The Record*, 7 April 2007) another author discusses what she sees as the popularity of movies and media coverage that offend and question Christian beliefs. She notes that she is a Christian, but still welcomes such coverage:

> Regardless of what I think about the motivation to attack the fundamental beliefs of over two billion Christians around the world, I do want to thank the people who do just that. Why? Because each time Christianity is questioned, it causes churches and individual Christians to study deeper and pray for those who are seeking to know the truth about Jesus. It helps Christians to wake up and pay attention to what others are saying about their faith—even if it is wild speculation and hearsay that is stretched thin.

In this case, the argument might be summarized as follows:

Conclusion: "Whatever the motivation of those who attack the fundamental beliefs of Christians, this is a good thing (something to be thankful for)."

First Premise: "Each time Christianity is questioned, it causes churches and individual Christians to study deeper and pray for those who are seeking to know the truth about Jesus."

Second Premise: "It helps Christians to wake up and pay attention to what others are saying about their faith—even if it is wild speculation and hearsay that is stretched thin."

Are these examples of *good* argument? That is a question we will put aside for now. Suffice it to say that assessing arguments is a two step process. The first step is identifying the components of an argument. The second is evaluating them. In this chapter, our focus is the first of these two steps.

EXERCISE 1B

1. Each of the following passages presents a simple argument. In each case, identify the premise(s) and conclusion.

    (i)* A clear increase in earthquakes and other natural catastrophes creates a compelling case for curbing our thirst for fossil fuels.
    (ii) Referendums bring out the worst impulses in a population. California's referendums have seriously weakened the educational system, and the Swiss have outlawed the building of mosques.
    (iii)* Feral cats are a major problem for urban centres. They carry disease, they fight, and they destroy wildlife.
    (iv) [From *The Windsor Star*, Editorial: "A One-term President?" by Toby Harnden, 17 September 2010, p. 8] "Obama is the first black American president, an established author, multimillionaire and acclaimed figure beyond American shores. It seems unlikely that he will decide not to run in 2012."
    (v)* [Adapted from a Letter to the Editor, *Popular Science*, March 2011, p. 12] In "Flapper Fashion" you state, "Last August . . . marked the first time a human-powered aircraft achieved sustained flight." No. Paul MacCready and Peter Lissman of AeroVironment, Inc. built the *Gossamer Condor*, which in 1977 won the Kremer Priveze for the first human-powered aircraft capable of controlled sustained flight.
    (vi) [From a CBC television report on the destruction of a house in Escondido, California, which was burned to the ground by authorities, November 2010] "A bomb squad concluded that it was too risky to send technicians into the house, because clothing and dishes were stacked next to volatile chemicals, and any knock against them could trigger an explosion."
    (vii) [From a discussion of a show on civil war drawings at the Virginia Museum of Fine Arts, in *American Artist: Drawing*, Winter 2011] The exhibition will be a boon to scholars and the public alike, as it gives viewers a chance to see how artists acted as eyewitnesses to history.

2. Explain the simple argument in each of the following by identifying the conclusion and reason(s) given.

    (i)   [From "Small business statistics on Canadian small business & the economy," http://sbinfocanada.about.com, accessed 29 April 2012]
          Small businesses are major contributors to the job market. Small businesses account for over two thirds of employment in five industries: the (non-institutional) health care sector (89 per cent), the construction industry (76 per cent), other

services (73 per cent), accommodation and food (67 per cent), and forestry (67 per cent). According to Statistics Canada's Survey of Employment, Payrolls and Hours (SEPH), on average in 2007, SMEs employed just over 6.8 million, or 64 per cent, of private sector employees covered by SEPH.

(ii) [From an article in *The Atlantic* magazine, October 2010, on the Junior Eurovision Song Contest, p. 30] Countries on the Continent's geographic and political periphery have started to see the junior circuit as a vehicle for mainstream acceptance—cultural, economic, and even strategic. Seven of the 14 countries that will compete at Minsk are ex-Soviet republics. Malta, Cyprus, Serbia, Croatia, and Macedonia are also regular contenders. Georgian President Mikheil Saakashvili, who desperately wants his country admitted to NATO and the European Union, dispatched his wife to Rotterdam in 2007 to attend Georgia's debut performance. Ukraine's president and prime minister both attended last year's festivities in Kiev.

(iii) [From "Health News" in *More* magazine, February/March 2011, p. 30]
"If you've been diagnosed with metabolic bone disease, you need to be tested for celiac disease," says Terry Moore, a gastroenterologist at St Michael's Hospital in Toronto. The reason? Osteoporosis is a known complication of celiac disease, an under-diagnosed intestinal disorder where the immune system goes on attack mode in the presence of wheat, barley or rye gluten, damaging the intestinal lining and preventing the absorption of key nutrients and minerals such as calcium.

(iv) [From an article in the same source as (iii)]
"Legumes don't get any respect," says Fall River, NS, registered dietitian and author Mary Sue Waisman. This is a shame, given that they offer cheap, filling, high-protein and high-fibre ways to avoid spikes in your blood sugar and are packed with folate, which some studies have linked to lowered blood pressure and depression risk in women.

3. Write a short paragraph that contains a simple argument for some conclusion. Identify your argument's premises and conclusion.

3   Arguers and Systems of Belief

Arguments are communicative acts (what are sometimes called "speech acts"), that are used in attempts to establish some point of view. In the communication this implies, the first party to an argument is the arguer who presents the argument. Usually this is an individual, but it could be a group of people or a corporate body of some sort—a company, a branch of government, or some other organization. When we construct arguments, we ourselves are arguers.

An arguer uses an argument to try and establish (or reinforce) a point of view with reasons that support it. These arguments are rooted in a system or "web" of belief. Some aspects of this system may be determined by our sex, race, and nationality. Others may reflect our education, our career, the organizations we join, and our personal reflections. The system may change over time. Many people retain the religious beliefs they grew up with; others reject or change their perspective in a way that has a dramatic effect on their world view. Because our various convictions and beliefs are integrated, it can be difficult to separate them and their origins. Together, they circumscribe our self-identity, constitute our personal perspective, and give rise to the various opinions we subscribe to. Our strongest opinions are the embryos from which our arguments typically develop.

Deeply held beliefs may influence our arguments in ways that are evident in the assumptions behind our reasoning and the consequences that follow from it. Consider the following excerpt from a famous essay by George Grant which appeared as "The case against abortion" (*Today Magazine*, 3 November 1981, pp. 12–13). In arguing against abortions for convenience, Grant introduces the following consideration into the debate (p. 13):

> Mankind's greatest political achievement has been to limit ruthlessness by a system of legal rights. The individual was guarded against the abuses of arbitrary power, whether by state or by other individuals. Building this system required the courage of many. *It was fundamentally based on the assumption that human beings are more than just accidental blobs of matter. They have an eternal destiny and therefore the right to rights.* But the large-scale destruction of human beings by abortion questions that view.

We have italicized the two sentences relevant to the present discussion. Our system of legal rights, Grant maintains, is "based on the assumption that human beings are more than accidental blobs of matter." This "more" is that human beings have a "right to rights" because they "have an eternal destiny." This implies a number of important propositions: that we are planned, that our existence is intentional, and that there is something eternal or immortal about us, presumably as individuals. All this makes us created rather than "accidental blobs."

But created by whom? Though no mention is made of "God," belief in a deity (a creator) is implied. In drawing out this meaning, we have moved beyond what Grant explicitly stated, but reasonably so. It shows that Grant's reasoning is grounded in a religious commitment: that he believes we are part of a divine plan. In a case like this, an element of our **belief system** can have a key influence on our arguments. It is important that we identify these influences as we go about attempting to convince others of our conclusions, for they may miss our point or reject our premises in view of these elements. In the case at hand, Grant's argument needs to be reinforced because his premises are unlikely to be accepted by people who do not share his religious point of view.

We cannot remove an arguer's belief system in order to prevent its influence, nor is it necessary or advisable to try to do so. But it is important to guard against its unconscious or illegitimate influence. In our own case, this requires self-evaluation. We need to ask ourselves what assumptions underlie our claims and make sure that these assumptions are defensible in an argument. Just because we believe something strongly, we cannot assume that others will, or that the next argument we see supporting it will be good. Even when the conclusion of an argument is true, the argument and premises offered for it may be weak. One of the best ways to strengthen a position is by pointing out the flaws in weak arguments for it, and by showing how those flaws might be remedied or avoided. Scrutinizing our arguments and assumptions will help us build a stronger system of belief.

In the case of other arguers, our scrutiny of their arguments may lead us to ask which beliefs and influences lead to the views that they propound. Beyond sex, race, religion, and nationality, this may entail reflections on their educational background, their political views, and their economic and social standing. Such reflections can provide a profile of an arguer's belief system that helps us understand why the arguer reasons in a particular way.

In some cases, the strength of arguments crucially depends on the credibility of the arguer—on their *ethos*, a Greek term that designates one's character and trustworthiness. In Chapter 12, we consider a whole family of arguments—called ethotic arguments—in which the assessment of the arguer plays a central role. Assessing the perspective and the credibility of arguers, ourselves included, is important in the process of learning to argue well.

EXERCISE   1C

1. Consider your own belief system, and construct a profile of its major features.

2. Pick someone who has a different system of belief than you do (blogs are a good source for this). Provide a profile of the belief system's major features. How does your subject's belief system differ from your own?

3. The following are quotations relevant to arguments. In each case, construct a profile of the writer by explaining some of the beliefs that can be attributed to them.

    (i)* [From *Skeptic* magazine, "What is Naturopathy," Vol. 16, No. 2, 2011, p. 4] Naturopathy arose in a pre-scientific environment, then lost popularity as scientific medicine developed effective treatments during the 20th century. It had a resurgence in the 1970s as part of the trend of so-called "alternative" medicine. It is currently taught in six schools in the U.S. and licensed in 15 states."

    (ii) [From the mission statement for the *Journal of Cosmology*] Most scientific journals are aimed at specific, narrowly defined areas of research; tailored to those specialists who devote their lives to learning more and more about less and less. The alternative, we are told, is to learn less and less about more and more, and thus "generalists" and interdisciplinary journals are rare indeed, for how many wish to discover how little they know? The interdisciplinary *Journal of Cosmology* is devoted to the study of "cosmology" and is dedicated to those men and women of rare genius and curiosity who wish to understand more and more about more and more: The study of existence in its totality.

    (iii)*[From "Judgment day: How Arnold Schwarzenegger might just have saved California," *The Atlantic*, October 2010, p. 28] Previously, California's gerrymandered districts rewarded loyalty to entrenched partisan factions. As a result, few Republicans would ever vote for a tax hike and almost no Democrat would take on the unions. Redistricting will recast many legislative districts, making them significantly less Democratic or Republican. And candidates running in a wide-open primary will have to rely on a broader base of contributors. The power of the unions, the shock jocks, the anti-taxers, will all be diluted.

(iv) [From *Popular Science*, March 2011, p. 100] Rick Tumlinson, the co-founder of the Space Frontier Foundation, a growing group of entrepreneurs who hope to use private enterprise to succeed where they believe a risk-averse and direction-less NASA has failed, maintains that we will settle the new frontier only when there is a compelling profit motive for it. He lists space tourism, extraterrestrial mining, and the beaming of solar energy from space back to Earth as the best financial reasons to leave the planet. "We achieve permanent human settlements when people are making money," he says. "No bucks, no Buck Rogers."

(v) [In 2011, a serious injury to a Montreal player hit by a player from the Boston Bruins ignited a controversy over violence in ice hockey. The following argument is adapted from a related *Globe and Mail* article "Hockey loving dad believes it's time for a change," by Roy MacGregor, 11 March 2011, who wrote about Dave Sasson, a well-known Quebec hockey enthusiast who won a court battle that repealed a law banning street hockey] This year discussions with NHL general managers will be preoccupied with the problem of concussions. This is the outcome of a 2011 that no one could have imagined: a year that has seen the NHL's greatest star, Sidney Crosby, sidelined with a concussion. There have been more than seventy players who have had to take time off because of concussions, gang fights on the ice, a 10-game suspension for one offender, advertisers questioning their sponsorship, and a commissioner who refuses to take the issue seriously. Dave Sasson is right to call for an overhaul of the culture of the game we all enjoyed as we grew up.

(vi) [An excerpt from another column on the same controversy, entitled "Face it, hockey fans live for brutality," by Cathal Kelly of the *Toronto Star*, 11 March 2011] What separates the NHL from other sports is full contact at high speeds and institutionalized fist fighting. That's it. Take cultural context out of the mix, and that's why Canadians watch hockey. Because it's fast and tough.

Asking people to mind their elbows at all times and pull out of hits on the boards isn't a little thing. It's a fundamental shift. It's mucking around with the basics. . . . The NHL understands this, but can't verbalize it in any way that won't get them crucified by opportunistic politicians and the usual set of hand-wringers who didn't like the game in the first place. . . .

No, players don't care; and fans care even less. How do we know? Because they continue to watch the game—in fact, TV ratings on both sides of the border are up. . . .

The NFL, which takes in grown men and spits out invalids, is turning over money like a Mexican drug cartel. The Ultimate Fighting Championship is sport's fastest comer overall. Pastoral pursuits like baseball and, increasingly, basketball are losing traction with young fans.

Elegance is out. Brutality is the growth industry.

Audiences

Arguers create arguments to convince an **audience**—someone or some group of people—of their conclusion. This makes audiences the second party to an argument. Sometimes we are our own audience. Sherlock Holmes probably acts as his own audience as he develops an argument in his mind. When he is satisfied, he addresses another audience—usually his partner, Watson. Sometimes, later in the story, he presents the argument to yet another audience, i.e. those who have hired him to solve the case he has resolved.

Poor reasoners tend to assume that whatever evidence convinces them of some conclusion will convince other audiences. When two people (say, Holmes and Watson) share similar systems of belief and points of view, this may be a reasonable assumption. But it is misleading in broader contexts in which we interact and argue with audiences who do not share our point of view. In these cases, it is egocentric to believe that our own convictions and beliefs are characteristic of the audience we address. The opposite should be expected, given that arguments are a means we use to convince people who have *different* points of view that they should share our conclusions.

Some Historical Examples

The role of audiences in argument is readily apparent if we look at historical examples of argument, for they were designed to appeal to audiences with attitudes, beliefs, and concerns other than our own.

Consider, to take a telling example, the content of cigarette advertisements in the following 1940s advertisement. It strikes us as peculiar, even bizarre, but many of these advertisements advocated for their brands by touting their medical benefits. In an advertisement for Philip Morris (which Morris refused to let us reproduce here), one reads that medical authorities—distinguished doctors and an authoritative medical journal—relying on clinical scientific studies concluded that Philip Morris was better for you than rival cigarettes. We would summarize the central argument in the advertisement as:

> **Premise:** Medical authorities know that Philip Morris is scientifically proven to be less irritating to the nose and throat.
>
> **Conclusion:** One should purchase (and smoke) America's "finest" cigarette, Philip Morris.

The premise in this argument is itself a conclusion of a sub-argument which features the premise: "Distinguished doctors, in clinical tests of men and women smokers—reported in an authoritative medical journal—found that substantially every case of irritation of nose and throat due to smoking cleared up completely, or definitely improved when smokers changed to Philip Morris."

The closest analogue to these statements today may be an attempt to market a "Vitamin E enhanced" cigarette by German Tobacco Group under the brand name

S.A.L.E. It features "an improved and soothing flavour" and is said to minimize the "irritation" that occurs when using conventional cigarettes. Though these claims might be compared to the Philip Morris's 1940 claim that its cigarettes were less irritating than other brands, there has been no attempt to promote smoking S.A.L.E. with appeals to scientific and medical authorities. At a time when health authorities have almost universally concluded that smoking is injurious to one's health, this is because no audience would accept an argument for a brand of cigarette that appeals to the findings of "distinguished doctors" and "medical authorities."

In the world in which we live, this is why the Philip Morris argument we have quoted has little impact. Instead of convincing contemporary audiences that they should smoke Philip Morris it is used by anti-smoking advocates as evidence for a very different conclusion: that cigarette companies and their advertisements should not be trusted. Partly in answer to these criticisms, Philip Morris, which still manufactures and sells cigarettes, has attempted to establish credibility in a way that makes more sense to contemporary audiences. To this end, its website www.philipmorrisusa.com emphasizes the *responsible* use of tobacco, and the ethics and integrity of its approach to sales. Philip Morris now promotes a *reduction* in the underage use of tobacco; provides advice on smoking cessation; and promotes itself as a company that "invests in our communities," "reduces our environmental impact," and "operates with compliance and integrity."

In the present context, the important point is that the difference between Philip Morris's approach to its public presence today and in the 1940s is attributable to the audience being addressed in each case. The 1940s advertisement we have quoted contains another feature that illustrates the significance of audience in a slogan that was printed alongside of it: 'Buy more war bonds." This was a common tag during World War II, when advertisers were concerned to address a population which was preoccupied with the war effort. This tendency is taken even further in an advertisement for Nestlé's chocolate bars in *Life* (11 November 1943) which advertises them under the title "U.S. troops fight on chocolate diet," emphasizing the fact that the American army included a Nestlé chocolate bar in its standard emergency rations.

Other historical advertisements illustrate the ways in which arguments assume and are directed to audiences with particular systems of belief. The Campbell Soup advertisement reproduced in Illustration 1.2—"A FEATHER in Mrs. Canada's Cap"—was addressed to women who read the magazine *Star Weekly* in the 1950s. It suggests that they should buy Campbell's Cream of Mushroom soup (*conclusion*) because it is "unusual and especially good" (*premise*), but emphasizes a different consideration which acts as the principle premise in the argument: i.e. the claim that it will win them praise and make a good impression on their families—and in this way be a "feather" in their "cap." Underlying the advertisement is the assumption that women are homemakers whose identity and satisfaction is tied to their ability to perform housework in ways that will earn the approval of their families. This reflects the view of women at the time (a view shared by the women who are the audience to whom the advertisement is directed), but one that is profoundly out of step with the attitudes, beliefs, and aspirations of popular audiences today.

Illustration 1.2   "A Feather in Mrs. Canada's Cap!"

We can highlight these differences by comparing the *Star Weekly* advertisement to advertisements today, which reject the view of women's identity that Campbell's soup appeals to. This does not mean that they always do so in a way that is not open to debate. The brand Wonderbra is known for an advertising campaign that offers a very different view of women's identity, emphasizing looks and sex appeal. One of their advertisements (which they would not give us permission to reproduce here) makes fun of the view of women in the 1950s advertisement we have looked at. It is a waist up photo of a voluptuous supermodel wearing only her Wonderbra, with the caption "I can't cook. Who cares?" The implied answer is that no one cares—because she is an alluring woman. Considered as an argument, the advertisement suggests that women should purchase Wonderbra (*conclusion*) because it will help them look sexy (*premise*). This rejects the view of women's identity highlighted in the 1950s advertisement, but it embraces a contemporary view which many would find equally offensive because it places so much emphasis on good looks and sexual appeal.

The image in the advertisement reproduced in Illustration 1.3 imitates another Wonderbra advertisement from the same campaign. The Wonderbra advertisement in question presents another supermodel in only her bra, with the caption "Regardez-moi dans les yeux. . . . J'ai dit les yeux. . . ." ("Look me in the eyes. . . . I said the eyes. . . ."). The point is that it is difficult not to stare at her chest adorned with her Wonderbra. Here again, the emphasis is on sexuality and good looks. In contrast, the advertisement we have reproduced (below) mimics that Wonderbra image, but in this case the model (Tanja Kiewitz) is a disabled woman with a missing limb. Inserted underneath the new image, the caption highlights our tendency to focus on her deformed limb rather than her good looks. CAP48, a Belgian group dedicated to disability awareness, used the advertisement to raise questions about our tendency to identify disabled people with their disabilities. It very successfully sparked a broad discussion of images of disabled in the media (for a sample, see the National Center on Disability and Journalism discussion at: http://ncdj.org/blog/2010/10/25/sizing-up-disability-in-the-media/).

One finds a more explicit rejection of the view of women one finds in the Wonderbra advertisements and the 1950s Campbell Soup advertisement in the cartoon from the *New Yorker* we have reproduced in Illustration 1.4. As in the first Wonderbra advertisement, the woman pictured—who is presented as a professional woman—frankly declares that she can't cook, but suggests that this doesn't matter for a very different reason: because she "can pay." One might see in this an implicit argument to the effect that cooking doesn't matter anymore, because a woman can establish her worth by being a professional and earning a good salary. In the present context, the three illustrations we have provided reflect different assumptions that appeal to different audiences who make different assumptions about the identity of women. The two contemporary examples explicitly reject the historical example we began with, but do so in different ways, appealing to different values: in the one case emphasizing good looks, in the other professional accomplishment.

REGARDEZ-MOI DANS LES YEUX…
…J'AI DIT LES YEUX.

POUR QUE LE HANDICAP NE SOIT PLUS UN HANDICAP. 000-0000037-37.

Illustration 1.3   "Regardez-moi. dans les yeux . . ."

"I can't cook, but I can pay."

Illustration 1.4   "I can't cook, but I can pay"

Different Kinds of Audience

The historical advertisements we have noted try to convince an audience at a particular historical moment that they should buy a particular product. They strike us as odd because we do not share the belief system of the intended audience. You can be sure that future audiences will find our own arguments and advertisements peculiar because they will assume some other, yet to be determined, system of beliefs and values.

In constructing an argument, an effective arguer considers the audience to be addressed. A *specific audience* shares some set of beliefs and commitments. If you want to successfully address such an audience, you need to recognize the beliefs that characterize its members and respond to them. This may mean that you use different variations of an argument when you address the different audiences made up of professional women; sports fans; property owners; renters; stay at home husbands; young people; seniors; automobile drivers; conservatives; atheists; Catholics; gay rights activists; attendees at a scientific conference; and so on. In each case, your argument will be most effective if you make an effort to respond to *their* convictions and concerns.

In gauging an audience's receptivity to a conclusion we want to propound, we distinguish three types of specific audience: audiences that are *sympathetic* to what we are arguing; those that do not accept our position but are *open* to considering it; and audiences that are *hostile* to it. Needless to say, a hostile audience is the hardest to convince, for it subscribes to attitudes and beliefs that are in some way opposed to the perspective we are defending. At the same time, this is the most important audience to argue with, for it is the audience that, more than any other, needs a *reason* to be convinced.

Consider an example. An audience made of people with a college or university education will probably be a sympathetic audience when one is arguing for the maintenance and support of post-secondary education. In addressing them, we can probably assume the value of a higher education. This is something they should have witnessed and experienced for themselves. The extent of their sympathy is likely to reduce the degree of evidence required to convince them of the importance of government funding, more scholarships, or lower tuition fees.

In contrast, more evidence will be required when one addresses an audience that is sceptical of post-secondary education. In this case, one might found one's argument on some other aspect of an audience's system of belief. One might, for example, begin with the premise that we need a flourishing economy and argue that a post-secondary education provides benefits for all, including those without a college or university education. Given this premise one could go on to argue that we should support higher education on the basis of the further claim that a strong economy depends on the innovation and creativity which higher education fosters, providing evidence for this.

Whenever one addresses a specific audience, the best argumentative strategy is to try and demonstrate that one's conclusion follows from some aspect of *the audience's own perspective*. This means meeting such an audience where they are, understanding the thinking on their side, and leading them from it to the conclusion one proposes. In extreme cases, this might mean that one needs to begin by arguing for a fundamental change in their system of belief.

The need to pay attention to a specific audience's system(s) of belief does not mean that one is entitled to exploit its sensitivities. In many cases, an audience's sympathy for a particular cause or position interferes with its critical assessment of the evidence for and against a particular conclusion. While many arguers exploit these inclinations, sometimes purposely so, this produces weak arguments that will not hold up to scrutiny when one is faced with a broader audience.

It is important to recognize specific audiences in many instances. When assessing someone else's arguments, the fact that they are directed toward a specific audience will be a relevant factor in what we expect of the argument. At times, we will focus on specific audiences, but they are not the primary focus of this book. If one develops a good argument that is addressed to a specific audience, then one should also be able to defend it in front of a broader audience that includes reasonable people who have different points of view. In theoretical discussions of argument, the audience that includes *all* reasonable people is commonly referred to as the *universal* audience. Arguments that attempt to satisfy this audience must meet the most stringent standards for good arguments, standards that are explored in this text.

The nature (and even the existence) of the universal audience has been the subject of much discussion. For our purposes, it is enough to say that we will, in most cases, assume a broad audience that includes people with many different points of view. This is the sort of audience that you would have to assume if you were arguing in a newspaper, in a political debate, or to specialists that embrace competing points of view. Even when you argue to convince a specific audience—a situation in which you must strive to understand their beliefs, the assumptions behind their perspective, and the particular knowledge they have—remember that you should be able to defend your perspective in front of a broader audience with many different (and contrary) points of view. Being able to satisfy both specific and universal audiences is an important way to test your arguments and your conclusions.

EXERCISE 1 D

1.* The following is a comment adapted from a letter to the editor that discusses legislation that would ban strikes by public employees. It contains an argument. What are the premises and conclusion? How has the writer failed to address their intended audience (the general readers of a newspaper)? What audience would be more appropriate for this particular argument?

> Bill 179 should be stopped. Not only does it take away the right to strike, it takes away the right to collective bargaining, through which both the employer and employee mutually agree to the terms and conditions under which they [employees] will work. As anyone who follows the news will know, the Pope has repeatedly stated that man has the right to demand what he feels is just compensation of his labours, including the right to strike.

2. Construct audience profiles for each of the following:

   Example: professional women
   Professional women are likely to be well-educated, to be strongly committed to equal rights for women, to value advancement in their profession, and to be sensitive to the issues that confront women in such careers.

   a)* university students
   b) Native North Americans
   c)* sports fans
   d) citizens of industrialized countries
   e) pet owners
   f) labour union members
   g) farmers
   h) media people

3. List the features you would include in the belief system of the universal audience.

4. In each of the following cases, identify the premises and conclusion in the argument, and discuss the audience to which it is addressed. Does it address the views of the specific and the universal audience?

   (i) [From a letter to the *National Post* newspaper, 10 December 2007] No amount of studies will change the fact that parallel private health care systems are splendidly efficient. One need look no further than the systems in place in Sweden, Switzerland and Japan. All these countries deliver timely health care, with comparable or better outcomes than we have in Canada and at a lower cost.

   (ii) [The following comes from a report on the Air France disaster in May 2009. "The riddle of flight AF447," The *Independent* newspaper, 10 June 2009] Airline disasters are meat and drink to conspiracy theorists. Several alternative explanations still exist for the Concorde disaster in Paris in 2000 and the terrorist bombing of a Pan Am jumbo plane over Lockerbie Scotland in 1988. The confusion and misinformation surrounding Flight AF447 will inevitably lead to similarly fevered speculation.

(iii) [From a Letter to the Editor, *The Globe and Mail*, Saturday, 1 September 2007, p. A20] "I am a carnivore," Jonathan Zimmerman twice proclaims in Why Is It A More Serious Crime To Kill A Dog Than Hit A Woman? (Aug. 29). If he thinks he's using the word effectively in its core sense, he's setting himself apart from the species, Homo Sapiens, to which I and most Globe readers belong. . . . True carnivores inflict cruelty and death on other creatures only out of necessity, unlike human beings.

(iv) [Jan Techau, head of the Alfred von Oppenheim Center for European Studies at the German Council on Foreign Relations, was one of a number of European leaders to comment in *Der Spiegel Online International* (11 May 2008) on the success of Barack Obama in the November 2008 American Presidential election] The manner in which the future American administration will treat its European counterparts will be all-important for constructive relations during the next four years. Europeans do not expect to find agreement on all policy issues with the U.S. Far from it—Europe itself finds it soberingly difficult to generate much-needed pan-EU unity, even on urgent policy issues. But Europeans expect to be treated without condescension and as nominally equal counterparts, even if it is true that the power imbalance between themselves and the U.S. is sometimes strikingly evident. In other words: a return to normal and established ways of diplomacy is much anticipated—and much needed. The new president could score easy points and make a huge difference by exercising old-fashioned, respectful leadership.

(v) [From the *National Post*, 8 December 2007. If you are unfamiliar with the Latimer case some quick research online will bring you the relevant details] Your letter writers claim there was a "miscarriage of justice" for Robert Latimer. I don't think so—Robert Latimer gassed his daughter to death. The words seem stark on the page, but they are true. He murdered her.

5. We have provided examples of argument that illustrate different views of women assumed by different audiences. Find two examples of argument (historical or contemporary) that illustrate different views of men and their identity. Discuss and contrast the views in question, and the audiences they appeal to.

5   Opponents and Proponents

The role of audiences in argument underscores the point that the presentation of an argument is not an isolated event, but a response to some issue, controversy, or difference of opinion. In many cases, it is a response to an argument that defends a contrary point of view. When you present your own argument, someone may respond by criticizing your reasoning, by requesting some kind of clarification, or by expounding an opposing argument. The give and take that this implies might be compared to a game of chess or some other game in which we move and counter-move in response to the moves of our **opponents**. In the case of argument, this process of exchange is called "dialectic."

We have already noted one instance of dialectic in our discussion of Philip Morris' 1940s advertisement. One might see this advertisement and others like it, as the first move in an exchange that produces criticisms from anti-smoking groups. In answer to these criticisms, Philip Morris has positioned itself differently. Its website www. philipmorrisusa.com makes the move and counter-move explicit, noting that "There are those who believe that a company that makes a dangerous and addictive product cannot be responsible," answering that "We believe that responsibility is defined not only by the products a company makes but also by the action it takes." Needless to say, the opponents of tobacco sales will themselves have a response to make to this answer to their concerns.

The dialectical exchange between proponents and opponents of particular points of view is a key dynamic in the history of ideas, where arguments and counter-arguments may shape debates that span centuries. An example rooted in the philosophy of Plato and Aristotle is the work of the Islamic philosopher, al-Ghazali, which is a critique of the views of Islamic thinkers who propound Platonic and Aristotelian points of views, most notably Ibn Sina (called Avicenna in the West). In answer to their views, al-Ghazali published a book entitled *The Incoherence of the Philosophers* (the *Tahāfut al-Falāsifa*) in which he becomes their opponent, criticizing key aspects of their arguments. The next step in the dialectic is evident in the work of another important Islamic philosopher, Ibn Rushd (known in the West as Averroes), who answers al-Ghazali in a work called *The Incoherence of the Incoherence*. The move and counter-move that characterizes these exchanges continues in the work of other philosophers who criticize Ibn Rushd, others who criticize them, and so on.

In situations which are explicitly designed to deal with arguments, the role of proponents and opponents is often formalized. In a court of criminal law, the prosecution propounds a case against the person accused of criminal activity. The defence acts as their opponent, criticising the prosecution's arguments and conclusion. In other processes of this sort, someone may be appointed as a "devil's advocate"—a role that makes them responsible for testing the arguments others propound. The term itself originates in the process of beatification which was once utilized in the Catholic church (the process by which someone is canonized and becomes a saint). Until Pope John Paul II changed the process in 1983, a devil's advocate was appointed to oppose (and in this way test) the arguments forwarded for the proposition that someone should be canonized.

Such processes underscore the role that opponents play in the development of argument, for their sceptical criticisms are an important way to test our reasoning. By definition, opponents are opposed to our arguments, but we still have an obligation to treat them fairly—in the same way that we have an obligation not to cheat competitors who oppose us in a game. Even when opponents are not included in our immediate audience, we are still obligated to develop our arguments in a way that tries to anticipate and answer their objections. If we are arguing for a public medicare system, this means that we should take seriously the objections to our arguments proposed by those who are opposed to publicly supported health care. If we are arguing against the use of animals in medical experiments, we should consider and respond to the views of those who think that it is justified because it is necessary for the development of new medicine.

A commitment to pay attention to the arguments of opponents forces us to take objections to our views seriously. In Judaism, a rabbi meeting with someone who wishes to convert must make three genuine attempts to persuade them that it is *not* a good idea. This is a powerful variant of the principle that one should take objections to one's conclusions seriously. It takes very seriously the idea that one is not ready to make a decision or hold a belief until one is certain enough not to be persuaded by objections to it. This is an ideal that we should aspire to in constructing arguments. Doing so will make our own arguments—and the conclusions they advocate—more compelling.

EXERCISE 1E

1.* Identify the arguments in the following excerpts from the lead article in the New Hampshire *Rockingham News* ("Dog-Fight Leader Gets Prison," 30 August 2002), which recounted the case of a man tried for cruelty to animals after he trained pit bull terriers to fight in matches, which he staged. For each excerpt, identify the premises and the conclusion of the argument, the specific audience, and the opponents of the view expressed.

   a) Judge Gillian Abrahamson said that the actions of the man who trained the dogs and staged the fights were disturbing because he had "inflicted such pain and torture on helpless animals for fun and profit."

   b) She held that the severity of the 37 counts of "Exhibition of Fighting Animals" justified a sentence in a state prison rather than a county jail.

   c) The attorney for the defendant asserted that the sentence handed down by Judge Abrahamson did not fit the crime because it was "unprecedented in its length."

   d) A coordinator for the Humane Society of the United States New England Regional Office supported the prison sentence, claiming that "the minor penalties associated with misdemeanour convictions are not a sufficient deterrent."

   e) They were not sufficient, she claimed, because "dog fighting yields such large profits for participants [that dog fighters] merely absorb these fines as part of the cost of doing business."

2.* A discussion of the dog-trainer's case above might easily evolve in a way that considers many related issues. Given that it is wrong to be cruel to animals, why is it permissible to kill them and eat them? Isn't killing animals a form of cruelty? Identify the position you would propound on the question whether it is permissible to eat animals. Construct a short argument responding to the views of your opponents in this context. Identify the premise and conclusion in your argument, and explain how it responds to the views of your opponents.

3. Someone defending dog fights might argue that we permit boxing, so we should permit dog fighting. Should these two sports be treated similarly? Why or why not? Construct an argument (with no more than three premises) for a conclusion one way or the other. Construct another argument that you would attribute to those who hold an opposing point of view. Construct a third argument that responds to these opponents.

4. Do you think that animals should be used in scientific experiments? Write a short (one paragraph) argument that supports your view. Imagine that your audience is the general public. Explain one way in which you might adapt your argument to take into account the position of your opponents.

5. Go to a newspaper or web blog and find an argument. Identify the arguer, the audience to which the argument is addressed, and the argument's opponents.

6 Summary

This chapter has introduced the basic ideas essential for a study of argument. We have considered the nature of arguments and how to recognize them. We have also looked at the other components of an argumentative situation: arguers and audiences. Both of these need to be understood in terms of the belief systems that comprise and motivate them. We have also considered different kinds of audience and what to expect with respect to each. Importantly, we have discussed specific and universal audiences, as well as the difference between opponents and proponents.

MAJOR EXERCISE 1M

1.* What is the argument in the following advertisement from *Family*, which features a large photo of a baby, accompanied by text? Who is the intended audience? How can you tell?

> YOU'RE THE ONE WHO HAS PROMISED TO PROTECT HER. PROTECT HER SCALP FROM IRRITATION WITH NEW IMPROVED JOHNSON'S BABY SHAMPOO, THE ONLY ONE CLINICALLY PROVEN HYPOALLERGENIC.

2. You are in the process of buying a new house. You must decide between three different options: (a) you buy a deluxe condominium on Lakeshore Boulevard; (b) you buy a modest bungalow on Northfield Road; (c) you decide to give up on the house and move into a downtown apartment. Option A will let you live the lifestyle you will most enjoy; option B will save you a significant amount of money; option C will place you within walking distance of a good grade school for your children. Pick an option and write an argument for it that is addressed to (a) your spouse; (b) your children; (c) your parents.

3. What is the argument in the following cartoon? Clearly identify the premise and conclusion.

Illustration 1.5   "I'm txting while drvng"

4. The following graph is entitled "Gender Equality Equals Mexico." Summarize the implied argument.

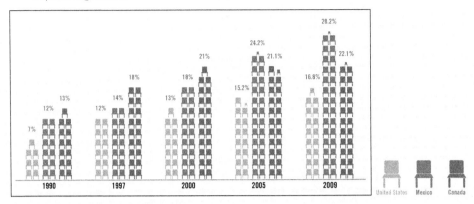

Graph 1.1 "Gender Equality Equals Mexico": Proportion of seats held by women in national parliaments (%)

Source: www.data.worldbank.org/indicator/SG.GEN.PARL.ZS/countries/MX-CA-US?display=default

5. For each of the following, discuss as many ideas from this chapter as the examples allow. Identify premises and conclusions; discuss the audiences involved with the beliefs that are assumed; and identify proponents and opponents.

    i)   [From an article entitled "Amazing Claims for Chlorophyll" posted on a website called *Quackwatch: Your Guide to Quackery, Health Fraud, and Intelligent Decisions*] What about deodorizing properties? Despite the sales hype, in products sold to the public, it doesn't have any. According to John C. Kephart, who performed studies at the laboratories of The National Chlorophyll and Chemical Company about 20 years ago, "No deodorant effect can possibly occur from the quantities of chlorophyll put in products such as gum, foot powder, cough drops, etc. To be effective, large doses must be given internally" (*Journal of Ecological Botany*, Vol. 9, No. 3, 1955).

    ii) [From a letter to *The Atlantic*, October 2010, in response to an article criticizing teachers and teachers' unions, pp. 21–22] Mr. Brooks's essay no more qualifies as a powerful idea than Senator Infhofe's observations about snow in Washington, D.C., qualify as a challenge to the facts of climate change.

         Mr. Brooks cites not one single fact to confirm his view that there has been "an absolute change in the correlation of forces" in relations between organized teachers and the communities they serve. He mentions only two proper names (one of which is General Patton) and provides not one quote in support of his argument.

    iii) [From "Health News" in *More* magazine, February/March 2011, p. 30] "There are so many changes that occur in women's lives from 40 to 60," says Marianna Golts, a psychiatrist at Toronto's Mount Sinai Hospital. "The stress of work, menopausal symptoms, aging parents, having kids or kids leaving—all these factors can contribute to your depression risk." . . . The safeguard is maintenance. "It's so important for women to put their needs first, get adequate sleep, exercise and have a life outside of family and work—all the normal things that usually get pushed aside at this point in a woman's life."

iv) [From *The Windsor Star*, p. A7, Opinion: "Keep phones out of class," by Cory Matchett, 24 September 2010] "The school board thinks it would be good for students and allow them to take notes on their phones. I think this is outrageous. I am a student at the university and have seen first-hand that many students just sit there and text all class. . . The world is far too complicated these days and the only way we are going to move in the right direction is by simplifying things. In my opinion, all you need to do well in school is paper, a pen and, most importantly, your mind."

v) [From *The Windsor Star*, Letters to the Editor, "Support for arts lacking in Windsor," by Mary Vasyliw, Monday, 7 March 2011, p. A7] "I would ask that every family with young children go out and actively support [the arts] before they are gone. Not only does it enrich the children's lives but brings many benefits to this city. To be a truly great city, there has to be a mixture of cultural and sporting activities for people of all ages."

vi) [From *More Magazine*, March 2011, pp. 52–53:] Singing can also nurture the body. A 2000 American study found that choral singing helps the immune system. The study measured the levels of immunoglobulin A and cortisol immediately after singing in a choir and after listening to choral music. The choir members had much higher levels of the immune-boosting chemicals right after singing

6. Connect each concept with its corresponding definition:

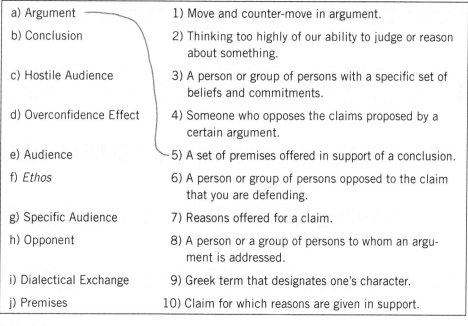

a) Argument	1) Move and counter-move in argument.
b) Conclusion	2) Thinking too highly of our ability to judge or reason about something.
c) Hostile Audience	3) A person or group of persons with a specific set of beliefs and commitments.
d) Overconfidence Effect	4) Someone who opposes the claims proposed by a certain argument.
e) Audience	5) A set of premises offered in support of a conclusion.
f) *Ethos*	6) A person or group of persons opposed to the claim that you are defending.
g) Specific Audience	7) Reasons offered for a claim.
h) Opponent	8) A person or a group of persons to whom an argument is addressed.
i) Dialectical Exchange	9) Greek term that designates one's character.
j) Premises	10) Claim for which reasons are given in support.

Table 1.1

For more online exercises, review questions, and quizzes related to the material in this chapter, please go to www.oupcanada.com/GoodReasoning5e

3

ARGUMENTS, WEAK AND STRONG

We evaluate arguments to distinguish those that are weak and those that are strong. In this chapter, we introduce the basic concepts of argument evaluation. You should emerge with an understanding of the following key concepts:

▶ burden of proof
▶ strong and weak arguments
▶ acceptability
▶ valid and invalid arguments
▶ argument schemes and counter-schemes
▶ contextual relevance
▶ fallacies
▶ red herring
▶ straw man.

We evaluate (or "assess") arguments to determine whether they are strong or weak or somewhere in between. We use the terms "strong" and "weak" to emphasize the point that the strength of an argument is not a black-or-white affair. A strong argument should convince a reasonable audience that its conclusion is plausible, but it will rarely be so strong that it cannot be strengthened or responded to. A weak argument may be so weak that it cannot be rehabilitated, but many weak arguments are better described as weak but capable of strengthening (by, for example, adding more premises). Argument evaluation encompasses a continuum from very weak to very strong that contains abundant, perhaps infinite, shades of grey. In this chapter, we explore the essential features of strong arguments.

1 Burden of Proof

Not every claim or situation calls for argument. In assessing arguments—or someone's failure to defend their claims with argument—this means that we must begin by understanding when we ought to argue. The answer to this question is tied to a notion called burden of proof. A "burden" is something that is carried. It might be an object—a backpack or a sack of coal—but it can also be something abstract, like the responsibility to take care of a difficult person or home. In circumstances where there is disagreement, the person who carries the *burden of proof* is the person who has an obligation, or *onus*, to defend (and in this way "prove") their views with argument.

In addressing a criminal court, the burden of proof rests with the prosecution, which accuses the defendant of a crime. In England, Canada, and the United States, this means that a defendant and his or her lawyer are not required to prove that the accused is innocent. Innocence is assumed, and the prosecution must proceed by trying to prove the defendant's guilt. The French legal system sometimes assigns burden of proof on some issues to the defendant, but generally also presumes the innocence of a person accused of crime. Internationally, the Universal Declaration of Human Rights places the burden of proof on the prosecution, stating that everyone has the right to be presumed innocent before the law.

Questions about burden of proof and an arguer's obligation to defend premises lie behind every argument, because every argument offers premises in support of its conclusion. In deciding such questions we must distinguish those cases in which the burden of proof rests with the arguer and those in which it rests with those who might challenge them. In the first case, the arguer will have to build sub-arguments that back their premises; in the second, the premises can be assumed without further argument.

We explore burden of proof in greater detail in Chapter 8. For now you should decide questions about burden of proof by asking whether it is reasonable to accept a premise, or whether it needs to be supported. In making such judgements, a key consideration will be the specific audience to whom the argument is directed, for different audiences will accept different premises without support. In a Spanish newspaper, one can assert without argument that bull fighting is a laudable cultural endeavour. In North America, where bull fighting is seen as cruelty to animals, the burden of proof reverses, requiring that those individuals who view it as a worthy endeavour defend their premises.

Over time, the burden of proof in a particular area changes as our view of the world changes. Economics is an established and revered discipline but the recent collapse of financial markets has raised questions about its credibility. James Galbraith, himself an economist, expresses this change in attitude in the following testimony, which he presented to the United States Congress on 18 May 2010:

> I write to you from a disgraced profession. Economic theory, as widely taught since the 1980s, failed miserably to understand the forces behind the financial crisis. Concepts including "rational expectations," "market discipline," and the "efficient markets hypothesis" led economists to argue that speculation would stabilize prices, that sellers would act to protect their reputations, that caveat emptor could be relied on, and that widespread fraud therefore could not occur. Not all economists believed this—but most did.

Such testimony challenges the assumptions that characterize standard economic theory, which assumes a model of behaviour which was unable to predict or properly account for the fall of the American housing market and the global financial crisis it precipitated. In the wake of these events, Galbraith is no longer willing to assign burden of proof in a manner that accepts without argument the standard premises that underlie traditional economic theory.

As this example shows, questions about burden of proof may themselves be the subject of argument. Some have argued that the practice of employment drug tests, instituted by some employers, is unfair (*conclusion*) because it places an unfair burden of proof on employees who must prove they are innocent of using illegal drugs (*premise*). In a much debated incident in 2006, Duke University expelled three players from its lacrosse team and cancelled the team's season when they were accused of sexual assault. When DNA evidence proved that they were innocent, the university and the prosecuting attorney were rebuked on the grounds that they had assumed the students were guilty, instead of assuming them innocent and placing the onus on those who alleged otherwise.

EXERCISE   3A

For each of the following arguments, discuss whether the burden of proof would lie with the arguer who puts forward the premises or with a challenger who might dispute them:

a)* [Lindsey Murtagh and David Ludwig, the authors of a commentary in *The Journal of the American Medical Association* entitled "State intervention in life-threatening childhood obesity," (2011, Vol. 306, No. 2, pp. 206–7), argued that in extreme cases the government should be allowed to intervene and remove children from their parents' custody. Their argument included the following premises] Ubiquitous junk food marketing, lack of opportunities for physically active recreation, and other aspects of modern society promote unhealthy lifestyles in children. Inadequate or unskilled parental supervision can leave children vulnerable to these obesigenic environmental influences.

b) [Bioethicist Art Caplan challenged some of the conclusions drawn in the above study, in comments reported in the *Toronto Star* (13 July 2011)] The debate risks putting too much blame on parents. Obese children are victims of advertising, marketing, peer pressure and bullying—things a parent can't control.

c) [The Omega watch company withdrew its advertising from *Vogue* magazine in protest over what it called distasteful pictures of an emaciated model in the June 1996 issue. The brand director of Omega argued as follows (source: the *New York Times*, 31 May 1996)] Since *Vogue* presumably targets an audience that includes young and impressionable females, its creators must surely be aware that they will inevitably be influenced by what laughably passes for fashion in these pages. It was irresponsible for a leading magazine that should be setting an example to select models of anorexic proportions.

d) [From the same news story. The publisher of *Vogue* responded] [The brand director's] comments appear to be motivated by sour grapes, because he had objected to the way Omega watches had been photographed for a feature on watches.

e) [Excerpted from a Letter to the Editor, *The Washington Times*, 6 June 2011, by the executive director of the International Climate Science Coalition based in Ottawa]

Referring to those of us who do not support the climate scare as "climate-change deniers" is both a mistake and a logical fallacy. It is a mistake because no reputable scientist on either side of the debate denies that climate changes. The only constant about climate is change—it changes all the time no matter what we do.

The term "deniers" is often used by supporters of the hypothesis that our greenhouse gas emissions are causing a climate crisis. They use it in order to equate their opponents to Holocaust deniers and so elicit negative emotions. This is the logical fallacy referred to as "ad hominem" in that it is against the man, not the idea. It is a common but offensive public relations trick and should be shunned by all honest citizens.

Use of the phrase "fossil-fuel industry-funded" to discredit our point of view is also a logical fallacy, by saying that we are funded by vested interests, appear to have a motive to lie, and, therefore, what we say is wrong is clearly illogical. It also implies that our scientific opinions can be bought and thus we are dishonest, which would again be an ad hominem logical fallacy. Besides, many skeptical scientists have nothing to do with the energy industry, fossil fuel or otherwise.

Strong Arguments

Burden of proof tells us when we are obligated to provide an argument. In doing so, our goal is a *strong* argument: an argument that provides evidence that will convince a reasonable audience that they should accept our conclusion. In the paradigm circumstance in which an argument is required—when we must address an audience that does not accept our conclusion—we might compare a successful argument to a journey which takes our audience from their current beliefs to the argument's conclusion. In doing so, a strong argument must satisfy two conditions.

(i) Premise Acceptability

One essential feature of good arguments is acceptable premises—i.e. premises the intended audience will (or should) accept. If they believe that the premises are false or misconceived or in some other way unacceptable, then the argument does not provide them with reasons for believing the conclusion. In a strong argument, the premises of an argument function like a vehicle that takes the audience to its conclusion. In an argument with unacceptable premises, the members of the audience might be compared to passengers who refuse to get on a bus which cannot, in view of this, take them to its destination.

When we say that an argument's premises should be "acceptable" we mean that they should be accepted as true by the audience it is addressed to. We leave for an advanced course in philosophy the complex questions raised by debates about the meaning of "true." In evaluating arguments, we hold that premises should be 'acceptable' rather than 'true' because there are many circumstances in which it is reasonable to rely on premises that are plausible or probable, or judged correct in some other provisional way. This is an inevitable aspect of many—perhaps most—arguments because they occur in circumstances characterized by uncertainty. Suffice it to say that the premises of a strong argument may be acceptable even though a reasonable audience might hesitate to go so far as to call them "true."

The kinds of issues raised by premise acceptability can be illustrated with a simple example we have taken from a debate in *Runner's World* magazine (December 2010). It features two experts who take opposite stances in response to the question whether one should listen to music while running. In the course of arguing the pro side of the debate, the expert who supports running with music argues as follows.

> **Premise:** Studies find that music reduces your perception of how hard you are running by about 10 per cent.
>
> **Conclusion:** Music can sometimes make running feel easier.

In gauging the strength of this argument, we must consider whether its premise is acceptable. What are we to make of its claim that scientific studies show that music reduces our perception of the effort we are making when we are running?

In the course of reading this debate, one might accept this claim on the grounds that it is offered by someone who is described as a "Ph.D., a sports psychologist, who has studied music's positive influence on athletes." In doing so, one grounds the premise on an appeal to authority of the sort we discuss in Chapter 12. This is a reasonable stance, but someone skeptical of the argument might adopt an opposing point of view. They might emphasize the point that the argument is offered in a context in which another expert—described as a "Ph.D., a sports sociologist and coach"—takes issue with the suggestion that it is a good idea to run with music. In such a situation, the skeptic may not be willing to accept a general claim about unspecified scientific studies, even if it is made by an expert. Without a more detailed account of the studies that are alluded to—one that allows them to check the credibility of the studies and their conclusions—they may find the premise unacceptable and maintain that the argument fails to provide compelling evidence for the conclusion that music can sometimes make running feel easier.

We will not attempt to resolve this debate. Our aim is to illustrate the kinds of issues raised by premise's acceptability, and the role it plays in evaluating arguments. Ideally, all the premises of a strong argument are acceptable, though there may be times when an argument is convincing even though it has some unacceptable premises.

(ii) Logical Consequence

Acceptable premises are the first component of good arguments. The second is a conclusion that is a logical consequence of its premises—i.e. a conclusion that "follows" from these premises. Put another way, the conclusion of a good argument is a conclusion we have good reason to accept if we accept its premises. If we think of an argument as a journey, the conclusion is the destination the argument is supposed to take us to. When the conclusion offered is not a logical consequence of the premises, the premises lead in the wrong direction. Even if they are acceptable, this means that they cannot lead us to the conclusion. In this case, the argument is like a bus which picks up its passengers but fails to take them to its intended destination.

We can illustrate the notion of logical consequence in terms of the example we have already outlined. Let's assume that we accept the conclusion that "Music can sometimes make running feel easier." In the context of the broader debate in *Runner's World*, this claim functions as a premise in support of running with music. We can summarize this argument as follows.

Premise: Music can sometimes make running feel easier.
Conclusion: Running with music is a good way to run.

When we evaluate this argument we need to ask whether its conclusion follows from (is a logical consequence of) its premise.

This is a more complex question than it might at first appear. Intuitively, one might think that conclusion of our new argument follows from its premise because it suggests that running with music will require less effort, and this seems to be a good idea. But one might argue for a very different point of view. In *Runner's World*, the expert who opposes running with music opposes it because listening to music distracts us from the signals our bodies send us when we are running—signals we should pay attention to if we want to avoid injury, over exertion, or an accident. As he puts it, "One big problem is that listening to music can remove you from the other sounds that running produces, such as breathing and foot strike, which are essential cues. They give you feedback on your effort." Looked at from this perspective, the premise "Music can sometimes make running feel easier" is a reason for thinking, not that you should run with music, but that one shouldn't do so—for it confirms the claim that listening to music interferes with our perception of our bodily state when we are running.

This makes the argument we are discussing an argument in which the second component of strong arguments—a conclusion that follows from the premises—is not present. Even when we assume that its premise is acceptable, it follows that the argument is weak without further backing. The latter might be provided by further premises or other arguments that qualify or elaborate the premise in a way that helps it establish the conclusion—by showing that listening to music makes running feel easier without interfering with our perception of the key signals we need to be attuned to if we are to run safely.

If we think of a strong argument as an argument that provides evidence that should convince its audience to accept the conclusion, and a "weak" argument as one that fails to, then the notions of premise acceptability and logical consequence allow us to more precisely elaborate the features of strong arguments in that:

A strong argument is an argument with (1) acceptable premises and (2) a conclusion that follows from them.

A *weak* argument is, in contrast, an argument without acceptable premises or with a conclusion that does not follow from them, and possibly both.

Argument Criticism

By definition a weak argument is an argument that fails to satisfy one or both of the criteria for strong arguments: i.e. an argument that has unacceptable premises or a conclusion that does not follow from its premises. Good argument criticism exposes one or both of these flaws.

We illustrate good argument *criticism* with an example from a talk radio show on CFRB Toronto. In it, host John Oakley responded to a Canada-wide speaking tour conducted by the well-known environmentalist, David Suzuki. Suzuki had emerged from his tour arguing that the Canadian government should institute a carbon tax on the carbon content of fuels. In support of this conclusion he said that he had consulted with Canadians across Canada and found them "overwhelmingly" in support of such a tax. One might summarize this argument as: "The people I have talked to overwhelmingly want a carbon tax (*premise*), which shows that Canadians overwhelmingly support such a tax (*conclusion*)."

Oakley was not convinced and took Suzuki to task for his claim that Canadians overwhelmingly want a carbon tax. Summarized, his position is that Suzuki's conclusion about Canadians does not follow from his premise. As we shall see when we look at polling in detail in Chapter 9, Suzuki's argument provides a paradigm example of a poor generalization. It is not surprising that the people he met and spoke to on his tour were overwhelmingly in favour of a carbon tax, for he is a famous environmentalist and it is people who support his strong environmentalism who are attracted to his talks. His experience talking to them does support the claim that these sorts of people are overwhelmingly in favour of a carbon tax, but it would be a mistake to conclude from this that the "average citizen" shares such views. On his own radio show, Oakley demonstrated the point by surveying his own listeners, finding that only 8 per cent of his respondents supported such a tax. Oakley's survey is no better proof of what Canadians believe (because there is no reason to think that those who like to listen to his views represent the views of most Canadians), but it does illustrate the problem of bias such generalizations involve, and this raises questions about Suzuki's claims.

Our criticism highlights problems with Suzuki's conclusion that Canadians overwhelmingly support a carbon task. This weakens the further argument in which this is used as a premise, which we can summarize as follows:

> The Canadian government should institute a carbon tax (*conclusion*) because Canadians overwhelming want a carbon tax (*premise*).

The issues we have already raised show that this argument fails to satisfy the first criterion of strong arguments—premise acceptability. There are, in contrast, no obvious problems with the link between the premise and the conclusion, for it is reasonable to assume that a government should do what the majority of its citizens want (there are, of course, all kinds of situations in which this does not happen, and for good reasons, but there is no obvious way in which they apply). In view of this, it is easy to see how the conclusion follows from the premise. It is the unacceptability of the premise, not its relation to the conclusion, which weakens this particular argument. Our two examples illustrate how good argument criticism assesses the two components of good arguments, premise acceptability and logical consequence. In responding to such criticism we can strengthen an argument by addressing the problems it highlights. In our second case, this would require the replacement of the weak premise we identified.

Our criticisms of Suzuki's arguments do not by themselves settle the question of whether Canada should institute a carbon tax. The arguments we have considered fail to show that this is so, but there may be other arguments that are more convincing (Suzuki himself enunciates many other arguments). A proper poll or vote would provide evidence establishing whether the majority of Canadians do support a carbon tax. Even if it doesn't one might argue that this is a situation in which the environmental consequences of a carbon tax are so important (for future generations as well as our own) that one should be instituted anyway.

In the course of evaluating arguments it is important to distinguish the criticism of a particular argument from an evaluation of the conclusion it presents. One may accept the conclusion of an argument without accepting the argument. The argument "Every intelligent person will read this book. You are intelligent, so you are reading this book," has a true conclusion but its first premise is (regretfully) implausible and makes this argument weak (our confidence in the second premise cannot remedy this flaw). A decision about the plausibility of any conclusion would require a comprehensive review of the evidence that might be marshalled for or against it.

EXERCISE 3B

1. The following examples of argument are derived (and in some cases adapted) from the debate on running with music we have already discussed. In each case, identify the premise(s) and conclusion of the argument and evaluate it as strong or weak, addressing the questions of premise acceptability and logical consequence.

   a) Running while listening to music also removes you from the environment you're in, which can be unsafe. You may not hear a car or person behind you. You may not hear thunder in the distance. And in races, it makes you oblivious of other runners and you can't hear the directions being given by officials.

   b) The ability to be at peace and be calm is something we've lost in our culture in favour of multi-tasking. We can recover this peace with running but I would argue that listening to music—or podcasts or audio books—while running is a form of multi-tasking. So find yourself by running without music.

   c) In the "flow state," which is complete immersion in the task at hand, time almost seems to stand still. You're enjoying what you are doing, you feel at one with yourself. But there's good research showing that music can help enhance flow state during running. So it can actually be part of this holistic experience, not necessarily detached from it or a detriment to it.

2. In each of the following examples, identify the premise(s) and conclusion of the argument and evaluate it as strong or weak, addressing the questions of premise acceptability and logical consequence.

    a)* [From Pliny the Elder, *Natural History* Book 7, Line 50] People may be born the same moment but have entirely different fates. So astrology is not reliable.

    b)* Cigarettes are the most flagrant example of drug pushing, since most tobacco is pushed on teenagers, who are led by advertising into thinking it's cool to smoke.

    c) University education should be free in the United States. It is free in Australia and many European countries that do not have the resources America has.

    d) It was once rare to find a professional with an MBA. Now they are a dime a dozen. Because value reflects scarcity, an MBA isn't worth what it once was.

3. Assess the following example of argument criticism, adapted from the "Citizen Tom" blog. Identify the premises and conclusion in both the argument in favour of compact fluorescent light bulbs (CFLs) and the argument against them.

It is true that CFLs use two-thirds less energy than standard incandescent bulbs to provide the same amount of light, and last up to 10 times longer. Environmentalists conclude that we should convert.

But the pros and cons of CFLs are not so simple. Why? Because there are, in addition to advantages, disadvantages to CFLs as well: i.e. because they contain mercury; because they are almost all made in China, which has poor environmental standards for production; and because light bulbs are used at night, which means that replacing all our household light bulbs will do little to reduce peak demand and mitigate the need for . . . power.

3   Logical Consequence: Deductive and Inductive Validity

The second criterion for strong arguments is logical consequence, which we have defined as "a conclusion that follows from the premises." Put in another way, a strong argument must have premises that *lead* to its conclusion. Those who study argument have debated the nature of this link between premises and conclusion. Some emphasize one kind of link that they attribute to all arguments, others differentiate between two kinds of links, and still others distinguish more than two. We will not pursue a theoretical account of these differences here, but we will refine our account of logical consequence by introducing the two most commonly distinguished ways in which a conclusion may follow from a set of premises.

In "deductive" arguments the link between premises and conclusions is so strong that the conclusion *necessarily* follows from the premises. In arguments of this sort, it is impossible for us to accept that the premises are true and still reject the conclusion. We call arguments of this sort deductively valid. Consider the following example:

(**Premise 1:**) The fetus, even in the case of a pregnancy resulting from rape or incest, is an innocent human being. (**Premise 2:**) The killing of innocent human beings is never permissible. (**Premise 3:**) Abortion kills the fetus. (**Conclusion:**) Abortion is never permissible.

In a case like this, someone who accepts premises 1, 2, and 3 must accept the conclusion, for as soon as you accept that the fetus is, in all cases of abortion, an innocent human being, that abortion kills the fetus, and that the killing of innocent human beings is never permissible, it is impossible to reject the conclusion that abortion is never permissible.

In deductively valid arguments, the link between the premises and the conclusion is as strong as it can be. Anyone who understands the argument must accept the conclusion if they accept the premises. If they do not, they have misunderstood the meaning of the statements that make up the argument or they are fundamentally irrational. The strength of the link between the premises and conclusion in a deductively valid argument means that it always satisfies the requirement that the conclusion of a strong argument must be a logical consequence of its premises. It does not follow that all deductively valid arguments are strong arguments, for they may not have acceptable premises.

In the example we have given, Premise 1 assumes that the fetus is a "human being"—a claim that has been widely debated. Premise 2 is also controversial, for it does seem to be permissible to kill innocent people in certain circumstances (in self defence and in times of war, for instance). Premise 3 is acceptable in our current circumstances but there might come a time in the future when it might be mistaken: if, for example, technological innovation allowed a doctor to remove a fetus from a pregnant mother without killing it (say, by placing it in an artificial womb). At the very least, such considerations show that the burden of proof in this case requires the arguer who forwards the argument to justify its first two premises (the third premise is acceptable in our current circumstances). Because they are not acceptable without further support, the argument is weak even though it is deductively valid.

Deductively *invalid* arguments contain a conclusion that does not necessarily follow from the premises. In these cases, one can reject an argument's conclusion even while accepting that its premises are true. This means that the link between an argument's premises and conclusion is not as strong as the link in deductively valid reasoning, but it does not mean that all deductively invalid arguments should be rejected. In the case of inductively valid arguments we can imagine that the premises of an argument are true and the conclusion false, but the premises still make the conclusion likely, and in this way provide reasonable support for it.

Consider an example from Vancouver, where the BC Court of Appeal ordered the city to amend their bylaws after it forced Falun Gong protestors in 2009 to take down a hut used in demonstrations outside the Chinese consulate. According to the court, this action violated the right to protest that is a key element of the freedom of expression that is essential in a democratic society. In response to the Court's decision, Vancouver's City Council discussed a new by law entitled "Structures for Public Expression on City Streets" in 2011. It was supposed to make room for protest structures, but the initial version of the law was widely criticized on the grounds that it was too restrictive: it would charge protestors $1200 to set up a structure; would prohibit structures in residential areas; would limit the size of the displays; and would require a traffic management plan for every structure. On the basis of these restrictions, some concluded that the law would inevitably lead to further court challenges that the city would lose.

We might summarize the latter argument as follows.

> **Premise:** The proposed "Structures for Public Expression on City Streets" is restrictive in a great many ways (by charging protestors $1200, prohibiting structures in residential areas; limiting the size of the displays; and requiring a traffic management plan).
>
> **Conclusion:** The law would lead to further court challenges the city would lose.

This is an argument which is not deductively valid, for we cannot say that the conclusion *necessarily* follows from the premise. The possibility that the city would lose future court challenges depends on many things: on the city's interpretation of the law; on the extent to which protest groups would be willing to invest the time and fiscal resources to challenge the law; on legal technicalities; and so forth. It is certainly possible that one or more of these factors would prevent future court challenges the city would lose.

This does not mean that the argument can be dismissed out of hand. The finding of the Appeal Court shows that it takes the issue of freedom of expression very seriously; the proposed law places many impediments that interfere with protesters' right to protest in public; and a number of incidents in the city's past suggest that protesters will zealously defend their right to protest. In such circumstances it is reasonable to suppose that a decision to pass the proposed law makes it plausible or likely that the city would lose further court challenges.

This is a good example of an inductively valid argument. Such arguments are characterized by a more tentative link between their premises and their conclusions. They function as an essential part of ordinary reasoning. We rely on them in many situations characterized by uncertainty in which they serve as an alternative to deductive arguments. In contrast, inductively *invalid* arguments are always weak, for their conclusions are not a logical consequence of their premises.

Relevance and Sufficiency

When judging validity, it may help to consider the premises of an argument from two points of view. First, we can ask whether the premises in an argument are *relevant* to the conclusion. We count a premise or group of premises as relevant when it provides some—that is, any—evidence that makes the conclusion more or less likely. Premises are *positively* relevant when they make a conclusion more likely and *negatively* relevant when they make it less likely. The following statements are all positively relevant to the claim that "University education is a way to build a better economic future":

- University graduates have, on average, much higher salaries than people who don't go to university.
- University graduates are more likely to occupy professional and managerial positions.
- University graduates are more likely to be promoted.

A strong argument proposes premises that are positively relevant to its conclusion. If it failed to do so, it would provide no support for this conclusion. But positively relevant premises do not guarantee a strong argument. In addition to positively relevant premises, a strong argument requires premises that are *sufficient* to establish that a conclusion is more likely than not. This implies something more than positively relevant premises, which may provide some support for a conclusion without providing *enough* support to convince a reasonable audience. We can, therefore, develop the notion of logical consequence by saying that an argument's conclusion follows from its premises if they are (1) relevant to the conclusion, and (2) sufficient to establish it as probable.

In a deductively valid argument, the premises are always relevant and sufficient to the conclusion, for it is impossible to accept the premises and reject the conclusion. One cannot have premises that are more relevant and sufficient than this. In an inductively valid argument the link between the premises and conclusion is weaker, but the argument may still be strong, and may provide sufficient evidence to convince us of its conclusion. In an inductively invalid argument, the link between premises and conclusion is too weak to do so.

Deciding when we have relevant and sufficient evidence for a conclusion can be a complex task. Consider a popular blog entitled "100 Reasons NOT to Go to Graduate School" (http://100rsns.blogspot.com). The author describes the blog as "an attempt to offer those considering graduate school some good reasons to do something else." The reasons given include the claims that:

- Graduate school is expensive and there are few jobs waiting for graduates.
- Graduate school forces you to put other important aspects of your life (e.g., marriage and a family) on hold.
- Universities use graduate students primarily as a source of cheap labour.

A full analysis of the overall argument would be a very complex endeavour requiring an assessment of the relevance and sufficiency of the 100 reasons given (and the relevance and sufficiency of the sub arguments provided in defence of each of the 100 reasons). To illustrate the notions of relevance and sufficiency, we consider just part of the evidence the blog provides for the claim that "The Smart People Are Somewhere Elsewhere"—the first reason it gives for not going to grad school.

> According to FinAid.org: "The median additional debt [the debt that graduate students pile onto the debt that they acquired as undergraduates] is $25,000 for a Master's degree, $52,000 for a doctoral degree and $79,836 for a professional degree. A quarter of graduate and professional students borrow more than $42,898 for a Master's degree, more than $75,712 for a doctoral degree and more than $118,500 for a professional degree." This is not intelligent behavior. The smart people are somewhere else.

Here the large debt that students accumulate in graduate school is used as a premise for the conclusion that going to grad school is not intelligent behaviour (and "The smart people are somewhere else").

Is this an argument that gives relevant and sufficient reasons for its conclusions? In addressing this question we would note that the premise tells us that a particular website,

FinAid.org, provides the figures it gives for graduate student debt. Certainly the statement on that website is relevant to the claim that graduate students acquire unreasonable debt, but is it sufficient to establish that this is so? One issue this raises is whether this website is a credible authority which is providing a reliable account of student debt—if the website is not credible, then there is no reason to accept its data as evidence for the claim that graduate student debt is unreasonable. To determine whether it is credible, we would have to learn more about FinAid.org and its claims. In the final analysis, this probably requires an assessment of the authorities *it* depends on when it makes its claims.

Assuming that the figures given can be established as reliable, the premise of our argument is relevant to the conclusion that it is not wise for most people to go to graduate school—for it isn't wise to accumulate large debts. But it does not provide sufficient evidence to establish the conclusion that going to graduate school is not an intelligent decision, for the wisdom of this debt depends, from a financial point of view, on the financial consequences of the decision to go to graduate school. If the result is likely to be a lucrative job with a high paying salary, then this may compensate for the expense that one occurs in graduate school. It may, to take one example, be expensive to become a medical doctor, but the ultimate financial rewards may outweigh the expense of doing so.

Of course, the argument for and against graduate school could continue. In answer to our analysis of one of its arguments, one might point out that the *100 Reasons* blog provides evidence for thinking that it is a mistake to imagine that most or even many of the graduates of graduate school will find lucrative jobs. We take no position on the question whether you should go to graduate school, but we would say that it behooves you to consider the arguments pro and con if you are thinking of doing so, and that they provide ample illustrations of the complexities that arise when we try to determine whether the premises of an argument are relevant and sufficient to establish its conclusion. This underscores the point that much more could be said about validity, and relevance and sufficiency, something we do in Chapter 8. Until we get there, our outline of validity and the criteria for establishing it will provide helpful background as we turn to the more complex aspects of argument analysis and evaluation.

EXERCISE 3C

In each of the following cases, identify the premise(s) and conclusion in the argument. Are the premises relevant and sufficient to establish the conclusion? Are the arguments deductively or inductively valid? Why or why not? Be sure to explain your judgements in each case. (Note that this exercise does not ask you judge whether the premises of the argument are acceptable. In this case you are asked only to consider whether the argument is valid or not.)

a)* Since large carnivores like grizzly bears and wolves are majestic creatures in their own right and are also critical to maintaining the health of the ecosystem, it is wrong to indiscriminately destroy them.

b) Medieval portrayals of Plato and Aristotle with haloes cannot be taken to mean that these two were seen as "saints." "Sainthood," and the attainment of it, is directly related to the following of Christ himself.

c)* We should not extend the status of the family to same-sex couples. There are two reasons for this. First, some discrimination is always necessary in complex societies. Secondly, a family by definition must have both a mother and father.

d) [From a Letter to the Editor, *The Globe and Mail*, 8 February 1997] An independent Associated Press poll (December 1995) showed that 59 per cent of the American public thought that it was "always wrong to kill an animal for its fur." A 1997 fur industry poll, specifically targeting fur coat wearers, found that a mere 17 per cent said that a fur coat represented fashion and 14 per cent said social status. From this information it follows that the public views those who wear coats as callous, showing arrogant disregard for the suffering of fur-bearing animals.

e) [From the *Wall Street Journal*, 4 June 2003, p. A3]

> **TAKE A CHANCE ON LOVE.**
> **NOT ON YOUR PRIVATE JET.**
>
> You have to throw caution to the wind when it comes to affairs of the heart. Purchasing a private jet, however, demands a rational approach. When you choose fractional jet ownership with NetJets, you'll have access to the world's largest fleet of business jets, which means you're guaranteed a plane in as little as four hours. The best-trained pilots in the industry assure your safety and it's all backed by the financial strength of Berkshire Hathaway. Maybe that's why people who can fly any way they want choose NetJets.
>
> **NETJETS. LEAVE NOTHING TO CHANCE.**

f) [From the *Wall Street Journal*, 4 June 2003, p. A8]

> Considering NetJets? If You Think Performance Matters, Call Flexjet.
>
> **BOMBARDIER FLEXJET'S HIGH PERFORMANCE FLEET STRETCHES YOUR HOURS.**
>
> Bombardier is a world-leading expert in the design and manufacturing of sleek, aerodynamically efficient aircraft. The superior speed advantage of Flexjet aircraft significantly shortens your trip time and delivers a lower cost per mile than NetJets. With Flexjet you'll fly faster, higher and more efficiently. So, you can use the hours you save towards more trips.
>
> Flexjet Gives You the Equivalent of 12% More Hours Per Year.
>
> Flexjet: Equivalent of 112 Hours
>
> Netjets: 100 Hours
>
> **Bombardier Flexjet**

 ## Contextual Relevance

The relevance of premises to the conclusion is not the only type of relevance that interests us when evaluating argumentation. We are also concerned to ensure that our own arguments and those we are considering are relevant to the contexts in which they arise. If a context assumes one understanding of an issue and then an arguer ignores or misrepresents that meaning, then the argument will be contextually irrelevant. Strong arguments will avoid this error and remain relevant to the appropriate context.

An argument that is contextually situated properly addresses whatever issue is at hand, responds appropriately to any prior argument it answers or builds upon, and anticipates reasonable objections from opponents. When arguments fail in this respect, they can exhibit the kind of weaknesses that have been traditionally identified as "fallacies." A fallacy is *a common mistake in argument*. The focus of this text is on *good* reasoning, so although we will have occasion to discuss several fallacies in the chapters ahead, we do so in terms of how arguments fail to meet the various criteria of strength that are our primary concern. In this chapter, however, we will illustrate specific kinds of weakness by introducing two fallacies of contextual *ir*relevance. They highlight problems that tend to characterize arguments that are not properly situated in their context.

Red Herring

A red herring is an attempt to shift debate away from the issue that is the topic of an argument. Instead of addressing the strength or weakness of the argument, it deflects attention to a new topic that is not relevant to the one at hand. The term "red herring" is commonly said to originate in the use of a real red herring (i.e. the fish) in fox hunting. Hunters who wanted to save an exceptional fox for another chase would drag a red herring across its scent, diverting the chasing hounds after the stronger scent of the red herring. Whether this is true or not, there is no doubt that the argumentative counterpart of this strategy is a common tactic in debate.

We take our first example from an Internet debate about Lance Armstrong, the seven time winner of the Tour de France. His status as a cancer survivor who has raised millions for cancer treatment has made him a hero to some, but others regard him as a fraud whose success was due to the use of illicit drugs. On the occasion of his retirement from cycling, *Velonews: The Journal of Competitive Cycling* posted an article on its website entitled "Armstrong's 25-year Journey is Over" (17 February 2011). It sparked an Internet exchange between readers who roundly criticized Armstrong, and others who rejected suggestions that he was guilty of doping. Here is a portion of that exchange:

road_bikerider

Can't anyone just be happy for Lance and enjoy all of the drama and excitement that he has given us over the years? He is a great athlete and has accomplished much in his lifetime, both before and after his cancer.

birillothedog

He's not a great athlete, he's a fraud, a cheat, and a liar. That's why not everybody is "happy for Lance."

lboogie6029

Jealousy is a bummer.

We can understand the first comment in this exchange as an argument. It suggests that we *should* "just be happy for Lance and enjoy all of the drama and excitement that he has given us over the years" (*conclusion*) because "He is a great athlete and has accomplished much in his lifetime, both before and after his cancer" (*premise*). The next commentator, birillothedog, answers with a different argument, maintaining that there is a good reason that "not everybody is happy for Lance" (*conclusion*) because "He's not a great athlete, he's a fraud, a cheat and a liar" (*premise*). Putting aside the question whether we should accept these arguments, we want to note the next contribution to the exchange, which abruptly dismisses birillothedog's argument, accusing him of jealousy.

In the next chapter, we will discuss how to detect the implicit argument behind assertions like this. Here, we will assume that lboogie6029 believes that the previous contributor is not a fan of Armstrong *because* he is jealous. This is a good example of red herring. For the topic at issue is the question whether Armstrong should, at the end of his career, be celebrated. The first commentator presents an argument for thinking so. Birillothedog provides an argument for the opposite conclusion. This second argument may be weak. If lboogie6029 wishes to reject it, then he or she should provide his or her own argument that shows that this is so. He or she could, for example, attempt to show that the premise is false, that the conclusion doesn't follow, or that there is other compelling evidence that shows that Armstrong should be celebrated. Instead of doing this, lboogie6029 changes the topic. The new topic is the question whether birillothedog is jealous.

This new question deflects attention away from the issue at hand: the question of whether Lance Armstrong should be celebrated. The new question is, moreover, a question that makes little sense as a topic for argument in the debate in which it is embedded. It is very difficult to see how lboogie6029 or anyone else could know that birillothedog is jealous by reading two sentences that might instead be taken as an instance of conviction, indignation, or anger. More importantly, it doesn't really matter whether birillothedog is jealous. In a debate about Lance Armstrong, the important question is whether his arguments criticizing Armstrong are strong or weak. This issue does not turn on the question whether he is jealous—even if he is, that cannot show that the argument he proposes must be mistaken. People who are jealous may still forward good arguments, so something more is needed if one wants to reject the argument he provides.

Straw Man

One kind of diversion that warrants special mention is called straw man. Historically, a "straw man" was a figure made of straw used to represent a man. Straw men were used in military drills that aimed to teach recruits how to fight with an opponent. In other circumstances, they were burnt as effigies to protest against leaders they were said to represent. In the world of argument, a *straw man* is a false account of an opponent's point of view. Presenting such an account violates our obligation to represent opposing positions fairly and accurately.

> ## RED HERRING
> The fallacy red herring is an attempt to shift attention away from the topic of an argument, in another direction that is not contextually relevant.

Usually, straw man arguments employ a weakened version of an opponent's position that is, like the straw men traditionally used in military training, more easily disposed of than their real counterpart. Within the scope of the argument in question, this makes it easier for an arguer to refute their opponents, but it is a false victory, for one has not defeated the real opponent, but a weaker replica that lacks the strength of the original.

In our discussion of proponents and opponents in Chapter 1, we noted the historical debate between al-Ghazali and Ibn Sina (Avicenna). In the context of straw man it is worth noting that al-Ghazali's critique of Avicenna's arguments was preceded by another book, titled *The Aims of the Philosophers* (*Maqasid al-falasifah*), which was a summary of Avicenna's philosophy. In the West, al-Ghazali was originally known for this work, because it was a superb guide to the tenets of Islamic Aristoteleanism—so good that al-Ghazali himself was at one point incorrectly thought to be an adherent. But as al-Ghazali himself said, one must be well versed in the ideas of others before setting out to refute them. This is the attitude we should all have when criticizing the views of our opponents. We should understand their views thoroughly (ideally, as well as they do), to ensure that our criticisms are not just fair and reasonable, but also telling, for this is the only way to ensure that our criticisms will themselves stand up to scrutiny.

Straw man arguments represent the other side of this spectrum, occurring when an arguer misrepresents the views of those he or she criticizes. To illustrate this, we return to the Internet debate about Lance Armstrong. The following is another contribution to the discussion posted by Samaway:

> Moral judgments of whether he doped, and whether his accomplishments are then somehow valid, are simply reflections of cultural constructs. . . . I can't condone doping, but nor do I get angry at riders who do. I think doping signals something much more troubling about our culture.

In answer to these remarks, "S" provides the following retort:

> So the end justifies the means? Whoever is the best at cheating wins and should receive our adulations? Who the hell cares about the guy who raced "clean" but came in 6th right?. . . It's about whether you won, placed or showed . . . anything less is for saps.

It should be evident that this seriously misconstrues Samaway's position. Samaway neither condones nor condemns (gets angry about) doping, which implies that they *don't* think "it's about whether you, won, placed or showed" and that "anything less is for saps." What Samaway suggests is something different: that the "troubling" issue that should be discussed and debated is what it is in our culture gives rise to doping. As they themselves write in response to this: "It seems that focusing on whether a cyclist is a cheater is a little short sighted, given the mix of political economy and cultural values that the sport embodies."

If S wishes to take issue with Samaway's views evidence should be provided that he or she is mistaken. This might be done by arguing that cheating is wrong no matter what cultural influences give rise to it, or by arguing that Samaway might as well argue that it is permissible to cheat on one's taxes or text while you are driving because our culture makes this a prevalent practice. Whether or not these are good arguments, they are arguments that respond to Samaway's real position, and that some such argument is what is needed if one wants to show that Samaway is mistaken. Instead, S constructs a straw man, dismissing Samaway's claims in a way that seriously misrepresents them.

We finish our discussion of red herring and straw man with an example from a Manitoba controversy that arose when a judge sentenced a convicted rapist to a conditional sentence—a sentence that meant the man would not spend time in jail. In explaining his decision, the judge described the case as a situation in which the defendant never threatened the woman and genuinely misperceived what the victim wanted. "This is a different case than one where there is no perceived invitation," he said. "This is a case of misunderstood signals and inconsiderate behaviour." ("Rape victim 'Inviting,' so no jail," *Winnipeg Free Press*, 2 February 2011, p. A3)

One might summarize the judge's main argument as the claim that the defendant should get a conditional sentence (*conclusion*) because (a) this was a case where he genuinely misunderstood what the woman wanted (*premise 1*) and (b) he never threatened the victim (*premise 2*). In a further account of the factors that were alleged to contribute to the miscommunication, the judge included the woman's attire—tube tops with no bra, high heels, and makeup; her suggestive comments; her willingness to accompany the man into the woods; and her flirtatious conduct, which included consensual kissing.

When the decision was reported, it produced a wave of comments and debate, which included many calls for the judge's dismissal. In less than a day, there were three hundred responses to the initial report on the website of the *Winnipeg Free Press*. Many of these responses focussed on the judge's comments about the woman's attire. A commentator called CDNinJPN wrote that:

> according to the judge "wearing tube tops with no bra, high heels and plenty of make up" means "let's have sex" no matter what the woman actually says. Seriously, I thought that kind of thinking went out the door with 8-tracks, rotary phones, and Betamax.

On the day following the report, the *Winnipeg Free Press* featured the following comment, by Denial Awareness, as the "Comment of the Day":

> The premises of this whole "she was wearing a tube top . . ." argument is that women control men's actions. If a woman is wearing a tube top, no bra, and make up, a man has absolutely NO control over himself and no responsibility for his actions. The woman MADE him rape her. He had no choice. He was forced by his uncontrollable

chemical reaction to seeing her in a tube top. This judge talks about "signals being misunderstood" as though "signals" are some sort of accurate way to communicate. I was once told by a guy that I had been "giving signals" that I wanted to have sex with him and he went on to describe how I lifted my arm and turned my head a certain way. It was ridiculous! I'm shocked that a judge even uses the term "signals" as a justification for vindicating a rapist!

In considering these comments, it is important to say that there are many ways that one might argue against the judge's decision—by arguing that it sets an unacceptable precedent, does not take the issue of sexual assault seriously enough, and so on. That said, the remarks that we have quoted are problematic because they seriously misrepresent the judge's explanation of his reasons for assigning the sentence he did. The following five problems with their characterization of the judge's argument may serve as premises in an argument for the conclusion that they are instances of the fallacy straw man.

- **Problem 1.** The judge did not argue that a man "has absolutely NO control over himself and no responsibility for his actions" when he sees a woman in a tube top. Nor does he hold that these are circumstances in which "The woman MADE him rape her. He had no choice. He was forced by his uncontrollable chemical reaction to seeing her in a tube top." Nothing in the judge's comments suggest that this is (as "Denial Awareness" suggests) a basic premise in his argument. His remarks imply the opposite: that the man *was* in a position to make a conscious decision to have—or not have—sex with the woman. The defendant was not given a mitigated sentence on the grounds that he could not help himself, but on the grounds that he misunderstood the woman and made a mistaken decision, not one that he could not have made otherwise.
- **Problem 2.** "Denial Awareness" incorrectly claims that the judge talks "about 'signals being misunderstood' as though 'signals' are some sort of accurate way to communicate." The judge very clearly thinks that that "signals" are *not* an accurate way to communicate, for this is implied by his suggestion that it is possible to misunderstand them and what they mean.
- **Problem 3.** It is unclear how the example that Denial Awareness gives from her own experience (when a "ridiculous" man told her that she was giving signals to have sex because she lifted her arm and turned her head) is relevant to the judge's assessment of this case. There is no reason to believe he would accept the claim of the man described, for the scenario in question shares little with the case before the judge.
- **Problem 4.** The claim that the judge uses the term "signals" as a justification for "vindicating a rapist!" greatly exaggerates the judge's views and actions. To "vindicate" means "to free from allegation or blame" but the judge found the defendant guilty, gave him a criminal record, and assigned a penalty that involved work in the community. It goes without saying that this may be too light a sentence (because the penalty does not include jail time) but one cannot equate it with vindicating the man in question.

- **Problem 5.** The judge did not say what CDNinJPN says he did, i.e. that "wearing tube tops with no bra, high heels and plenty of make-up means let's have sex." He listed these as factors that *contributed* to a miscommunication, and said that this *plus* other aspects of the situation (the kissing, the suggestive remarks, etc.) resulted in the alleged misunderstanding. One might compare the meaning of other claims qualified in a similar way: if an astrobiologist says that the presence of carbon is one of the factors that contributes to the possibility of life, then we would seriously misrepresent his or her position if we described it as the claim that "the presence of carbon means the presence of life." In the case at hand, the judge maintained that it was a series of factors *and still other* aspects of the situation (notably, the lack of threatening behaviour) that warranted the conditional sentence.

When we describe the comments we have quoted as instances of straw man, that does not mean that the judge's own argument is a good one. That remains to be established. The important point is that straw man criticisms of the judge are weak criticisms because they fail to address his real views. If we want to forward strong (even devastating) criticisms of the judge—or any other opponent, then we must do so in a way that carefully and accurately presents their views. When we fail to do so, our arguments become contextually irrelevant.

The examples of red herring and straw man we have given are not extraordinary. In the give and take of ordinary argument, it is common for arguers to deflect attention from the issues at hand. Often this is done by misrepresenting their opponents, typically by ignoring the nuances of their position and creating a simplified version of it that is easily derided. Especially when arguments are heated and the stakes are high, it is easy for our reactions to push us in this direction. Resisting this inclination is one way to establish yourself as an accomplished arguer and ensure you produce strong arguments.

STRAW MAN

The fallacy straw man is a type of diversion that attempts to shift attention from the proper topic of an argument against an opponent's point of view by misrepresenting the views that are the subject of criticism.

EXERCISE   3D

Assess each of the following examples in terms of how well the arguers comply with the requirements of contextual relevance. Identify the arguments, and in the case of fallacies of irrelevance explain what has gone wrong and why.

a) The government's healthcare bill is designed to pass the costs onto the public and this is a bad idea. The post office is a similar example of government mismanagement. It is extremely inefficient compared to private couriers, losing taxpayers billions of dollars a year, and there is no incentive to improve matters because of the government monopoly.

b)* The government's healthcare bill promises much but will likely deliver very little. It's impossible to believe it will make Americans healthy overnight. It should therefore be defeated.

c) A: Why are you not willing to support the gun-control legislation? Don't you have any feelings at all for the thousands of lives that each year are blotted out by the indiscriminate use of handguns?

B: I just don't understand why you people who get so worked up about lives being blotted out by handguns don't have the same feelings about the unborn children whose lives are being indiscriminately blotted out. Is not the sanctity of human life important in all cases? Why have you failed to support our efforts concerning abortion legislation?

d) [From "Europes elites are destroying the grand project" (*Der Spiegel* Online International, 9 June 2009, http://www.spiegel.de/international, which attempts to account for the poor turnout in European Parliamentary elections. The center-left political party *Süddeutsche Zeitung* is being quoted]

All opinion polls show that the majority of European's value the EU, that they would not like to do without it, that they appreciate the advantages of the community and that they would like to see more Europe when it comes to dealing with the big questions of the present and future such as climate change, energy supplies or foreign and security policy.

Why then does this majority not turn out to vote? Because no one has convinced them that it is important. Almost every party in every country in the EU has failed in the task of encouraging the voters to take part in the decision-making process.

e) [From a Letter to the Editor, *The Peterborough Examiner*, 20 May 1992, p. A3]

I am concerned by the recent letters to the editor that portray the Women's Health Care Centre as an abortion clinic I would like to point out that the Women's Health Care Centre provides many valuable services . . . pregnancy non-stress testing; colposcopy clinic; lactation consultant (breastfeeding support); counselling and information on a wide range of health issues of concern to women and their families; workshops covering PMS, menopause, body image, living alone, and many others.

I feel that the services provided by the Women's Health Care Centre work in conjunction with physicians and provide comprehensive information and support for the women of Peterborough and the surrounding areas.

⑤ Schemes and Counter-Schemes

In judging arguments, we can distinguish questions of acceptability from questions of validity. In many cases, we judge the validity of an argument by relying on our intuition—on our intuitive appreciation of what does and does not follow from a set of premises. This is what Sherlock Holmes tends to do when he reflects on his investigations and announces the unexpected verdict that "So-and-so committed the crime." In response to Watson's quizzical response, he claims that his reasoning is "Elementary, my dear Watson." By this, Holmes means that the conclusion is easy to see once his argument is properly understood. Typically, Holmes goes on to explain his argument in a way that clearly demonstrates that its conclusion follows from the evidence at hand.

We have all listened to and proposed many arguments. This gives us an intuitive appreciation of what makes sense and what does not which we can use to determine whether a straightforward and uncomplicated argument is valid or invalid. This is in some ways an easier task than judging whether premises are acceptable, for we can judge the relationship between premises and conclusion without having to marshal evidence for and against the premises. We rely on this intuitive skill when we follow Holmes's step-by-step explanation of his conclusions. Like Holmes, we use this skill when we try to demonstrate that our own inferences are valid.

Consider a simple example. In working through the exercises in this text, you wonder whether the answer to a particular question is included in the answers collected on the website that supports this text. In the process, you might employ the following reasoning:

> **Premise 1:** All the starred exercise questions are answered on the text website.
> **Premise 2:** Exercise question number 5 is starred.
> **Conclusion:** Exercise question number 5 must be answered on the text website.

This argument is deductively valid. If you are unsure why, try to imagine that you accept the premises but reject the conclusion. This would mean that exercise question number 5 is, contrary to the conclusion, not answered on the text website. But it would also mean that premise 1 is true—i.e. that all answered questions are starred. It would necessarily follow that question 5 is not starred, but this contradicts premise 2. This "mental experiment" shows that it is impossible for the conclusion to be false when the premises are true—i.e. that the argument's conclusion deductively follows from the premises.

Consider another example. Let's suppose you have an interest in nuclear science. You have heard that the person who discovered radioactivity won two Nobel prizes. You discover that this person is Marie Sklodowska Curie. You argue with a friend over the date when she discovered radioactivity. To settle the matter, you ask a professor and go back to your friend and say, "Marie Curie discovered radioactivity in 1898. Professor Szabo, who studied this in graduate school, told me so." Your argument is inductively rather than deductively valid, but it is a strong argument. Professor Szabo could have slipped up and confused this date with another one, but he is an expert in the matter, has studied the issue you have asked about, and betrayed no doubts when you asked him. In all likelihood, you and your friend will intuitively see that your conclusion should be accepted.

Relying on intuition is one way to judge whether an argument is valid or not. It will work in many cases, but it is difficult to intuit whether a long extended argument is valid, especially as intuitions may prove to be mistaken. Clearly, the principle "Trust your intuition" is not a sure guide to the strength of arguments, for people do present weak arguments and this is a situation in which the argument seems intuitively valid to at least one arguer—i.e. the arguer who proposed it. In these and many other cases, argument evaluation must provide us with a way to choose *between* competing intuitions.

In developing a more systematic approach to argument, and one that can tell us how to construct valid arguments, we can rely on the observation that individual arguments come in a variety of repeating patterns that can be identified in terms of the kinds of premises and conclusions they involve. We call these patterns **argument schemes**. By isolating particular schemes that apply to different kinds of argument, we can distinguish strong and weak patterns of reasoning, and judge arguments accordingly.

The last two examples we have given can illustrate this approach. The inductively valid argument that established the conclusion that Marie Curie discovered radioactivity in 1898 is an instance of a scheme called "appeal to authority." Arguments employing this scheme provide the word of an authority or expert as evidence for a conclusion (we discuss this scheme in detail in Chapter 12). The previous example, about exercise question 5, was an instance of a scheme that deduces a **particular affirmative** from a **universal affirmative**. We discuss this and similar schemes when we examine syllogisms in Appendix 1.

When we define schemes, we do so in a way that lets us separate the scheme from the particular instance of it conveyed in a specific argument. In the case of our argument about starred exercises, we can do this by letting "X" stand for "starred exercise questions," by letting "Y" stand for "questions answered on the text website," and by letting "z" stand for "question number 5." On this basis, we can represent the scheme of our example as follows.

SCHEME 1 (UNIVERSAL INSTANTIATION)
Premise 1:   All X are Y.
Premise 2:   z is X.
Conclusion: z must be Y.

This scheme is sometimes called "universal instantiation."

Once we identify this scheme we can see that the example we have given shares its structure with many other arguments that can be represented in the same way. For any groups X and Y, and any individual z, an argument that has the same form of Scheme 1 will be deductively valid. Scheme 1 is, for example, implicit in the following argument about BMW automobiles:

All luxury cars are expensive vehicles. Your BMW is a luxury car, so it must be an expensive vehicle.

If we let X = luxury cars, Y = expensive vehicles, and z = your BMW, you will see that this new argument is an instance of scheme 1. Our ability to represent both arguments in terms of this same scheme shows that they share a common structure even though their contents are different.

It is easy to build other arguments that are examples of universal instantiation. To do so, we only need to let X, Y, and z represent different groups and individuals. If we let X = logic professors, Y = people who read a lot, and z = Jan, then this produces the following argument of this form:

> All logic professors are people who read a lot. Jan is a logic professor. So Jan must read a lot.

Here again the result is a valid argument, for it is impossible for the conclusion to be false (i.e. for Jan *not* to read a lot) if its premises are true.

In developing our account of argument evaluation we have often compared an argument to a journey that takes one from accepted premises to a destination that is the conclusion. In understanding schemes and how they work, we might compare the distinction between an argument's scheme and its content to the distinction between directions and a particular location. If we say you need to go south 10 kilometres, then go east seven kilometres, this will take you to a different location depending on where you start. The same directions may, in view of this, take us to drastically different places: to a location in Saskatoon or Alaska or Singapore. Some directions will almost always make sense ("The location is 10° west and 10° south of you") and others not ("Turn left and right at the next traffic light"). The directions function in the same way in each case, but take us to very different destinations. In a similar way, a scheme of argument is a pattern or structure that can take us to a variety of conclusions.

When we embark on an analysis of complex arguments, it is helpful to identify any scheme of argument they incorporate, for different schemes have different criteria that can be used to assess the strength or weakness of instances of the scheme. These standards tell us what kinds of "critical questions" we should ask when evaluating an argument that is an instance of the scheme. In judging an appeal to authority, for example, we will need to ask questions about the authority's credentials, trustworthiness, and any bias they might have that might interfere with their judgement in this instance. These kinds of questions help us distinguish valid and invalid instances of the scheme.

"Counter-schemes" are schemes that are used to criticize arguments of a particular type, by showing that the premises in question are unacceptable or that the argument is not valid. The counter-scheme "argument against authority" is used to criticize appeals to authority. Some of the arguments we have to deal with in our reasoning will not correspond to any scheme or counter-scheme. In other cases, arguments are so complex that identifying an argument scheme requires a substantial amount of interpretation. That said, an understanding of schemes and how they work will significantly improve your ability to assess and create all types of arguments. The most common schemes are discussed in Chapters 9, 10, 11, and 12.

EXERCISE   3E

Discuss each of the following argument schemes. Do you think they are schemes that define deductively or inductively valid arguments? In each case, construct three arguments that are instances of the scheme.

   a)* All X are Y, all Y are Z, therefore all X are Z.
   b) After a thorough search, we have not been able to find any evidence of hypothesis X, so it is probably false.
   c) If X, then Y. If Y, then Z. So if X, then Z.

6   Summary

In Chapter 1 we introduced the notion of argument. In this chapter we looked at the difference between strong and weak arguments and how to evaluate them. In particular, we have explored how strong arguments must have conclusions that follow from premises, and learned that those premises must be acceptable. These two criteria will be developed in important ways in later chapters. We have also considered that strong arguments must be relevant to the contexts in which they arise. In this respect, we have looked at two failures of this requirement characterized by certain weak arguments, these are the Red Herring and Straw Man arguments. Finally, we have introduced a key tool that will be the focus of our accounts of argument: argument schemes and counter-schemes. These are regularized patterns of reasoning that can be evaluated according to specific ways in which the criteria for strong arguments arise for each scheme.

MAJOR EXERCISE 3M

   1. For each of the following topics, construct short arguments that adequately satisfy the two basic criteria for strong arguments. Be sure to consider and meet your obligations with respect to the burden of proof. Once you have done this, exchange your arguments with another member of your class and constructively evaluate each other's efforts. Discuss the results.

   a)* Appropriate email etiquette.
   b)   The right to smoke in enclosed public spaces.
   c)   Publicly funded health care.
   d)   The best student restaurant in town.
   e)   The danger of a world wide flu pandemic.
   f)   Our obligations to help with the AIDS epidemic in Africa.

   2. [The following arguments explore both sides of the controversial practice of factory farming. They are adapted from International Debate Education Association, www.idebate.org, accessed 20 June 2011. For each example, identify the argument, consider whether it is contextually relevant, and then assess it using the two basic criteria for strong arguments]

a)* Factory farming sees animals as "products," "commodities" for production and sale just like bricks or bread. But animals are conscious and aware and know pleasure and pain.

b)* Unless the state is going to impose vegetarianism (and that's not being proposed here) the business of food will continue, and that business should be efficient and productive like any other—that's in the interest of the producer, who makes a profit, and the consumer, who gets a low price.

c) Health risks to humans are also greatly magnified by factory farming, with epidemics swiftly spread between overcrowded animals and antibiotic resistance encouraged by medicated feed.

d) This intensive type of farming brings meat down to a price affordable to the poorest in our community on a regular basis. Without factory farming the poor will have an even worse diet.

e) Factory farming is very cruel. Confinement to the point at which suffocation is commonplace is the norm. Many animals never touch the ground or see direct sunlight. Chickens are bred selectively and genetically modified until the birds cannot stand up and their bones cannot support their weight. Battery hens are crammed into tiny cages and to stop them doing damage when they attack each other (as they inevitably do in such unnatural conditions) their beaks and toes are cut off. Pigs, highly social animals, are kept singly in cages they can't turn around in—and a number of diseases are very common because of the cramped conditions.

f) There is very little cruelty or suffering in factory farming—certainly no more than in traditional forms of farming. Foie gras has been produced since time immemorial by the force feeding of geese. Animals have always been herded together, confined, branded, killed and eaten. This is not the fault of the modern intensive (or "factory") industry, it's just the way things are when people eat meat.

3. For each of the following arguments from *The Sporting News* (24 July 1995), identify the argument and assess it as a strong or weak argument. Explain your decisions.

a)* [Dave Kindred, arguing against major league baseball's decision to institute new rules designed to speed up the game] There is pleasure knowing that events and not an expiring clock will decide when the evening's entertainment is done.

b) [Mike Schmidt, talking about the content of his speech on his induction into baseball's Hall of Fame] Children and their dreams must have positive reinforcement from parents, coaches, and friends. I truly believe that this reinforcement is not only important, but imperative. . . . Without parental encouragement to reach their goals, it is more difficult for children to develop self-esteem and become successful.

c) [Letter to "Voice of the Fan"] So Rockets' general manager John Thomas . . . doesn't think changing the logo after back-to-back titles won't hurt their luck? Well, I subscribe to Crash Davis's theory, as stated in the movie *Bull Durham*— "Never (mess) with a winning streak." . . . Ask the Penguins if they're sorry they changed logos. They did after their second consecutive Stanley Cup title but haven't made it past the second round since.

4. For each of the following arguments, say whether the argument is deductively or inductively valid. Explain your decision.

   a)* The conclusion of the argument can be false when the premises are true, so the argument is invalid.

   b) Most people find that their logical abilities improve with practice. So you should do fine if you work regularly on the exercises in this book.

   c)* In order to avoid the intricacies of theories of truth, we will rely on our earlier remark that the objective of an argument is to convince an audience. If this is so, then it is sufficient for our purposes that the premises of a good argument be accepted as true by both us and our audience. So this is what we will aim for.

   d)* [Greg Gutfeld, in "Be a jerk," *Men's Health*, 1995]
   A long time ago, I had this health problem. . . . Almost immediately, my doctor laid my worries to rest. He told me to relax. He sat with me and we talked for a long while. . . .We bonded. We became pals. . . . Over the course of a few months, I began to look forward to my visits. . . . But there was a small problem. I was still sick.

   Finally, I gave up and went to see another doctor. He was not a pleasant guy, more like a scowl in a white jacket. He took one look at me and spat out a diagnosis. . . .

   A week later I was cured.

   I learned something valuable here: When it comes to your health and other important matters, you can usually count on a jerk . . . .

   e) [From the same article] Nice bosses can ruin your career by not challenging you to do better. They won't tell you when your ideas stink, your work has been slacking or your fly is down. . . . A nice-guy boss will happily nod as you explain how elevator shoes for dachshunds is the wave of the future.

5. Provide argument criticism for each of the following passages. Begin by deciding whether the passage contains an argument. If it contains an argument, identify the conclusion and premise(s), and indicate the audience and opponents. For any arguments that you find, discuss where the burden of proof lies and whether contextual irrelevance has been avoided. Then assess whether they are strong arguments by applying the two basic criteria.

   a)* Certain non-human primates have been known to exhibit grief at the loss of a family member. But if they do that, then they are capable of abstract thought, and creatures with those capabilities must have a self. So, certain non-human primates must have a sense of self.

   b)* Certain non-human primates have been known to exhibit grief and be capable of abstract thought. And if they have those kinds of capabilities, then they are demonstrating some of the key indicators of personhood. Therefore, certain non-human primates are moral agents, since if they exhibit indicators of personhood then they are moral agents.

   c) [From a Letter to the Editor, *Wired* magazine, January 2003]
   Current chipmaking processes may require dangerous substances, but those cited in "Cleaning up clean rooms" are hardly carcinogenic franken-chemicals.

Hydrogen peroxide is what our mommies had us rinse our mouths with (albeit in diluted form) and pour into our ears (full strength) to help remove wax. Isopropyl alcohol we swab on cuts and abrasions.

Sometimes just the word chemical frightens people, so we need to be cautious. After all, dihydrogen oxide keeps us alive, but a few years ago a survey revealed that people were terrified of it and would want the FDA to ban it from foods.

d) [The following is a response to a news item (April 2008) that researchers in the United Kingdom had produced hybrid embryos, part-human and part-animal. The embryos did not survive beyond three days. The response is from Dr David King of Human Genetics Alert, http://news.bbc.co.uk, accessed 3 May 2010] For anyone who understands basic biology, it is no surprise that these embryos died at such an early stage. Cloning is inefficient precisely because it is so unnatural, and by mixing species it becomes even more unnatural and unlikely to succeed. The public has been grossly misled by the hype that this is vital medical research. Even if stem cells were ever to be produced, like cloned animals, they would have so many errors of their metabolism that they would produce completely misleading data.

e) [Robert F. Hartley, in *Business Ethics: Violations of the Public Trust*, 1993, Hoboken, New Jersey: J. Wiley] Lest we conclude that all takeovers involving heavy borrowing are ill-advised, reckless, and imprudent, let us look at a positive example. A&W root beer is part of America's motorized culture. . . .In 1986, Lowenkron engineered a leveraged buyout for $74 million, with $35 million in junk bonds. . . . By 1989, the company's sales surpassed $110 million, more than triple what they were before the buyout; profits reached $10 million, compared to a small loss in 1986.

f) [Al Bugner, on his heavyweight fight with Frank Bruno, in *Facing Ali: The Opposition Weighs In*, by Stephen Brunt, 2002, Alfred A. Knopf, Toronto, p. 160] The fight was the most disgraceful affair ever in a boxing ring. . . . I was rabbit-punched eight or ten times in the back of the head. Even in the eighth round when I was on the ropes he was doing it. There's no doubt in my mind that the whole affair was rigged. It was a set-up.

g)* [From *Life Extension* magazine, December 2002, p. 75] Carnosine may play a role in improving and increasing exercise performance. A study examined 11 healthy men during high-intensity exercise for concentration of carnosine in their skeletal muscle. . . . Carnosine was able to significantly buffer the acid-base balance in the skeletal muscles, which becomes unbalanced by the overproduction of hydrogen ions occurring in association with the build-up of lactic acid during high-intensity exercise.

h) [From "No chicken in this game," *Star Weekly*, 3 October 1959] Cock-fighting is one of the oldest and bloodiest sports in the world. The natural spur of the cock is replaced by one of steel, two inches long, which is tied on with leather throngs. The spurs are needle sharp and can do terrible damage. Matches are sometimes over in a few seconds or they may last for over an hour. The fight is always to the finish.

i) [The following is from a Letter to the Editor, *The Windsor Star*, 1 February 2007, by the chief electoral officer of Leamington, Ontario] Mail-in balloting is not a threat to democracy. . . . This form of balloting makes voting more accessible to many voters and promotes participation in our democratic process. And it is a system that is greatly appreciated by the many voters who have to manage mobility and accessibility issues.

j) [From an article on automated chicken catching machines, "Poultry in motion," in *The Wall Street Journal*, 4 June 2003] Human catchers are expected to snag as many as 1,000 birds an hour. As the men tire during eight-hour shifts, they accidentally slam birds against the cages, breaking wings and legs. Up to 25 per cent of broilers on some farms are hurt in the process. By contrast, a recent study in the British scientific journal *Animal Welfare* found that a mechanical catcher in use in Germany reduces some injuries by as much as 50 per cent. That's good news for the birds, and also for the industry.

k)* [From a personal email on "why to stop drinking Coke"] In many states the highway patrol carries two gallons of Coke in the trunk to remove blood from the highway after a car accident. You can put a T-bone steak in a bowl of coke and it will be gone in two days. The active ingredient in Coke is phosphoric acid. Its pH is 2.8. It will dissolve a nail in about four days.

l) [Excerpted from "At Risk: Vaccines: How a legal case could cripple one of modern medicine's greatest achievements," by Paul A. Offit, the *Boston Globe*, 3 June 2007] No single medical advance has had a greater impact on human health than vaccines. Before vaccines, Americans could expect that every year measles would infect four million children and kill 3,000; diphtheria would kill 15,000 people, mostly teenagers; rubella (German measles) would cause 20,000 babies to be born blind, deaf, or mentally retarded; pertussis would kill 8,000 children, most of whom were less than one year old; and polio would paralyze 15,000 children and kill 1,000. Because of vaccines all of these diseases have been completely or virtually eliminated from the United States. Smallpox—a disease estimated to have killed 500 million people—was eradicated from the face of the earth by vaccines. And we're not finished; vaccines stand as our only chance to prevent pandemic influenza, AIDS, and bioterror, and our best chance of preventing certain cancers.

m) [From an editorial on how to deal with the proliferation of nuclear weapons, in *The Wall Street Journal*, 4 June 2003, p. A16] For our part, we don't have much faith in UN inspections, which tend to see only those things the host nation wants to be seen. North Korea hid its clandestine uranium program for years, even as IAEA inspectors "safeguarded" its plutonium program. Then Pyongyang simply shut off even those TV cameras and booted the inspectors out of the country.

n) [From a 2007 advertisement for Broil King barbecues] Unlike folded steel, cast aluminum ovens retain heat for superior cooking performance and have no seams for heat and drippings to escape. Most importantly, the thick aluminum will NEVER rust, and even features a Lifetime Warranty.

6. Go to your local newspaper or your favourite magazines and find five examples of simple arguments and assess them as strong or weak.

For more online exercises, review questions, and quizzes related to the material in this chapter, please go to www.oupcanada.com/GoodReasoning5e

DRESSING ARGUMENTS

We have already introduced the key components of arguments and the concepts that we apply when evaluating them as weak and strong. Our account has focused on **simple arguments** because the fundamental elements of arguments are more easily distinguished in such cases. In this chapter we turn to more complex arguments and questions of interpretation they raise. In doing so, we discuss:

▶ simple and extended arguments
▶ explanations
▶ inference indicators
▶ argument narratives.

In a discussion of argument and argument analysis, John Woods has distinguished between arguments "dressed" and "on the hoof." These are terms normally used to refer to meat as it appears in a grocery store or butcher's shop, and on a live animal before it is butchered. Arguments on the hoof are arguments as they actually appear in the exchange that characterizes the use of arguments in science, social commentary, political and philosophical discussion, and so on. "Dressed" arguments are arguments as they appear after we clarify and delineate their structure, recognize their premises and conclusions, and label and identify them and their component parts. Woods's terminology underscores the point that it takes some significant work to dress an argument on the hoof, and that the result often looks different than the argument did before this work began.

Learning to dress arguments is a key part of learning to understand, construct, and evaluate them. Doing it well allows one to present an argument in a way that clarifies its structure, and prepares the way for a detailed evaluation. But dressing can itself be a difficult task and requires an understanding of a number of the complications that arise when we present and express arguments in the contexts in which they naturally occur.

1   Simple and Extended Arguments

So far, we have restricted our discussion of arguments to simple arguments. A simple argument has one conclusion supported by one or more premises. We contrast a simple argument with an extended argument—an argument which has a main conclusion supported by premise(s) and some premise(s) that are supported by other arguments. In an extended argument, sub-arguments support the premises that support the argument's principal conclusion.

Philip Yancey is a Christian author who wrote a book expounding the Christian notion of grace (P. Yancey, *What's So Amazing about Grace?*, Zondervan, 2002, p. 247). In it, he writes that the church has "for all its flaws" dispensed grace and justice to the world. "It was Christianity, and only Christianity, that brought an end to slavery, and Christianity that inspired the first hospitals and hospices to treat the sick. The same energy drove the early labour movement, women's suffrage, prohibition, human rights campaigns, and civil rights." This passage is naturally interpreted as a simple argument. It presents a claim—that the Christian church has, despite its flaws, dispensed grace and justice to the world—and backs it with reasons for thinking that this is so: that it was only Christianity that brought an end to slavery, inspired the first hospitals and hospices, and so forth.

Yancey's argument appears in a book written for Christian readers. His argument may convince—or rather reinforce—his audience's conviction that there is something valuable and worthwhile in the Christian church. But it is easy to imagine how his simple argument would have to evolve into an extended argument when it is presented to a broader audience; for those skeptical of his point of view (atheists, agnostics, adherents of non-Christian religions) are unlikely to accept his premises without debate. They are, for example, likely to need some evidence before they are willing to accept the claim that it was only Christianity that brought an end to slavery or that Christianity made women's suffrage possible.

In turning Yancey's simple argument into an extended argument, someone who advocates his views might back the claim that Christianity brought an end to slavery by providing evidence that shows that the abolitionists who succeeded in eliminating slavery were motivated by their commitment to Christian religious beliefs. It is in this way that a simple argument naturally evolves into an extended argument.

In analyzing such an argument (in dressing it for evaluation) we need to recognize (a) a principal argument that establishes the arguer's main conclusion, and (b) the various sub-arguments that are used to back the premises of the principal argument. In each case, we will need to identify the premises and conclusion of the arguments involved. In many cases, we will have to go even further, for the sub-arguments backing the premises of the principal argument are themselves extended arguments which have premises backed by further arguments.

> A simple argument is an argument that has one conclusion supported by one or more premises. An extended argument is an argument that has a main conclusion supported by premises, some of which are conclusions of subsidiary arguments.

1. Dentists, medical researchers, and health activists have debated the risks of "silver" amalgam fillings. The principal ingredient in these fillings is mercury, which is toxic to human beings. Those opposed to amalgam fillings argue that the mercury in the fillings does not remain inert and enters the body, where it can cause serious illness and multiple side effects. Those committed to amalgam fillings (including professional dentistry associations) have argued that there is no convincing evidence to back these claims. Identify and analyze the argument put forward in the following excerpt from the website of the American Dental Association, www.ada.org/news/881.aspx, (accessed 29 July 2009). How would one go about turning it into an extended argument?

    ### Are dental amalgams safe?
    Yes. Dental amalgam has been used in tooth restorations worldwide for more than 100 years. Studies have failed to find any link between amalgam restorations and any medical disorder. Amalgam continues to be a safe restorative material for dental patients.

2. Take any potential topic for argument and construct first a simple argument and then an extended argument that results when you back some premises of your simple argument with sub-arguments.

3. In each of the following cases, identify the argument as a simple or extended argument. In the latter case, identify the premises and conclusion in the principal argument and the sub-arguments that support its premises.

    a) The death penalty process is inherently flawed and broken, and can thus never be administered fairly, quickly, and with good faith that all the fail-safes are effectively employed. Given this, it should be abandoned in all societies that profess to be established on humane principles.

    b) The quality of political campaigns has been seriously degraded by the increase in attack advertisements because they detract voters from the real issues and focus attention on issues of personality.

    c) We should be grateful when people choose to care for ailing relatives. Not only does that choice allow the sick person to remain in more comfortable surroundings, it also alleviates the burden on hospitals, nursing homes, and an inadequate home care system.

    d) [From *The Vancouver Sun*, Opinion, "No reason to delay warnings, help line on cigarettes," 7 October 2010, www.vancouversun.com] Of all the risks we can do something about, smoking is the most clearly defined. There is no argument about the health effects of tobacco. There are no offsetting benefits, and we can easily see the needless suffering and loss of vitality caused by tobacco-related illness.

    e) [Adapted from a Letter to the Editor, *The Los Angeles Times*, November 5, 2010, www.latimes.com, accessed 5 November 2010] McDonald's spends tens of millions of dollars a year on advertising that uses toys to get kids to prefer junk food and demand it from their harried parents. What parent wants to constantly compete against that?

Most Happy Meals contain fatty meat, fatty fries, sugary drinks and white flour. That's pretty much the opposite of what kids should be eating. As the kids grow older, they almost certainly will graduate to the restaurants' bigger burgers and drinks, while graduating into overweight adolescence and obese adulthood.

Inference Indicators: Distinguishing Arguments and Non-Arguments

We have defined an argument as a conclusion and a set of statements ("premises") offered in support of it. The first step in learning how to deal with arguments "on the hoof" is learning how to recognize arguments and their components in the contexts in which they naturally occur. In doing so, it is important to remember that the claim that something is an argument must not be confused with the claim that it is a good argument. Arguments on the hoof may be strong or weak, plausible or implausible, convincing or unconvincing. We leave a further discussion of these distinctions for later chapters. In this and the next chapter, our only concern is recognizing, identifying, and dressing arguments and their components. In passing we will note that you are likely to be a more adept arguer if you learn to separate the attempt to dress an argument from the attempt to evaluate its strength.

Some people are poor reasoners because they fail to recognize arguments and their components. But some enthusiastic (or pugnacious) arguers go too far in the opposite direction, interpreting almost anything as an argument. This is a mistake. In looking for arguments and creating them, remember that many claims and remarks are not properly understood as attempts to provide evidence for some conclusion. We use communication for many purposes—to convey our feelings, to report facts, to ask questions, to propose hypotheses, to express our opinions, and so on. Arguing is only one of the ways in which we communicate. It is a pervasive practice, but the first step in learning how to analyze and assess arguments on the hoof is, learning how to distinguish arguments and non-arguments.

In deciding whether or not a set of sentences is an argument, it is important to remember that arguments, even when they are explicit, may be expressed in a variety of ways. Sometimes the conclusion comes first and is followed by premises. Sometimes the premises come first and are followed by the conclusion. At other times, some of the evidence is given first, followed by the conclusion, followed by further evidence. In many cases, the premises and conclusion are interspersed with opinions, questions, and judgements that are background or comment on the argument itself. Our first task in dressing arguments will be recognizing them and extracting their premises and conclusions in a way that makes the argument clear.

Inference indicators are words and phrases that tell us that particular statements are premises or conclusions. The words "consequently," "thus," "so," "hence," "it follows that," "therefore," and "we conclude that" are conclusion indicators. When you come across these and other words and phrases that function in a similar way, it usually means that the statement that follows them is the conclusion of an argument. Consider the following examples:

> All the senior managers here are members of the owner's family. *So* I'll have to move if I want to get promoted.
>
> A human being is constituted of both a mind and a body, and the body does not survive death; *therefore*, we cannot properly talk about personal immortality.

In cases as simple as these, we can easily identify the premises of an argument, for they are the statements that remain after we identify the conclusion.

In other cases arguments are designated by **premise indicators**. Common premise indicators include the expressions "since," "because," "for," and "the reason is." The argument in our last example can be expressed with a premise indicator rather than a conclusion indicator as follows:

> *Since* a human being is constituted of both a mind and a body, and the body does not survive death, we cannot properly talk about personal immortality.

The following simple arguments also employ premise indicators:

> Nothing can be the cause of itself, *for* in that case it would have to exist prior to itself, which is impossible.
>
> Sheila must be a member of the cycling club, *because* she was at last week's meeting and only members were admitted.

In these and cases like them, premise indicators identify the reasons offered for some conclusion. The conclusion is the statement they support. In the last case, the conclusion is "Sheila must be a member of the cycling club."

Arguments may contain both premise and conclusion indicators, but this is unusual. An argument with a premise indicator *or* a conclusion indicator is usually a clear argument. In constructing arguments, you should always use inference indicators so that other people can clearly recognize both that you are forwarding an argument and the evidence you are offering for what conclusion.

COMMON INFERENCE INDICATORS

Premise Indicators

Since	Because	For
As can be deduced from	Given that	The reasons are

Conclusion Indicators

Consequently	Thus	Therefore
So it follows that	Hence	We conclude that

EXERCISE   4B

For all of the following examples, either (a) identify all premise and conclusion indicators and the structure of the argument they inform (i.e. what premises lead to what conclusions) or (b) insert premise or conclusion indicators, and revise the sentences in any other way that clarifies the argument, the premises, and the conclusion.

1.* We have defined an argument as a unit of discourse that contains a conclusion and supporting statements or premises. Since many groups of sentences do not satisfy this definition and cannot be classified as arguments, we must begin learning about arguments in this sense by learning to differentiate between arguments and non-arguments.

2. In other cases, indicator words are used, but not to indicate premises and a conclusion. When you come across indicator words that have more than one use, you must therefore be sure that the word or phrase is functioning as a logical indicator.

3. [Clara explaining why she isn't ready to go to school] "Because there's a blizzard outside and they close Detroit schools whenever there's a blizzard."

4. Sun Tzu's famous book *The Art of War* tells us that a successful military force must act swiftly and cannot sustain a military operation for a protracted period of time. But Hitler's decision to attack Russia inevitably committed him to a long war. Because of this, he was bound to fail once he decided to attack Russia.

5. It is important that you be alert to variations from the usual indicator words, for the richness of our language makes many variations possible.

6. We have already seen that an argument is a unit of discourse consisting of a group of statements. However, genuine questions are not statements but requests for information. As such, a genuine question cannot serve as a premise or conclusion.

7. Misinterpreting someone else's thinking is a serious mistake. It's important to proceed with caution when we are trying to decide whether a particular discourse is or is not an argument.

8.* [From a travel brochure] You'll like the sun. You'll like the beach. You'll like the people. You'll like Jamaica.

9. [Adapted from "The world needs our military, but we need to shed some burdens'," Commentary, *The Globe and Mail*, www.theglobeandmail.com, accessed 30 October 2010]

   The belligerents today are often warlords, terrorists or militia groups that rarely play by anyone else's rules. Canada has a moral duty to help where help from the international community is desperately needed. Canada can no longer be a nation of traditional peacekeepers, because the world needs something else.

10. [From a Letter to the Editor, *The Globe and Mail*, 19 August 2004] A.B. implies that hunting is unethical because it is akin to killing. If this were true and killing were wrong, then we would all be walking contradictions. Finding, killing, and consuming life of all kinds is a requirement of life, human and non-human alike. Therefore, there is not much hope for those who believe unconditionally that killing is wrong.

11. [Adapted from a Letter to the Editor, *The Walrus*, April 2007] Great architecture involves sophisticated engineering and material experimentation. It must negotiate the social relationships of the day. It must perform well in its urban infrastructure. Great architecture is more than nifty aesthetics.

12. [Aristotle, *Metaphysics*, 1084a] Number must be either infinite or finite. But it cannot be infinite. An infinite number is neither odd nor even, but numbers are always odd or even.

13. [A variant of the second proof of God's existence in St Thomas Aquinas's *Summa Theologica*: sometimes called the "argument from first cause"] The second proof of God's existence is from the nature of cause and effect. In the world we find that there is an order of causes and effects. There is nothing which is the cause of itself; for then it would have to be prior to itself, which is impossible. Therefore things must be caused by prior causes. So there must be a first cause, for if there be no first cause among the prior causes, there will be no ultimate, nor any intermediate cause, for to take away the cause is to take away the effect. If there were an infinite series of causes, there would be no first cause, and neither would there be an ultimate effect, nor any intermediate causes; all of which is plainly false. Therefore it is necessary to admit a first cause, to which everyone gives the name of God.

14. [From the *New York Times*, Opinion, "In vitro fertilization," by Robin Marentz-Henig, 6 October 2010, www.nytimes.com/2010, accessed 6 October 2010] Science fiction is filled with dystopian stories in which the public blindly accepts destructive technologies. But in vitro fertilization offers a more optimistic model. As we continue to develop new ways of improving upon nature, the slope may be slippery, but that's no reason to avoid taking the first step.

3   Arguments without Indicator Words

Inference indicators are signposts that help us identify arguments. But many arguers do not use inference indicators in their arguments. They simply assume that their meaning is clear, even when this is not the case. In some specific contexts, the argumentative purpose of claims is understood in a way that makes inference indicators less important. Many editorials, political cartoons, and advertisements contain no inference indicators, though they are clear attempts to convince us that we should accept one conclusion or another.

In dealing with cases such as these, we need to be able to determine when arguments occur without premise or conclusion indicators. When you come across a group of sentences without an indicator, you can start by considering whether it appears in a context in which something is in dispute or controversial. Ask yourself whether this is a circumstance in which we would expect someone to justify their claim(s) by offering reasons in support of it. Consider the following excerpts from negative reviews of the film *What Women Want*, taken from www.rottentomatoes.com:

Shallow characters the audience cares little about, an unbelievable situation rather than a potent plot, and, for those who don't find men-in-pantyhose or poodle-poop jokes hilarious, not many funny lines.

Susannah Breslin, TNT ROUGH CUT

Women are from Venus; men are from the gutter. That's more or less the view of things at work in *What Women Want*, a sporadically funny, rigidly formulaic romantic comedy about a chauvinistic man's man named Nick Marshall (Mel Gibson) who suffers a standard-issue comedy-fantasy freak accident that gives him telepathic access to the thoughts of women. Nick may be a male chauvinist, but the film verges into misandrism. . . . In *What Women Want*, no male character ever does anything noble or generous or compassionate . . . (except of course for the ultimately-redeemed Nick of the last act), and no female character ever does anything self-serving or insensitive or underhanded.

Steven D. Greydanus, Decent Films Guide

Both of these comments forward arguments. In part we know this because they are excerpts from film reviews. Film reviews are inherently argumentative, for they function as assessments of films in which the writer provides reasons for their judgment that the film is outstanding, not worth seeing, a must see, disappointing, and so on. In the present case, we do not need to be told that both reviews conclude that the film *What Women Want* is a "rotten tomato": that is indicated on the website visually, via the splattered tomato that appears beside the review 🍅 (some other reviewers make this judgement in another visual way, with a "thumbs up" or a "thumbs down"). In the first case, three reasons are given for thinking that this is so: (a) shallow characters the audience cares little about; (b) an unbelievable situation rather than a potent plot; and (c) not many funny lines (for those who don't find men-in-pantyhose or poodle-poop jokes hilarious). In the second case, the reviewer criticizes the film makers of a simple-minded sexism against men (misandrism). In both cases we have clear arguments even though these passages do not contain premise or conclusion indicators—no "therefore," "since," or "because."

It is important to recognize argumentative contexts, for we should approach them with a critical attitude to the arguments they present. It is especially important to be critical when the arguments are not explicit, for this might easily lull us into an uncritical acceptance of the reasons and conclusions they suggest. When we consider whether we will download Mary Gordon's *Joan of Arc* to an e-reader, we need to recognize that the praise for her other books noted on a publisher's announcement is an attempt to persuade us to purchase it. In such a context, the critical reader will ask how strongly quotes from a handful of selected newspaper reviews (a handful of reviews out of possibly thousands, in a context in which reviewers often disagree radically) support the conclusion that we should buy this book.

Context is one factor that can help us decide whether a set of sentences with no inference indicators should be classified as an argument. In making this decision, other clues may be found in the wording of the sentences themselves. Consider the following paragraph from a letter on the history of South America:

The artistic motifs that characterize the ruins of ancient Aztec pyramids are very similar to those found in Egypt. And the animals and vegetation found on the eastern coasts of South America bear a striking resemblance to those of West Africa. From all appearances, there was once a large land mass connecting these continents.

These sentences do not contain indicator words. Yet the first two report observational data that appears to justify a speculative third statement—a statement that is the sort of statement that needs to be supported. This reading seems confirmed by the expression "from all appearances," which suggests that the first two sentences appear to lead to the third. In this way, the internal clues in this passage convince us that this is a case in which the author offers the first two statements as premises for the last.

Borderline Cases

The ability to detect arguments on the basis of context and internal clues is a skill that everyone has to some degree, but it is a skill that improves with practice. Your skill will improve as you spend more time looking for, detecting, and analyzing arguments. But no amount of skill will resolve all of the issues raised by borderline cases, where it is difficult to know whether something should be interpreted as an argument. In a typical case, we must decide whether a set of statements is an argument or simply an expression of opinion. This is a key decision for expressions of opinion and arguments call for different responses. In the first case we may agree or disagree with the opinion (and may construct an argument for or against it). In the second case, we need to go further and dress the argument embedded in the statements. This requires us to identify its premises and conclusions in a way that prepares the way for an evaluation that assesses the argument as strong or weak.

The following example is adapted from a letter to the *Hamilton Spectator*, written on the occasion of a strike by steel workers in the city:

> Haven't we had enough letters to the editorial page of the *Spectator* every day from cry-baby steel workers talking about how the Stelco strike is killing them? I am sure there are hundreds of pro-union letters going into the *Spectator* office, but only the anti-union ones are printed. I would not be a bit surprised if Stelco and the *Spectator* were working together to lower the morale of the steel workers who chose to strike for higher wages.

It is not easy to say whether this passage contains an argument. Certainly an opinion is expressed. But does the author offer reasons to support it?

If we want to distil an argument from the letter, we might dress it as follows:

Premise 1: We have had enough letters to the editorial page from cry-baby steel workers talking about how the Stelco strike is killing them.

Premise 2: I am sure there are hundreds of pro-union letters going into the *Spectator* office, but only the anti-union ones are printed.

Conclusion: There is reason to believe that Stelco and the *Spectator* are working together to lower the morale of steel workers.

This interpretation of the letter contains some linguistic adjustments. The final sentence in the published letter reads like a privately held suspicion. We have reworded it so that it carries the impact of a conclusion (but have tried to preserve the tentative tone of the author's comments). Given that the writer has decided to express such a controversial claim publicly, it is plausible to suppose that she wants to persuade readers that it is true on the basis of her claims about letters to the editor. For this reason, we have interpreted "I would not be a bit surprised if . . ." as the claim, "There is reason to believe that . . ."

In creating our first premise, we have put into statement form what appeared in the letter as a question, changing "Haven't we had enough letters . . . ?" to "We have had enough letters . . ." This is not an arbitrary change. It highlights a common stylistic feature shared by many ordinary language arguments. Genuine questions are not statements but requests for information. They cannot function as a premise or conclusion in an argument. But not all questions are requests. Some are implicit statements or assertions that are expressed as questions for "rhetorical" effect. They ask the person who hears or reads them to answer the question in a suggested way. We call such questions rhetorical questions. In the case at hand, the writer is not genuinely asking whether there have or have not been enough letters to the editorial page. Rather, her question is a way of asserting that there *have* been enough letters. Our revised wording clarifies this meaning.

We could have constructed a more complex representation of the chain of reasoning that seems to be contained in this letter about steel workers. In this and many other cases, one may interpret a set of sentences in more than one way. The question remains: Does the writer argue? Does she assert a claim and provide evidence for it? Do our proposed premises and conclusion capture reasoning in the letter? Is this a situation in which the author has given reasons for some conclusion? There are no definitive answers to these questions. There is no way to exactly discern the author's intentions, for she does not make them clear. On the one hand, this is a context in which an argument would be appropriate—the letter is, after all, published in the context of a debate about the steel workers' strike—but one might also hold that this is a context in which she might reasonably express an opinion instead of arguing for one. If an argument is intended, she would have done better to make this clear by using explicit or even oblique indicator words

In dealing with borderline cases, it is best to recognize the uncertainty of one's interpretation. In the present cases, we can do so by recognizing that there is no certain way to establish whether the author of the letter intended it as an argument. We might, for example, respond to the *Hamilton Spectator* letter by remarking that:

> The author of this letter suggests that the *Spectator* is acting in collusion with Stelco. She appears to believe that this is so on the grounds that . . . If this is her reasoning, then . . .

Here the expressions "She appears to believe" and "If this is her reasoning" clearly recognize our uncertainty in a way that nonetheless allows us to deal with the argumentative issues raised by the letter. Dealing with these issues in this manner is the proper way to further the discussion and debate.

In cases where we wish to analyze a possible argument but are unsure of our interpretation, we can note the uncertainty of the arguer's intention by introducing our discussion with a statement like the following:

> It is not clear whether the author intends to argue for the claim that . . . He appears to think that this claim can be justified on the grounds that . . . If this is what he intends, then it must be said that . . .

We can go on to outline the tentative argument we wish to discuss and analyze it as we would analyze other arguments. The simple fact that someone might interpret the claims in question as an argument warrants this discussion.

Whenever we attempt to identify and assess arguments, it is important to be conscious at the risk of misinterpreting someone's claims. When you construct your own arguments, aim to construct them in a way that prevents misinterpretation. In dealing with other people's claims, avoid interpretations that turn their claims into bad arguments they may not have intended. In the midst of controversy and debate, remember that the attempt to avoid misinterpretation is no reason to avoid issues raised by someone's remarks. If it is unclear what some potential arguer intends, say so, but go on and discuss whatever issues are raised by their remarks.

EXERCISE   4C

Are the following passages arguments? Borderline cases? For any possible argumentative passages, how would you identify the premises and conclusion if you were responding to it?

1.* [Excerpted from a Letter to the Editor, from The Royal Canadian Legion, Ottawa, to *The Petrolia Topic*, June 2011, www.petroliatopic.com/ArticleDisplay.aspx?e=3175744&archive=true]

Sir: As the combat mission in Afghanistan transitions into other military activities, The Royal Canadian Legion would like to extend a heartfelt thanks to those service men and women, and their families, who have served with distinction and sacrificed on behalf of Canadians during these past several years.

Their contribution to the well-being and care of another country's populace is a tremendous reflection of Canada's efforts toward maintaining global peace and we are proud of the way you have represented us.

2. [Stephen Brunt's book *Facing Ali: The Opposition Weighs In* (Alfred Knopf, New York, 2002) consists of interviews with the opponents who boxed against Muhammad Ali. On the back of the jacket cover, one finds three quotes under the heading *Praise for Facing Ali*. The following is attributed to Bert Sugar, identified as the "co-author of *Sting Like a Bee* and former editor and publisher of *Ring Magazine*."]

Just when you think that everything about Muhammad Ali and his career has been written, re-written and over written, along comes Stephen Brunt to give us a valuable new perspective to the Ali story in this extraordinary look at the parties of the second part: his opponents. *Facing Ali* has "winner" written all over it. And through it.

3.* [From a letter to *National Geographic*, November 1998] The laboratory where I am a consultant obtained a hair sample of an alleged 1,200-year-old Peruvian mummy. Our analysis revealed levels of lead, cadmium, and aluminum 5 to 13 times higher than would be acceptable in the typical patient of today. . . . consensus was that he received the contaminants from improperly glazed clay pottery.

4. [Martha Beck, in "Looking for Dr Listen-Good," *O: The Oprah Magazine*, January 2003, p. 42] You can steer clear of all these nightmare councillors by remembering Goethe's phrase "Just trust yourself, then you will know how to live." Rely on this truth at every stage of the therapeutic process. Trust yourself when your aching heart tells you it needs a compassionate witness. Trust yourself when your instincts warn you that the therapist your mother or a minister recommended isn't giving you the right advice. Trust yourself when, sitting in a relative stranger's office, you suddenly feel a frightening, exhilarating urge to tell truths you've never known until that very moment.

5.* [From *PC Gamer*, December 2002]. In Battlefield 1942, airpower is a strong weapon, . . . but it comes with high dangers. Ground-based anti-aircraft guns can chop you to pieces with flak, and enemy fighters are a constant dogfighting threat. But when you land your payloads, it's a devastating blow to the enemy.

6. [From the same article] American, British, Russian, German, and Japanese forces are all modelled. Each map pits two forces against one another in a re-creation of a historic battle.

7. [From an interview, "Ayaan Hirsi Ali on Islam, Catholicism and democracy," *El País* (Spain), 13 February 2008, www.eurotopics.net, accessed 25 September 2008. The former Dutch deputy Ayaan Hirsi Ali is analyzing the links between democracy and religion in an interview with Jose Maria Marti] As a group of principles, Islam is very consistent, very coherent, very simple and not at all compatible with liberal democracy. The principles of liberal democracy consider human life an end in itself, whereas Islam says that a satisfactory life can only be obtained by submitting oneself to the will of God . . . Catholicism isn't compatible with democracy either, but Christian societies have established a separation between Church and State. As a result, this religion does not have the power to punish those who fail to respect its principles.

8. [From a letter to the *National Post*, 10 December 2007] No amount of studies will change the fact that parallel private health care systems are splendidly efficient. One need look no further than the systems in place in Sweden, Switzerland, and Japan. All these countries deliver timely health care, with comparable or better outcomes than we have in Canada, and at a lower cost.

4   Arguments and Explanations

Attempting to distinguish arguments from non-arguments can sometimes be confusing when the words that can be used to indicate premises and conclusions are used in other ways. The "since" in the sentence "Since you arrived on the scene, my life has been nothing but trouble" is not a premise indicator but rather used to indicate the passage of time. The "for" in the sentence "I work for IBM" is not a premise indicator, and "thus" does not signal a conclusion in "You insert the CD in the CD-ROM drive thus."

In such cases, it is obvious that we do not have an argument. In other cases, this is less clear, especially where indicators like "so," "since," "therefore," and "because" are used in *explanations*: attempts to provide the reasons why something is the way it is. To understand how indicator words function within explanations—and to appreciate the difference between arguments and explanations—we need to separate two different meanings that can characterize our talk of "reasons." When we talk of "reasons" in the context of arguments, we mean "reasons for believing." It is in this sense that premises are reasons for believing some conclusion. In contrast, the word "reasons" means "causes" when we are discussing explanations. In this context, the *reason* something happened is the *cause* that brought it about.

Hugh Rawson begins a book on folk etymology (*Devious Derivations*, Castle Books, 2002, p. 1) with the remark that: "One of the most basic of all human traits is the urge to find reasons for why things are as they are. Ancient peoples heard thunder and created gods of thunder. They witnessed the change of seasons, and devised stories to explain the coming of winter and the miraculous rebirth of spring. The tendency is universal, appearing in every aspect of human thought and endeavor." Here the reasons alluded to are those things that bring about—i.e. cause—thunder, the seasons, and everything else that humans aspire to explain.

The kinds of contemporary issues we typically want to explain might include catastrophic weather patterns; the fall of the Greek, Irish, and Portuguese economies; the reasons that some people manage to live so long; mad cow disease; and how bird flu moved from birds to humans. In explaining such phenomena, we often use indicator words in their causal sense. We say that global warming is intensifying *since* we burn too much fossil fuel; that Aunt Sally lived so long *because* she didn't drink or smoke or engage in arguments; that the virus that causes bird flu is destroyed by cooking, *so* we cook chicken and eggs thoroughly.

In deciding whether indicator words are being used to indicate an explanation rather than an argument, you must consider the status of the claim that is backed by the "reasons" given. If "X, therefore Y" is an argument, then it is Y (the conclusion) that is in dispute. If it is an explanation, then the issue in dispute is whether X caused Y. In an explanation, we know what happened. What we are trying to establish are the reasons (causes) for it. In an argument, we know the reasons (premises). What we are trying to establish is a conclusion that is in doubt.

In the statement that "The house burnt down because they were smoking in bed," the indicator word "because" is used to indicate an explanation, not an argument. It would be an obvious mistake to interpret it as the argument:

Premise: They were smoking in bed.
Conclusion: Their house burnt down.

Something similar can be said of the following remarks in which an expert witness explains to a court what happened in an accident:

> The minivan was carrying a load in excess of the maximum recommended and was hauling a trailer that had been improperly attached to the vehicle. Consequently, when the driver veered suddenly to the left—trying to avoid a stalled truck—he lost control of the vehicle and crashed into the oncoming vehicle.

These remarks give the reasons why (according to the expert) the accident occurred. No one doubts that the crash occurred, so it is not a matter of dispute.

It goes without saying that the expert's explanation in this case might be debated. It probably will be if it is testimony in a trial that accuses the minivan driver of breaking the law. In such a context, an explanation may generate an argument. But this does not change the fact that it is not an argument. It would be a mistake to interpret it as one because it contains a word ("consequently") that is frequently used as a conclusion indicator.

In most cases, you can distinguish arguments and explanations by putting them into the general scheme "X, therefore Y" (or "Y because X") and asking whether they are an attempt to explain the cause of Y or an attempt to argue for Y. If Y (the conclusion) is in dispute, the sentences are an argument. If the question whether X (the set of reasons) caused Y is in dispute, they form an explanation. In the case of an explanation, Y must be a present or past fact or event. If it is a prediction, an evaluation, a recommendation or a classification, then the passage is an argument.

Arguments within Explanations

Explanations complicate our attempts to identify and dress arguments, because they use indicator words in a different way than arguments. Still more complex cases arise in situations in which explanations contain arguments because they outline a chain of reasoning, or because arguments themselves may act as causes (causing people to believe and do the things they do). This means that there will be times when an explanation incorporates an argument that we will, in the process of recognizing and dressing arguments, need to recognize and analyze.

Consider the following comment from a business article in the *New York Times* entitled "Shares fall on lower oil and commodities prices" (12 April 2011). It appeared in the wake of a major tsunami that severely damaged the Japanese nuclear reactor in Fukushima.

> Analysts cited several reasons for Tuesday's decline in the oil and commodities markets, including expectations of lower demand in Japan as that economy slows in the aftermath of the earthquake, the tsunami and the nuclear crisis.

In this case, the word "reasons" in the first sentence indicates an explanation. But this is a situation in which the explanation suggests that a particular argument—one implicitly attributed to investors—has led to the decline in the oil and commodity markets. We might summarize this extended argument as follows.

> **Premise:** The Japanese economy will slow in the aftermath of the recent earthquake, tsunami, and the nuclear crisis.
> **Conclusion 1:** This will mean less demand for oil and commodities.
> **Conclusion 2:** This is not a time to invest in these markets.

The passage we have quoted alludes to other arguments that have influenced investors, but this is the only one that it makes explicit. In doing so, the commentator provides an explanation which incorporates an argument that can be isolated, identified, and discussed.

Another example can illustrate the difference between arguments that do and do not contain arguments. In a history lesson, someone might forward the hypothesis that "Germany lost World War II because Hitler turned his attention to Russia when he had England at his mercy." Some would criticize this as a simplistic explanation of Germany's turn of fortune. The important point is that this is a paradigm instance of an explanation which is not an argument. The statement that Germany lost the war is not a matter of dispute. The speaker offers a controversial explanation why it happened but he has not attempted to provide evidence to back it. This makes this a case where "because" indicates an explanation *rather* than an argument.

We may, however, easily imagine someone challenging the proposed explanation of Germany's defeat. Let us suppose that the initial speaker answers such a challenge as follows:

> Sun Tzu's famous book *The Art of War* says that a successful military campaign must move swiftly. No army can sustain a war for a protracted period of time. Hitler ignored this. His decision to attack Russia committed him to a long and protracted war. Because of this, he failed.

In this remark, our interlocutor offers a more detailed *explanation* of the reasons that led to Hitler's fall. But this is now a case in which his explanation incorporates an argument. For it indicates a chain of reasoning that should, if it is correct, cause one to believe that Hitler was bound to lose the war when he decided to turn his attention to Russia. We can dress this chain of reasoning as follows:

> **Premise 1:** Sun Tzu's famous book *The Art of War* tells us that a successful military campaign must move swiftly—no army can sustain a military operation for a protracted period of time.
> **Premise 2:** Hitler's decision to attack Russia ignored this wisdom, committing him to a protracted war.
> **Conclusion:** Once Hitler decided to attack Russia, he was bound to fail.

Once we recognize and dress the argument incorporated in the explanation we have cited, it should prompt a variety of questions. Does Sun Tzu say what our speaker claims? Is the proposed principle of military success debatable? Are there counterexamples? Did the decision to attack Russia inevitably mean a long war? Were there other factors that extended it? It is in this way that recognizing and dressing the argument is a first step toward a rational scrutiny of the issues that it raises.

An argument is a set of reasons forwarded as premises for a conclusion. Most explanations present reasons in a different sense—i.e. reasons that are the purported cause of some event or circumstances. That said, there are times when an explanation of the cause of something incorporates an argument. Typically it will do so by providing a chain of reasoning within the explanation, or by suggesting an argument as the reason for some belief or behaviour. In identifying and dressing arguments, and in distinguishing between arguments and non-arguments, this means that we need to carefully distinguish between explanations that do and do not incorporate an argument.

EXERCISE   4D

Identify any argument (or explanation) indicators in the following passages. Put the reasoning in each case into "X, therefore Y" (or "Y because X") form and discuss whether it is an explanation and/or an argument. In the case of arguments, identify the premises and conclusion.

  a) The company lost a lot of money last year, so we are not getting a wage increase this year.

  b)* Drugs should be legal because the attempt to ban them creates more problems than it solves.

  c) The debt crisis in Greece is no mystery. Various studies, including one by the Federation of Greek Industries, have estimated that the government loses as much as $30 billion a year to tax evasion.

  d) Everybody inside and outside Afghanistan is aware of the high illiteracy rate, particularly within the Afghan police. Moreover, this fact about a high illiteracy rate has been known for years. In particular it is known for years among the Afghan ministers in charge! How can this not be seen as an internal Afghan problem which it should be a top priority to address?

  e) [Adapted from a Letter to the Editor, *Times Literary Supplement*, 17 January 2003] Galileo was faced with the choice of whether to recant the Copernican theory or face almost certain death by torture at the hands of the Inquisition. He chose the disgrace of recanting, rather than an honourable death as a martyr to science, because his work was not complete. He was subsequently able to develop, among other things, a physics involving concepts of constant velocity and acceleration that were crucial to Newton's development of the laws of motion.

  f) [From a Letter to the Editor, *Skeptic* magazine, Vol. 4, 2006, p. 13] Many accident reports include claims like "I looked right there and never saw them". . . . Motorcyclists and bicyclists are often the victims in such cases. One explanation is that car drivers expect other cars but not bikes, so even if they look right at the bike, they sometimes might not see it.

  g) [From About.com, http://autism.about.com, accessed 12 January 2011] Do vaccines cause autism? Two theories link autism and vaccines. The first theory suggests that the MMR (Mumps-Measles-Rubella) vaccine may cause intestinal problems leading to the development of autism. The second theory suggests that a mercury-based preservative called thimerosal, used in some vaccines, could be connected to autism. The medical community has soundly refuted these theories, but a very passionate group of parents and researchers continues to disagree, based on anecdotal evidence.

h)* [From Peter King's web site http://users.ox.ac.uk/~worc0337/note.html, accessed 19 December 2002] The smug and offensive (and ignorant) tone of this [comment from another web site] gets up my nose, and is a sure-fire way of ensuring that I don't include a link to the site in question.

i) [From *Life Extension* magazine, December 2002, p. 32] the fact is that millions of women all over the world don't need Premarin because they don't get the [menopause] symptoms Western women get. By now most people have heard that the Japanese have no word for "hot flash." But did you know that the Mayan and Navajo indigenous peoples don't either? The women in these cultures don't get "hot flashes." In fact, they get virtually no menopausal symptoms at all. And it's not because they have strange rituals or odd lifestyles. They simply eat differently. Sounds boring, but these women incorporate things in their diet that keep menopausal symptoms away.

5 Argument Narratives

The most obvious examples of arguments are directly conveyed to us by the words of the arguer. Most of the examples in this book are arguments of this sort. But we will end our chapter on the complications that arise in arguments on the hoof by noting that there are cases in which arguments are conveyed in a way that does not use the words and expressions of the actual arguer.

Consider the novel *Redwork*, in which Michael Bedard describes a liaison between one of his main characters, Alison, and a philosophy Ph.D. student she nicknames "Hegel." When her liaison with Hegel leads to pregnancy, "His solution to the problem was as clear, clean and clinical as a logical equation—get rid of it. Instead, she had got rid of him. She hadn't had much use for philosophy since" (p. 24). In this passage, the narrator provides a second-hand account of reasoning—what we will call an "argument narrative." We do not have the reasoning attributed to Alison expressed in her own words, but it is clear that it was her negative experience with her boyfriend that convinced her that she had no use for philosophy. We might summarize the argument as "Hegel is a philosopher who deals with human situations in the way of a philosopher (as clean and clinical as a logical equation), so philosophy is of no use to me."

Like borderline cases, the arguments implicit in argument narratives have to be treated with care, for they represent cases in which we do not have the original arguer's actual words, and it is always possible that the person who narrates the argument may not present it accurately. This is a significant disadvantage when one wants to accurately capture the details of an argument, but it is still useful to consider the arguments conveyed in narratives for they may be important topics to discuss. Consider, for example, the following CBC report of the reaction of Elizabeth May, the leader of the Green Party of Canada, after a federal leader's debate from which she was excluded (14 April 2011).

Green Party Leader Elizabeth May, excluded from Tuesday's leaders debate by the broadcast consortium, blasted the event as a "sad spectacle of a partial leaders' debate" . . . May said the list of issues left out of the debate is long, including First Nations issues, Canada's position in Libya, food policy, homelessness, energy policy, arts funding and the environment.

This is an argument narrative. It does not exactly present May's words, but it still outlines an argument for the conclusion that the debate was a "sad spectacle." It includes this conclusion and the premise that the list of issues left out of the debate is long, including First Nations issues, Canada's position in Libya, food policy, homelessness, energy policy, arts funding and the environment. We cannot be sure what words May used to convey this argument and it is always possible that the reporter has missed some nuance in her comments, but this is still a worthy argument for analysis—one which usefully highlights some of the key issues raised by the debate.

In dealing with argument narratives, it is important to recognize that we are working with someone else's summary of an argument, and that this has limitations, which we acknowledge. In particular, we need to guard against the possibility that a criticism of an argument as it is described in an argument narrative may be a straw man argument because the person reporting the argument has not done so accurately. Provided we recognize this possibility, we should be able to avoid it. We can still usefully analyze the arguments we find in argument narratives, and should bear in mind that doing so may shed light on some of the significant issues we need to explore and understand.

EXERCISE   4E

Identify the arguments reported in the following argument narratives:

a) [From "Prayful science," *Skeptic* magazine, 2006, Vol. 12, No. 4, p. 11] The issue of intercessory prayer was recently in the news again when a study reported no significant health benefits among those who received prayer . . . In 1999, the medical journal *Lancet* published a critical report that analyzed studies from around the world on the efficacy of prayer and the role of religion in medicine. The researchers found that nearly all studies lacked proper scientific controls, or their conclusions were too broad and inconsistent to be useful.

b) [From *The Expositor* newspaper, 12 April 2007, p. A7] Ontario's Liberal government asked Transport Canada Wednesday to release the latest studies on seatbelts in school buses following an accident in Brampton, Ont., that left several children injured. But an official with the federal agency said there is no need to do so, as all studies show that children are much safer in buses that are designed to protect them in the event of an accident than they would be with seatbelts holding them rigidly in place.

c)* [From *Xinhua*, 13 April 2007, http://news.xinhuanet.com/english/2007-04/13/content _5971431.htm] In the 1993 Oscar-award-winning movie *Jurassic Park* and again in the 2001 *Jurassic Park III* flick Sam Neill, portraying the character of dinosaur expert Dr Alan Grant, expounds the theory dinosaurs really never went extinct, they just evolved into birds. . . .

Once again, science fiction becomes science fact.

Now a team of scientists from North Carolina State University have extracted collagen tissue from a 68-million-year-old T. rex thigh bone and found protein that is structurally similar to chicken protein, offering further evidence of the evolutionary link between dinosaurs and birds.

d) [The following is taken from a news report titled "Opinion polls undermine trust, says Dutch minister" in *NRC Handlesblad* newspaper, 26 September 2008. Dutch home affairs minister Piet Hein Donner (Christian Democrat) was speaking at a conference on "the economics of trust"] Donner said opinion polls undermine trust in the government, parliament and official authorities. He was referring only to regular surveys that indicate confidence in politicians and the government, and mentioned a recent poll by RTL News which concluded that 70 percent of Dutch people do not have faith in the current Christian-Labour cabinet. He referred to academic studies which show that the results of voter surveys can be disputed. Answers to questions concerning people's confidence in the government depend on a variety of factors, he said. They are based on a combination of personal preferences and general sentiment at the time.

 ## Summary

Chapter 4 has dealt with more complex questions surrounding the identification and treatments of arguments. In particular, we have moved beyond the simple arguments of earlier chapters to look at extended arguments. A further complexity has been the similarity between argument and explanation, and here we have discussed the differences between these two types of discourse. We have also explored further tools for identifying arguments, like the presence of indicators words, and discussed how to proceed when such aids are absent. Finally, we have looked at argument narratives.

MAJOR EXERCISE 4M

1. Provide two examples of each of the following:
    a)* extended argument
    b) inference indicator
    c) premise indicator
    d)* rhetorical question
    e) conclusion indicator
    h) argument narrative

2. Identify the argument forwarded by each of the following editorial cartoons.

a) [An Anthony Jenkins cartoon from *The Globe and Mail*, November 2011, in preparation for the Christmas shopping season]

Illustration 4.1   "Turbulence"

b) [A comment on the BC Reform Party's opposition to photo radar]

Illustration 4.2   "All opposed to photo-radar . . . ?"

3. Explain why you are reading this book. Since this explanation will have to explain your reasoning, it will contain an implicit argument. Identify the premises and conclusion in the argument.

4. For each of the following, decide whether an argument and/or explanation is present, and explain the reasons for your decision. (Some examples may contain non-arguments that are not explanations.) Be sure to qualify your remarks appropriately when dealing with borderline cases. In the case of arguments, dress them (i.e. identify their premises and conclusions).

    a)* Religion is nothing but superstition. Historians of religion agree that it had its beginnings in magic and witchcraft. Today's religious belief is just an extension of this.

    b)* [A comment by an observer who visited the seal hunt on the east coast of Newfoundland] The first time I went out onto the ice and saw the seal hunt, it sickened me. I could not believe that a Canadian industry could involve such cruelty to animals and callous brutalization of men for profit.

    c)* The island of Antigua, located in the Caribbean, boasts secluded caves and dazzling beaches. The harbour at St John's is filled with the memories of the great British navy that once called there.

    d) [Overheard at a train station] These trains are never on time. The last time I took one, it was two hours late.

    e) [From an advertisement for Ceasefire, the Children's Defense Fund and Friends, 1995] Each year, hundreds of children accidentally shoot themselves or someone else. So if you get a gun to protect your child, what's going to protect your child from the gun?

    f) [From a Letter to the Editor, *The Globe and Mail*, 14 July 2011] One reason waitlists for orthopedic surgeons are so long is the number of inappropriate referrals from general practitioners who don't have enough specific training in orthopedic injuries.

    g)* [Donald Wildmon, an American United Methodist minister, quoted in *Time* magazine, 2 June 2003] Could somebody have a husband and a woman partner at the same time and be a Christian? . . . I doubt that seriously.

    h) [From Robert Wilson, *The Hidden Assassins*, (Harper (Re-issue) edition), 2009, pp. 86–7]

    "Why are you certain that this could not have been a gas explosion?"

    "Apart from the fact that there's been no reported leak, and we've only had to deal with two small fires, the mosque in the basement is in daily use. Gas is heavier than air and would accumulate at the lowest point. A large enough quantity of gas couldn't have accumulated with anybody noticing," he said. "Added to that, the gas would have had to collect in a big enough space before exploding. Its power would be dissipated. Our main problem would have been incendiary, rather than destruction. There would have been a massive fireball, which would have scorched the whole area. There would have been burn victims. A bomb explodes from a small, confined source. It therefore has far more concentrated destructive power. Only a very large bomb, or several smaller bombs, could have taken out those reinforced concrete supporting pillars. Most of the dead and injured we've seen so far have been hit by flying debris and glass. All the windows in the area have been blown out. It's all consistent with a bomb blast."

i)*   [Richard Stengel, *You're Too Kind: A Brief History of Flattery*, New York: Simon & Schuster, p. 14] In many ways, flattery works like a heat seeking missile, only what the missile homes in on is our vanity. And vanity, as the sages tell us, is the most universal human trait. . . . Flattery almost always hits its target because the target—you, me, everybody—rises up to meet it. We have no natural defense system against it.

j)*   [From *Time* magazine, 2 June 2003, p. 4] As a single father who, when married, held down a demanding job and fully participated in child rearing and household chores, I was offended by Pearson's fatuous attempt to mine the worn-out vein of humour about useless males. She defines a husband as "a well-meaning individual often found reading a newspaper." None of the fathers and husbands I know come anywhere close to this stereotype. I was dismayed that *Time* would publish such tired pap and think it's funny or relevant.

k)   [From an advertisement in *University Affairs*, March 2003, p. 51] UBC hires on the basis of merit and is committed to employment equity. We encourage all qualified people to apply. There is no restriction with regard to nationality or residence, and the position is open to all candidates. Offers will be made in keeping with immigration requirements associated with the Canada Research Chairs program.

l)   [From a Letter to the Editor, *The Globe and Mail*, 14 July 2011] A history with a powerful US neighbour in many ways pushed Canada to work at alternative ways of addressing conflict. This, along with the deep roots and influence of aboriginal culture—and its ethos of acceptance and enlarging the circle—had far more of a profound impact on what Canada is today than military action. For these reasons, Canadians always have been uncomfortable with the use of military force.

m)   [Hugh Rawson, in *Devious Derivations*, Castle Books: Victoria, BC, 2002, p. 2] False conclusions about the origins of words also arise . . . as a result of the conversion of Anglo-Saxon and other older English terms into modern parlance. Thus a crayfish is not a fish but a crustacean (from the Middle English crevis, crab). A helpmate may be both a help and a mate, but the word is a corruption of help meet, meaning suitable helper. . . . Hopscotch has nothing to do intrinsically with kids in kilts; scotch here is a moderately antique word for a cut, incision, or scratch, perhaps deriving from the Anglo-French escocher, to notch or nick.

By the same token, people who eat humble pie may have been humbled, but only figuratively. The name of the dish comes from umbles, meaning the liver, heart, and other edible animal innards.

n)   [From a local, Brantford, Ontario, church pamphlet, 2006] None of us on the Leadership Team, here at Brant Community Church would claim to have received an infallible picture of the future, but we do believe that forecasting and planning is part of the job that God has called us to do.

o) [A quote from "Midwifery on trial," *Quarterly Journal of Speech*, February 2003, p. 70] The difficulty I find with the judge's decision [to dismiss a charge against a midwife] . . . is that these people are completely unlicensed. They are just a group of people, some with no qualifications, whose only experience in some cases is having watched five or six people give birth. They have no comprehension of the complications that can arise in childbirth . . . we are about to embrace totally unqualified people . . . I think the judge is out of his mind.

p) [The *Expositor* newspaper, Brantford, 12 April 2007] As I drove to a school for my volunteer work this morning, I once more noticed some truly dedicated people. These men and women occupy busy street corners three times per day in all sorts of weather, while most of us look out the windows from warm rooms. Their role is to protect our children from dangers—traffic and otherwise . . . . So, a big thanks to the crossing guards. Be sure to wave as you go by (with all five digits) and when you have an opportunity, say thank you!

q) [From the Disability Discrimination Act of the United Kingdom, available online at www.parliament.the-stationery-office.co.uk/pa/ld200102/ ldbills/040/ 2002040.htm, accessed 8 January 2003] Where (a) any arrangements made by or on behalf of an employer, or (b) any physical feature of premises occupied by the employer, place the disabled person concerned at a substantial disadvantage in comparison with persons who are not disabled, it is the duty of the employer to take such steps as it is reasonable, in all the circumstances of the case, for him to have to take in order to prevent the arrangements or feature having that effect.

r)* [From a Letter to the Editor, in *National Geographic*, May 1998, which is a comment on an article on the aviator Amelia Earhart, who disappeared on a flight over the Pacific in July 1937] I was sorry to see Elinor Smith quoted, impugning Amelia's flying skills, in the otherwise excellent piece by Virginia Morell. Smith has been slinging mud at Earhart and her husband, George Putnam, for years, and I lay it down to jealousy. Amelia got her pilot's license in 1923 (not 1929 as Smith once wrote) and in 1929 was the third American woman to win a commercial license.

s) [John Beifuss, in "Timing's right for Kissinger portrait," a review of the film *Trials*, at gomemphisgo.com, "Movie reviews," www.gomemphis.com/mca/ movie_reviews/ article/ 0,1426,MCA_ 569_ 1592636,00.html, accessed 24 December 2002] At the very least, Trials serves as an overdue corrective to the still active cult of Kissinger. Even viewers who aren't convinced that the former national security adviser, Secretary of State and Nobel Peace Prize winner fits the definition of "war criminal" likely will emerge shocked that presidents still call for advice from the man who may have been responsible for such clandestine and illegal foreign policy initiatives as the 1969 US carpet bombing of Cambodia, the 1970 overthrow and murder of democratically elected Chilean president Salvador Allende and the 1972 "Christmas Bombing" of North Vietnam, which Hitchens, in an onscreen interview, describes as "a public relations mass murder from the sky." As journalist Seymour Hersh comments: "The dark side of Henry Kissinger is very, very dark."

t)   [An exchange attributed to a reporter interviewing a former Miss Alabama] Question: If you could live forever, would you and why? Answer: I would not live forever because we should not live forever because if we were supposed to live forever then we would live forever but we cannot live forever which is why I would not live forever.

u)   [A controversy connected with the Internet resource Wikipedia has been the practice of Alphascript Publishing to collect related articles from the site and publish them as stand-alone books. This has resulted in a lot of criticism. The following is an extract from an interview between a journalist of the *Guardian* newspaper and a representative of Alphascript. It can be found on Alphascript's site: www.alphascript-publishing.com, accessed 1 June 2011]

   Q: . . . do all of Alphascript's books take their content from Wikipedia?

   Alphascript: Yes, since we believe that the quality of the Wikipedia articles is so good that it is worthwhile creating books with them. Wikipedia themselves give an impulse for this. The articles published on their sites are free in every respect and without any limitations as to further use. All authors participating in texts of Wikipedia know this or should at least know it.

   The vice-versa procedure by now seems to have become "normal." For years Google has been scanning books and published them in internet.
   Of course there are also protests, but then the rights for the material concerned are still with the author or the publishing house.

v)*   [From a Letter to the Editor, *New Woman* magazine, July 1995, in support of a commitment to cover New Age issues] When I was going through a recent bout with depression, I discovered the "goddess spirituality" movement. I chose Artemis as the goddess I would seek comfort in . . . I built an altar to her in my room, burned incense, and meditated, and I found comfort in these ritualistic practices. I think this type of paganism can be an important tool for women to discover their inner strengths.

w)   [From a *New York Times* editorial, "A virus among honeybees," www.nytimes.com, visited 11 September 2007 Two other factors may also have played a role in this die-off [of honeybee populations]. One is drought, which in some areas has affected the plants that bees draw nectar and pollen from. The other—still unproved—may be the commercial trucking of bees from crop to crop for pollination, a potential source of stress. These may have made bees more vulnerable to the effects of this virus.

   In some ways, this newly reported research seems all the more important given all the speculation about what has been killing off the honeybees. These hive losses have inspired a kind of myth-making or magical thinking about their possible environmental origins. The suspected culprits include genetically modified crops and cellphones, to name only two.

x)   [From a Letter to the Editor, *National Post*, 27 November 2007] I wanted to share a recent experience that shows how draconian the Ontario Provincial Police's new approach to speeding really is. I received a ticket for driving 20 kilometres over the limit, on a straight stretch of highway outside of built-up areas in light traffic. I was not driving aggressively and I had been following other traffic at a safe distance for several kilometres. When I questioned the officer, he seemed to accept that my speed wouldn't normally be a problem, but he said he had to write the ticket because "we have a new commissioner now and he has changed the rules and he wants us to crack down on this type of speeding craziness."

Is driving 20 kilometres an hour over the limit with the flow of traffic in safe conditions really the type of "speeding craziness" we need to crack down on?

y) [What is the argument propounded in the following advertisement?]

Illustration 4.3　"It's a small world"

4. An earlier example was excerpted from the current debate over the safety of traditional dental amalgams (so called "silver fillings"). Go to the Internet and explore this debate, finding sites that discuss the safety of amalgam fillings. Extract three arguments on the issue, identifying their premises and conclusions.

For more online exercises, review questions, and quizzes related to the material in this chapter, please go to www.oupcanada.com/GoodReasoning5e

ARGUMENT DIAGRAMS

One of the most effective ways to represent arguments is by "diagramming"—by constructing diagrams that identify their premises and conclusions, and illustrate the relations between them. The present chapter introduces diagramming and how it works. The key concepts are:

▶ argument diagrams
▶ linked and convergent premises
▶ supplemented diagrams
▶ diagramming in argument construction.

We have already introduced the distinction between arguments dressed and "on the hoof." In dressing arguments, we identify their premises and conclusions and, in the case of extended arguments, the sub-arguments that support the premises that lead to their main conclusion. Up to this point we have been dressing the arguments we discuss by labelling their premises and conclusions. This is one way to dress arguments, but it is a clumsy way to present the structure of complicated arguments and does not represent different premises in a way that makes it clear when they may provide different strands of evidence for a conclusion. To provide a more precise and effective way of dressing arguments, this chapter introduces a method of diagramming that does not have these shortcomings. As you continue to practise argument analysis, you will find it a convenient way to map the structure of an argument and in doing so prepare the way for evaluation.

Argument Diagrams: Simple Arguments

Once we recognize something as an argument, we need to dress it in a way that delineates its structure. This is the first step in deciding how we should assess it. As we have already seen, the task of dressing arguments is not always easy, for arguments on the hoof are frequently confusing. A conclusion may be stated first or last, or sandwiched in between the premises. Premise and conclusion indicators may not always be used, and the same ideas can be repeated in a number of different ways. Extraneous comments, digressions, and diversions (insinuations, jokes, insults, compliments, and so on) may be interspersed with the content that really matters to the arguer's attempt to provide evidence for a conclusion.

In analyzing arguments, we call the remarks and comments that accompany but are not integral to an argument *noise*. Your first step in dressing an argument is eliminating noise. Sometimes noise exists in the form of introductory information that sets the stage or background for an argument that follows. Sometimes it consists of statements that are intended only as asides—statements that have no direct bearing on the argument but may add a flourish or a dash of humour. In discarding noise, you must be careful to ensure that you do not, at the same time, discard something that is integral to the argument.

We can discard the noise that accompanies an argument by drawing an argument "diagram" that maps and clarifies the argument's structure. Diagramming is an especially important tool when you are first learning how to understand an argument (your own or someone else's), for it shows you how to isolate the essential components and plot their relationship to each other. Even when you have developed your logical skills, diagramming will be an invaluable aid when dealing with complex arguments or with arguments presented in confusing ways, something that is common in ordinary discourse.

Having extracted noise, we proceed to diagram an argument by extracting its components. It is easiest to start with the conclusion, because it is the point of the whole argument. After we determine the conclusion, we can identify the premises by asking what evidence is given to support the conclusion. When we are constructing a diagram, we create a "legend" that designates the argument's premises as P1, P2, etc., and the conclusion as C. In an extended argument, we list the intermediary secondary conclusions as C1, C2, etc., and designate the main conclusion as MC. Once we have constructed a legend for a diagram, we use the legend symbols (P1, P2, MC, C1, etc.) to represent the argument's premises and conclusion and connect them with arrows that indicate what follows from what.

We will illustrate the fundamental principles of argument diagramming with some examples of simple arguments. The argument "Thinking clearly and logically is an important skill, so all students should study the rudiments of logic," we construct a legend as follows:

P1 =   Thinking clearly and logically is an important skill.
C =   All students should study the rudiments of logic.

Once we have this legend, we can diagram the argument as:

This diagram portrays the essential structure of our argument. It shows it to consist of one premise that leads to one conclusion. Together with our legend, the diagram shows the argument's components and their relationship. The only thing that might seem missing is the conclusion indicator "so," but this is represented by the arrow in the argument, which tells us the direction of the inference.

Many arguments can be represented by the same diagram. If we let:

P1 =   We have over 150 hotels in nearly 30 countries, and even more are on the way.
C =   Wherever you go, we're already there with a great stay in big cities, on the beach, by the airport and in the suburbs.

then our diagram represents the following argument, found in a flyer in a hotel room in the Four Points by Sheraton (hotel): "We have over 150 hotels in nearly 30 countries, and even more are on the way, so wherever you go, we're already there with a great stay in big cities, on the beach, by the airport and in the suburbs." Once we dress the hotel's argument with this diagram, we may proceed to argument evaluation and consider whether its premise is acceptable and its conclusion follows.

Consider another example. The following argument is taken from an article about one of the CEOs at RIM (Research In Motion, the makers of BlackBerry) published in *PC Magazine*, 13 April 2011:

Today the co-CEO of RIM, Mike Lazaridis, got upset and cut short a BBC interview after the reporter asked him a (fair) question about the company's issues with security in India. This comes shortly after he played Rodney Dangerfield to the New York Times, complaining about how his company doesn't get any respect . . . What's got Lazaridis so rattled?

In this case the question at the end of the passage is a rhetorical question which functions as a way of introducing a conclusion and inviting us to reflect on it. The conclusion is that Lazaridis is rattled, which is used as an opening for a discussion of the reasons this is so: reasons that have to do with RIM's position in the market and the success of their competitors. Keeping this in mind, we can diagram the argument in the passage as follows:

P1 =   Today the co-CEO of RIM, Mike Lazaridis, got upset and cut short a BBC interview after the reporter asked him a (fair) question about the company's issues with security in India.
P2 =   This comes shortly after he played Rodney Dangerfield to the New York Times, complaining about how his company doesn't get any respect.
C =   Lazaridis is rattled.

In this case our diagram shows that our commentator offers two premises for the conclusion they offer, i.e. two pieces of evidence that support the claim that Lazaridis is rattled.

EXERCISE   5A

Diagram each of the following arguments:

1.* [An argument from Aristotle's *Nichomachean Ethics*] Politics appears to be the Master Science because it determines which of the sciences should be studied in a state. . . .

2. It seems that jurors are more willing to convict for murder when the death penalty is abolished, so maintaining the death penalty makes it more likely that more murderers will roam the streets.

3. The beach is the best place to go to really relax. The sound of the surf is one of the most soothing sounds I know.

4. [From *Adbusters* magazine, March/April 2007] Al Jazeera [Television] is a breath of fresh air. . . . There are half the number of commercials, no pro-war or anti-war bias, and a fearlessness no longer seen at the other networks. And it does it all in style.

5. [Excerpted from *The Windsor Star*, "A one-term president?" by Toby Harnden, 17 September 2010, p. A8] Obama is the first black American president, an established author, multimillionaire and acclaimed figure beyond American shores. It seems unlikely that he will decide not to run in 2012.

2   Diagramming Extended Arguments

These first examples of argument diagrams dress simple arguments, but it should be readily apparent how the same diagramming can be extrapolated to apply to extended arguments. Consider a case where someone uses our first argument—"Thinking clearly and logically is an important skill, so all students should study the rudiments of argument"—as support for the further conclusion that "Courses on critical thinking should be mandatory." In this case, the corresponding diagram would be a "serial" diagram, where:

P1 = Thinking clearly and logically is an important skill.
C1 = All students should study the rudiments of logic.
MC ["Main Conclusion"] = Courses on critical thinking should be mandatory.

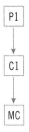

Our third argument—the argument for the conclusion that "Lazaridis is rattled"—might also be made the basis of an extended argument. We will relabel this conclusion C1. If we imagine a situation in which the value of RIM stock has declined rapidly in the last week, we can further imagine someone combining this observation with C1 to establish the new conclusion that "I should sell my RIM stocks." Using the legend that we have previously established, and allowing MC to represent our new main conclusion, this new argument can be diagrammed as:

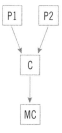

As this illustrates, the diagram of an extended argument will incorporate the diagrams of the simple arguments it contains.

A Complex Example

When diagramming arguments, especially extended ones, you will often need to make minor (and sometimes major) linguistic adjustments to clarify the argument. We have already seen that we delete inference indicators, since the arrows and symbols in our diagram perform the task of indicating premises and conclusions and the ways in which they are connected. A more difficult task is eliminating sentences that repeat ideas, as well as remarks, words, and phrases that are, for some other reason, properly classified as noise. In many cases, changes in the wording (but not the meaning) of an argument's premises and conclusion will make the structure of the argument clearer. Sometimes, we may need to change verb tenses and reformulate exclamations, rhetorical questions, and sentence fragments so that they are easily recognizable as statements that function as a premise or conclusion.

The following excerpt illustrates the kinds of linguistic changes that may be necessary in order to diagram the kinds of arguments that we may find "on the hoof." It is taken from an article entitled "$40,000-plus for eggs of clever, pretty women," by Kate Cox, posted on the *Sydney Morning Herald* web site www.smh.com.au, 15 December 2002). Consider, in particular, the argument it attributes to Shelley Smith:

> Karen Synesiou, a director of Egg Donation, Inc., said women [in Australia who are willing to donate their eggs to American couples] could earn up to $US25,000 ($44,000), although the average payment was between $US5,000 and $US10,000. American fertility specialist and former model Shelley Smith, who runs the Egg Donor Program in the US, said it was unethical for US agents to tout for business overseas. "I vehemently oppose what they do," she said. "We work frequently

with Australian couples, more and more over the years because they just can't find donors there. But we don't import Australian donors.

It's just terrible that they purposely take a woman from there and bring them here when there are dozens of couples desperately needing donors in their own country. It's a roundabout way . . . and it really exploits everybody, the girls and the couples. Everybody gets hurt."

Ms Smith said recipient couples would most likely receive less information about their donor, and Australian egg donors would be offered less than US citizens get paid for their eggs, not have adequate access to counselling services, and possibly regret it later.

The controversial nature of the egg donor issue and Smith's explicit opposition to the practice of employing Australian donors suggest that the criticisms she makes of this practice function as premises in an argument. Once we recognize that this is so, we can proceed to diagram the argument in question.

In this and other cases, we recommend that you begin your analysis by trying to identify the principal point the arguer is trying to establish. This will help you cut through the noise the argument contains. In the case of an argument the main point will be the argument's main conclusion. In this passage, Smith's main conclusion is indicated early in the excerpt, when she is attributed the claim that it is unethical for American agents to use Australian egg donors. We take the following statements:

"I vehemently oppose what they do."
"[I]t really exploits everybody, the girls and the couples. Everybody gets hurt."
"[W]e don't import Australian donors."

as another way to make this same point. As the discussion is focused on the use of Australian women donors, we will identify the main conclusion as:

MC =   It is unethical for American companies to solicit human egg donations from Australia.

Having established this main conclusion, we need to ask what evidence Smith gives in support of it. We detect a number of premises.

P1 =   It's just terrible that they purposely take a woman from Australia and bring her here when there are dozens of Australian couples desperately needing donors.

P2 =   American couples involved in such transactions will most likely receive less information about their donor.

P3 =   Australian egg donors will likely be offered less money than US citizens get paid for their eggs.

P4 =   Australian egg donors will not have adequate access to counselling services.

The last of these premises is included in Smith's suggestion that "Australian egg donors would not have adequate access to counselling services and possibly regret it later." We think that this is plausibly interpreted as a sub-argument, for it suggests that Australian women may regret their decision later *because* they will not have adequate access to counselling services. In order to capture this aspect of the reasoning we will include a sub-conclusion in our legend, which we will identify as:

C1 =   Australian egg donors who donate to American couples may regret their decision later.

This completes our legend, allowing us to diagram the argument attributed to Smith:

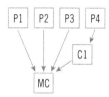

This example is more complex than our other examples, and better illustrates the complexities that arise when we "translate" ordinary language arguments into diagrams. It is especially important to observe the way we constructed a clear diagram by eliminating background information, digressions, and significant repetition of the original. In this case, the first sentence in the excerpt is noise that provides background information rather than the content of an argument: it explains the context of Smith's argument, but it is not a part of it. Hence it contains nothing that needs to be included in our diagram. The finished diagram presents a well dressed argument that provides the key information we need to evaluate the reasoning: it shows us how many lines of support there are for the main conclusion and how many of those lines are also supported.

Since diagramming is a skill that improves with practice, it is by completing exercises with examples such as this one that you will learn how to make the linguistic adjustments that will allow you to clearly represent an argument in a diagram.

DIAGRAMMING: A SHORTCUT METHOD

In most cases in this book, we will present a diagram by defining our legend in the way we have already outlined. But in dealing with arguments on a more casual basis, we can use a quicker method. Instead of writing out each premise and conclusion, we circle the relevant statements in a passage and number them consecutively. We can then sketch a diagram that shows the relationships between the numbered statements. Those sentences or words that can be considered "noise" can be crossed out or left unnumbered. The following is a simple example:

I have spent some time thinking about university education. What should a student should study when they go to university? (Thinking clearly and logically is an important skill) so (all students should study the rudiments of logic.)

In diagramming with this shortcut method, our first example might be diagrammed as follows:

This shortcut method of diagramming can help you complete practice exercises much more quickly than the long method, which requires you to write out an argument's premises and conclusion in full. Use the shortcut when it is convenient, as we will on occasion, but be aware that there are cases in which this method is unsuitable. In these cases, the premises and/or conclusion of the argument need to be identified by making revisions to the actual statements that the arguer uses (in order to eliminate "noise," to clarify the arguer's meaning, to recognize the argument's implicit components, or for some other reason).

EXERCISE 5B

1. Diagram each of the following extended arguments (use the long method or the shortcut method as you prefer):

    a)* The conservative government did the right thing when it abolished the Canadian Firearms registry in 2012, because it wasn't an efficient instrument for fighting crime, since criminals are the people least likely to register their firearms.

    b) [From a *National Geographic*, July 2011, article on species extinction "Food ark" found at: http://ngm.nationalgeographic.com/2011/07/food-ark/siebert-text] Food varieties extinction is happening all over the world—and it's happening fast. In the United States an estimated 90 percent of our historic fruit and vegetable varieties have vanished. Of the 7,000 apple varieties that were grown in the 1800s, fewer than a hundred remain. In the Philippines thousands of varieties of rice once thrived; now only up to a hundred are grown there. In China 90 per cent of the wheat varieties cultivated just a century ago have disappeared. Experts estimate that we have lost more than half of the world's food varieties over the past century. As for the 8,000 known livestock breeds, 1,600 are endangered or already extinct.

        Why is this a problem? Because if disease or future climate change decimates one of the handful of plants and animals we've come to depend on to feed our growing planet, we might desperately need one of the varieties we've let go extinct.

c) Wikipedia is no substitute for serious research in a library. The articles on Wikipedia have no guarantee of reliability because what is written may only just have been entered without anyone else checking what is said. Moreover, Wikipedia articles rarely have the depth of information available in good libraries.

d) [From *The Windsor Star*, Editorial, "All-year school: At least, let's discuss it," 8 October 2010, p. A6] Do children benefit from attending school all year long? Studies show they do, for one obvious reason: Lots of valuable facts can be lost during that two-month gap called summer vacation.

e)* [Adapted from an editorial in *The Globe and Mail* (14 July 2011) responding to the proposal of Shawn A-in-chut Atleo, the National Chief of the Assembly of First Nations, that the Indian Act be repealed and the Department of Aboriginal Affairs abolished] An entity smaller than a department might not be an improvement because the needs of First Nation communities are so great, and so urgent. The provinces have more political power in relation to Ottawa and vastly more revenues of their own than first nations communities. Thus, the breakup of the Department of Aboriginal Affairs could result in a dangerous neglect of aboriginal policy.

3 Linked and Convergent Premises

In order to make diagrams a more effective way to represent the structure of an argument, we draw them in order to distinguish between premises that are "linked" and those that are "convergent." **Linked premises** work as a unit—they support a conclusion only when they are conjoined. **Convergent premises** are separate and distinct and offer independent evidence for a conclusion.

Some simple examples can illustrate the difference between linked and convergent premises and the ways in which they can be represented in a diagram. Consider, as a first example, the Sherlock Holmes argument we discussed in Chapter 1. It can be diagrammed as follows:

P1 = Although the living room window is open, there are no footprints outside despite the softness of the ground after yesterday's rain.

P2 = The clasp on the box was not broken but opened with a key that had been hidden behind the clock.

P3 = The dog did not bark.

C =   The crime was committed by someone in the house.

The premises in this argument are convergent: each premise has a separate arrow leading to the conclusion, indicating that it provides an independent reason for that conclusion. You can see this by imagining that the only premise in the argument is either

P1 or P2 or P3. In each case, our reasoning would be weaker, but the single premise would still provide some evidence for C. The premises do not require each other to provide support for the conclusion.

The situation would be very different if Sherlock Holmes used the following reasoning to conclude that the crime could not have been committed by the butler, George:

> It is clear that the crime was committed by someone who is very strong. But George is singularly weak. So he cannot be the culprit.

In this new argument, the premises are linked: they provide support for the conclusion *only* if they are considered as a unit. The first premise—the claim that the crime was committed by someone very strong—provides *no* support for the conclusion that George "cannot be the culprit" unless we combine it with the second premise—that George is singularly weak. Similarly, the second premise provides no support for the conclusion unless it is combined with the first.

In an argument diagram, we recognize the linked nature of these two premises by placing a plus sign (+) between them, drawing an underline beneath them, and using a single arrow to join the two of them to the conclusion. Our finished diagram looks like this:

P1 =   The crime was committed by someone very strong.
P2 =   George is singularly weak.
 C =   George cannot be the culprit.

We can easily imagine Sherlock Holmes combining this argument with further reasoning. If he has already decided that "Either George or Janice is guilty of the crime," he may now conclude that Janice is the culprit, for the argument above has eliminated the only other possibility. In this case, Holmes's entire chain of reasoning may be diagrammed by extending our initial diagram:

P1 =   The crime was committed by someone very strong.
P2 =   George is singularly weak.
C1 =   George cannot be the culprit.
P3 =   Either George or Janice is guilty of the crime.
MC =   Janice is guilty of the crime.

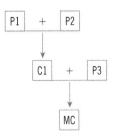

In this new diagram, C1 and P3 are linked premises for the main conclusion, for they support it only when they are combined.

In drawing diagrams, it is important to make sure that you distinguish between linked and convergent premises, for this distinction will determine how you assess particular premises. If you have difficulty deciding whether some premise P is linked to other premises, ask yourself whether P provides any support for the conclusion when it is considered independently of the other premise(s). Some premises need to be considered together, others not, and when you diagram your argument you need to group them accordingly. To some extent, this is a judgement call. You must be prepared to defend your decision to link premises by showing that one of those premises could not serve as support for the conclusion unless it is combined with at least one other premise.

Some Examples

To better acquaint you with argument diagrams, we have designed the following examples to illustrate the application of our diagramming method to particular arguments.

EXAMPLE 1

Argument

The ruins of ancient Aztec pyramids are very similar to those found in Egypt. Also, animals and vegetation found on the eastern coasts of South America bear a striking resemblance to those of West Africa. From all appearances, there was once a large land mass connecting these continents. This implies that the true ancestors of the indigenous peoples of South America are African.

Diagram

P1 = The ruins of ancient Aztec pyramids are very similar to those found in Egypt.

P2 = Animals and vegetation found on the eastern coasts of South America bear a striking resemblance to those of West Africa.

C1 = There was once a large land mass connecting these continents.

MC = The true ancestors of the indigenous peoples of South America are African.

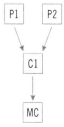

EXAMPLE 2

Argument

[In a famous incident in Homer's *Odyssey*, Odysseus and his men land on an island inhabited by one-eyed giants called "Cyclops." When Odysseus speaks to a Cyclops inside a cave, he reminds him that Zeus requires the Cyclops to treat guests well. The Cyclops responds with the following argument] "Stranger, you must be a fool, or must have come from very far afield. For you warn me to take care of my responsibilities to Zeus and we Cyclopes care nothing about Zeus and the rest of the gods. . . ."

Diagram

P1 = You warn me to take care of my responsibilities to Zeus.
P2 = We Cyclops care nothing about Zeus and the rest of the gods.
 C = You must be a fool or have come from very far afield.

EXAMPLE 3

Argument

[Adapted from a Letter to the Editor, *The Globe and Mail*, 9 October 1998] Re. Lord Elgin's Greek Marbles: Robert Fulford advocates that the sculptures should be kept at the British Museum. He's wrong. I can think of three reasons why the marbles should be returned to Greece. They are part of the cultural heritage of Greece, not Britain. They were taken from Greece with the consent of the Ottoman empire, which had no cultural claim on the antiquities. And there is no evidence that the marbles were in danger of "destruction or dispersal," as he puts it, when Lord Elgin shipped them off to Britain.

Mr Fulford should think again.

Diagram

P1 = The Elgin Marbles are part of the cultural heritage of Greece, not Britain.
P2 = The Elgin Marbles were taken from Greece with the consent of the Ottoman empire, which had no cultural claim on the antiquities.
P3 = There is no evidence that the marbles were in danger of "destruction or dispersal" (as Fulford puts it) when Lord Elgin shipped them off to Britain.
C1 = The marbles should be returned to Greece.
MC = Robert Fulford is wrong when he advocates that Lord Elgin's Greek marbles should be kept at the British Museum.

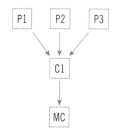

DIAGRAMMING AN ARGUMENT

1. Determine the main conclusion of the argument: the major point the arguer is trying to establish.
2. Mark the text into blocks that have a unified logical purpose, such as stating a premise or drawing a conclusion.
3. Cross out digressions and noise.
4. Express the content of each block in statement form. In doing so, try to capture the author's intended meaning.
5. Create a legend listing the premises as P1, P2, etc., the subsidiary conclusions as C1, C2, C3, etc., and the main conclusion as MC.
6. Join each independent premise to the conclusion it supports with an arrow.
7. Conjoin linked premises with a plus sign (+) and an underline, and connect them to the appropriate conclusion with an arrow.

EXERCISE   5C

Diagram the following arguments, using the bracketed words to define premises and conclusions:

a) [Thinking requires the capacity for abstraction], so [computers cannot think].

b)* [White Jaguar automobiles are unusual in this area]. [The defendant owns a white Jaguar]. And [the car from which the shots were fired has been identified by several witnesses as a white Jaguar]. Therefore, [there is reason to believe that the defendant is guilty of the drive-by shooting].

c) Because [the hospital has been in debt for over a decade] and [all debt-ridden public institutions should be closed], [this hospital should be closed]. Besides, [the technology in the operating rooms is outdated].

d)* [The sun is bigger than the Earth]. It follows that [the Earth revolves around the sun], due to the fact that [smaller objects revolve around bigger objects and not vice versa].

e) [Explanations depend on the laws of nature, either explicitly or implicitly], and [they seek to tell a story of how something came to be the way it is]. In distinction, [arguments don't depend on the laws of nature in any way], and [they don't tell a story of how something came to be]. We must conclude that [arguments are not explanations].

f)*   [It is fair that anyone who intentionally takes another's life should forfeit their own]. Hence, [capital punishment is not wrong]. In addition, [it is cheaper to execute someone than to keep them in prison for 50 years], and [society has a right to save money whenever it can]. Also, [executing murderers serves as a deterrent to others who might be contemplating similar crimes]. Thus, [society should execute murderers].

g)   [University graduates tend to occupy a higher place in society than those who do not graduate from a university]. Hence, [if university were a privilege, it would become a means of perpetuating an elitist society]. Therefore, [university should be a right and not a privilege], since [all means of perpetuating an elitist society should be avoided] because [elitist societies are unjust societies]. Moreover, [elitist societies are economically inefficient].

Supplemented Diagrams

A diagram is an efficient way to summarize the content of an argument. Its legend presents the premises and conclusion(s). The diagram provides a visual representation of the relationships that exist between them. When we want to assess an argument, constructing a diagram is a good way to begin our assessment of the reasoning it contains.

It is important to remember that, as useful as they may be, diagrams do not, in themselves, provide all the information we need to assess any argument. We have already noted that there is more to an argument than premises and conclusions. Arguments are situated in a context of communication that includes arguers, audiences, and opponents. A careful analysis of an argument must frequently discuss these parties. In order to prepare the way for this discussion, we may, in drawing the diagram for an argument, decide to identify one or more of them. In discussing the strength of the argument, this information may provide the basis for a discussion of the arguers (which may address their credibility or our past experience in dealing with their arguments, etc.), the audiences for whom the argument is constructed (which may explain aspects of the argument that might otherwise make little sense), or the opponents (for we may need to assess the extent to which the arguers have adequately dealt with objections to their views).

A *supplemented* diagram is a diagram of an argument to which has been added information about the arguer, the audience to which the argument is directed, or those who oppose this point of view. A *fully supplemented* argument contains information on all three. The following advertisement for Scotiabank illustrates the construction of a fully supplemented diagram. It appeared in a variety of university newspapers in an effort to promote the bank among students:

Being a student has its advantages. With Scotia's student bank account—*Student Banking Advantage*® Plan for post-secondary students, there is no monthly fee and no transaction limits.

PLUS other free benefits include:

- 2,000 SCENE®* rewards points[1] (2 free movies) and an additional 1 point for every $5 you spend on debit purchases. You may never have to pay for movies again!
- *Bank the Rest* ®—turn debit purchases into savings automatically by rounding up[2] each purchase to the next multiple of $1 or $5.
- Access to your accounts 24/7 via Scotia Online, smart phone, telephone, Interac Online, or one of Scotiabank's 3,000 ABMs.

Speak to your local branch for details.

® Registered trademarks of the Bank of Nova Scotia.
®* Registered trademark of SCENE IP LP, used under license.

[1] 1,000 SCENE points will be added to your SCENE membership account when you obtain a SCENE® *ScotiaCard*® debit card on a new Student Banking Advantage® Plan. This bonus points offer will be awarded once per customer per SCENE membership. For joint accounts, if at the time of awarding either offer, each customer has registered an eligible individual SCENE membership, points will be split equally. This offer does not apply to existing SCENE-eligible Scotiabank account holders. Additional 1,000 points will be added to your SCENE membership when you transfer your payroll or two pre-authorized debits/credits.

[2] *Bank the Rest* savings program can only be set-up on Personal *ScotiaCard* bank cards. Conditions apply.

To construct a fully supplemented diagram for this argument, we proceed by preparing a standard diagram, combining it with an account of the arguer, the audience, and the opponents. When we do so, the resulting account of the argument might look like this:

> The *arguer* is Scotiabank.
>
> The *audience* is students, for this particular advertisement speaks only to students, not to other potential customers.
>
> The *opponents* include competing banks, who are likely to argue that their banks are as student-friendly as Scotiabank, as well as those who might oppose banking in a more fundamental way. The latter may believe that there are moral reasons that show that we should not use banks and should support credit unions in their place.

> P1 = With Scotia's student bank account—Student Banking Advantage Plan for post-secondary students, there is no monthly fee and no transaction limits.
>
> P2 = Other benefits include 2,000 SCENE®* rewards points[1] (2 free movies) and an additional 1 point for every $5 you spend on debit purchases.
>
> C1 = You may never have to pay for movies again.

P3 = If you have a Scotia student bank account, *Bank the Rest* will allow you to turn debit purchases into savings automatically by rounding up[2] each purchase to the next multiple of $1 or $5.

P4 = You can access your Scotia accounts 24/7 via Scotia Online, smart phone, telephone, Interac Online, or one of Scotiabank's 3,000 ABMs.

MC = You should speak to a Scotiabank branch about Scotiabank's student account.

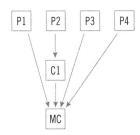

This fully supplemented diagram provides a very complete background for argument analysis. On the one hand, it clearly delineates the premises and conclusion of the argument and the pattern of support within the reasoning. At the same time, it provides us with the information on the arguer, the audience, and the opponents that may play an important role in our attempt to determine whether this is a good argument. For example, the recognition that the arguer is Scotiabank is not inconsequential, for this is a case where the arguer has an obvious vested interest, where there are financial benefits that accrue to Scotiabank if the intended audience accepts its conclusion. This is something we may need to consider in deciding whether the argument is biased in a way that reflects this vested interest.

In dealing with most arguments, we will not provide fully supplemented diagrams. Why? Because this is a time-consuming task, especially if we are analyzing a whole series of arguments. Instead of providing fully supplemented diagrams, we will normally provide diagrams that are supplemented only with whatever information about the arguer, the audience, or the opponents we believe is relevant to a critical assessment of the argument. We suggest you do the same, while keeping in mind that someone who fully understands an argument should be able to provide a fully supplemented diagram that discusses the features of argument we have outlined in this and the previous chapter. Even when you don't provide a fully supplemented argument, you should, in principle, be able to do so.

EXERCISE 5D

1. Illustrate each of the following concepts with two examples of your own:

    a)* diagram legend

    b) linked premises

c) convergent premises

d) supplemented diagrams

2. Decide whether each of the following passages is an argument. If it is an argument, provide a supplemented diagram that illustrates its structure.

a) Since everyone has a right to free access to the best health care and few could afford the high costs of private health care, it would be wrong to move to a predominantly private system, and hence the government has an obligation to fund all health care programs.

b) Not only does having an on-line presence give academics exposure to new audiences, it is also fundamental to their role as educators. How can academics be relevant to students if they are not engaged with the most powerful research medium ever? Students use social media, and if teachers want to understand their students, they must understand social media. And the only way to do that is to use it.

c) [Richard Stengel, in *You're Too Kind: A Brief History of Flattery*, Simon & Schuster, 2000, p. 234] Compliments, favours, and self-enhancement aren't good bets when ingratiating upward, because they seem manipulative and even impertinent.

d) [Hillary Clinton, quoted by David Heinzmann in the *Chicago Tribune*, 28 October 1999] "[I]n many ways, the story of Chicago blues is the story of the African-American experience," she said. "The blues found its beat with the polyrhythms of Africa; gained words and form and pain and emotion on the plantations of the South; travelled up the Mississippi; collaborated with white musicians and discovered electricity, volume and fame right here in the Windy City."

e)* [Adapted from www.openair.org, (accessed 4 June 2003)]
Urge Hillary Clinton to Save Maxwell Street, An American Treasure
Hillary Clinton has an appreciation for and understanding of the blues and played an instrumental role in ensuring that the Chess Studios have been saved and rehabbed. If preserving the Chess Studios is essential to the legacy of the blues, certainly Maxwell Street must be preserved also. Blues is, at root, a folk idiom. Its creation comes from the folk at the grassroots street level. The music got recorded at Chess, VJ, and other labels but it got created on Maxwell Street.

f) [From a university debate over the proposed North American "missile shield," which would protect North America from incoming missiles] The proposed missile defence system would be the first step toward weapons in space. So far, space has been preserved as a military-free zone. It is important—for the safety of us all—that we keep it that way. So we should reject the proposed missile shield.

g) [Robert Sullivan, "Adventure: An attempt at a definition" in *LIFE: The Greatest Adventures of All Time*, Life Books, Time Inc., 2000, pp. 8–9] We will not deny that when the Norwegian Viking Leif Eriksson sailed to Vinland in the year 1000, . . . he had quite an adventure. We will not deny that when Marco Polo traveled the Silk Road at the end of the 13th century, he had many adventures. We will not deny the adventurousness of Christopher Columbus. . . . But adventurers first? We would argue not. Most were explorers, principally, while others were variously conquistadors, missionaries and mercenaries. Among their reasons for venturing, adventure was low on the list. . . . Yes, on paper an explorer may look quite the same as an adventurer. They share several traits—boldness, stoicism, strength. But the reason for the enterprise is fundamentally different, and an adventurer is, therefore, a very different beast.

h)* [From *Time* magazine, 2 June 2003, p. 23] Swing voters have always been elusive creatures, changing shape from election to election. . . . This axiom is proving true again with that most-talked-about slice of American political demography: the Soccer Mom. Since 9/11, polls suggest she has morphed into Security Mom. . . . The sea change in these women has already reshaped voting patterns. Their new attitude helps explain why the gender gap that had worked to the Democrats' advantage since Ronald Reagan was in office narrowed sharply in last year's congressional elections.

i) There are several key reasons to not use social media for marketing. First of all, it's all hype. If you explore the issue, you'll find that very few companies have successfully followed this route. Also, it doesn't generate profit. If it did, then everyone would be on the bandwagon. But the biggest reason is that social media is just too distractive. Because of this, it is easy to waste time, and wasted time means low productivity.

j) [Excerpted from a Letter to the Editor, *The Globe and Mail*, 19 August 2004] Vancouver—A.B. implies that hunting is unethical because it is akin to killing. If this were true and killing were wrong, then we would all be walking contradictions. Finding, killing, and consuming life of all kinds is a requirement of life, human and non-human alike.

Therefore, there is not much hope for those who believe unconditionally that killing is wrong and who subscribe to Kantian ethics.

5   Diagramming Your Own Arguments

Our examples have already demonstrated that diagramming is a useful tool when we need to plot the structure of someone else's argument. We will end our discussion by noting that diagramming can also be used to analyze and construct arguments of our own. How extensively you use diagrams will depend on your own inclinations. Some people find a diagrammatic representation of an argument an invaluable tool in argument construction. Others who are not inclined to visual representations may not make extensive use of them. Though you will need to decide what works for you, there are two ways in which a supplemented diagram can help you construct an argument, especially if you feel some trepidation as you approach the task before you.

First, a diagram will provide you with a precisely defined set of premises and conclusions and illustrate the way in which the premises support particular conclusions. Because the structure in a diagram is clear, using one will encourage you to plot straightforward patterns of argument with clear lines of reasoning. Second, diagramming will help you see for yourself whether the premises you provide work independently to support a conclusion or rely upon each other to provide support.

Once you sketch a diagram, turning it into a written or a spoken argument is a simple task. It requires only that you substitute premise or conclusion indicators for the arrows in the argument and make any minor adjustments that the sense of the argument requires. If there are sub-arguments, you will want to include them as separate paragraphs (or separate sections) in a written argument. The argument that results will have a clear structure because it has been built upon a structure that was clearly delineated in your diagram.

A supplemented diagram is an especially useful tool when preparing an argument, because it requires you to think about the audience for and opponents of your argument and their own beliefs and attitudes. This can help you develop an argument that takes them into account. A long extended argument should appeal to the beliefs, convictions, and concerns of the audience and should address counter-arguments that opponents to your position are likely to raise. The ability to prepare supplemented diagrams will be important to your development as a reasoner.

To illustrate this use, consider one of the most controversial contemporary debates—that of embryonic stem cell research—and consider how you might use diagramming in constructing a position in this debate. This will be an issue that recurs in examples throughout the text and will form the context for an extended argument in the final chapter. Imagine that you want to defend the position that human embryonic stem cells should *not* be used in research. You have the main conclusion, so you need to decide what central lines of support to provide for it: these will form the sub-arguments in your diagram. You also need to consider the audience and the opponents. The *audience*, we will assume, is the public, since this issue is a broadly discussed issue which is discussed in the public media. Your *opponents* would be those who do favour using embryos in research. Identifying this group helps us to focus on what their principal argument might be for that position (addressing this argument should form part of the argument you construct).

Let's take as reasons for your conclusion the following:

Premise 1:	All humans are subject to respect and dignity
	And (+)
Premise 2:	The embryos in question are human by nature.
	Furthermore,
Premise 3:	there are other means to achieve the outcomes for which embryonic stem cells are to be used.

The corresponding diagram has two linked premises and a third premise converging on the conclusion. But now you need to consider where the burden of proof lies with respect to these three premises. Premise 1 seems relatively uncontroversial in Canadian society (your target audience), so you can leave this without further support. The burden of proof lies with someone who would challenge it. But premise 2 could be deemed controversial and needs some support if only by way of clarification. Perhaps you could offer the following: P4: "Anything composed of human material is human by nature." This makes P2 a conclusion (C1) and expands your argument so that it is now extended rather than simple. Likewise, P3 needs to be supported, because this is the premise that most directly addresses the position of your opponents. They believe that the use of embryonic stem cells is essential for developing remedies of major diseases like, for example, Parkinson's disease. P3 says there are other means to achieve some positive ends. What are they? A review of the issue would indicate that a lot of people put their trust in research using *adult* stem cells. So P5: "Research in adult stem cells promises important results" would be support for P3, making that in turn C2. Now you have a more complex argument and diagramming it shows where your lines of support lie.

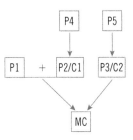

Of course, this argument could be developed further and it still has several points that would be vulnerable to counter-argument. But the point of the exercise has been to show how diagramming can serve as an aid to argument construction.

The arguments you present should be ones that can easily be diagrammed; it should not be difficult for someone who wishes to diagram it to identify your premises and conclusions in a legend. Premise and conclusion indicators will make clear which premises are tied to which conclusions, allowing an observer to easily determine how arrows connect the different components of the argument and whether premises should be linked in the diagram or left to converge on the conclusion.

EXERCISE   5E

1. Go back to exercise 1M. Pick four arguments in the exercise. In each case, dispute the argument's conclusion by providing a supplemented diagram (specifying an audience and an opponent) for a simple argument for the opposite conclusion. Present the argument in a paragraph.

2. Construct and diagram simple arguments supporting or disputing five of the following 10 claims. In each case, let the audience be the general public, and define some group of likely opponents. Present the argument you have diagrammed in a paragraph.

    a)* A college education is a privilege rather than a right.
    b)* Genetic experiments should be banned.
    c)* Capital punishment is wrong.
    d) The threat of terrorism justifies greater security measures in airports.

e) Climate change is the number one challenge facing our generation.
f) Water is a resource that should be protected from commercial exploitation.
g) Newspapers should not exploit their position by supporting causes.
h) Research using embryonic stem cells should be permitted.
i) The right to bear arms does not extend to assault weapons designed for killing humans.
j) University education should be free for all who qualify.

A Cautionary Note

Having extolled the virtues of diagramming, we offer you a few words of caution and some practical suggestions. In diagramming—and in constructing arguments—aim for simplicity. Plot the structure of your argument so that it is relatively simple and stands out as clearly as possible. Do not defeat your purpose by creating a small-scale version of a confusing city map, with myriad roads and intersections. Do not push the possibilities for diagramming to extremes. All you need is a diagram that shows clearly the role that each premise plays in the total scheme of your argumentation. Too much elaboration tends to be confusing.

Illustration 5.1 "Not a successful diagram"

PREPARING ARGUMENTS

1. Decide on your conclusion.
2. Pick your premises and diagram your argument.
3. Diagram an argument against likely objections.
4. Keep your diagrams as simple as possible.
5. Base your finished argument on your diagrams.

6 Summary

This chapter has introduced a diagramming method as a tool for constructing and evaluating simple and extended arguments. We have looked at how such diagrams can depict the relationships between components of an argument. We have introduced serial diagrams, as well as linked and convergent diagrams. All extended diagrams are composed of these basic structures. We have finally discussed supplemented diagrams, which involve adding information about the arguer, audience, and opponents.

MAJOR EXERCISE 5M

Decide whether each of the following contains an argument, and explain the reasons for your decision. Diagram any arguments you find. In at least four cases, provide a fully supplemented diagram of the argument.

a)* The room was sealed from the inside. Hence, no one could have left it. Therefore, the murderer was never in the room.

b) Few monographs are successful in introducing readers to the manifold benefits of a new theory or idea while at the same time making clear its weaknesses and limitations. The author is to be commended for what she has accomplished here.

c)* Literacy skills are essential for the development of productive citizens. This program has been teaching people basic literacy skills for over two decades. Providing continued funding for the program is clearly justified.

d) Active euthanasia, or assisting someone to die, is a practice that will come to be accepted in the future. For when people become old or debilitated by illness, they may lack the strength to end their own lives. Such individuals may try many times, unsuccessfully, to end their own lives, causing themselves and others great suffering. Therefore, the need to have assistance in ending terminal pain is becoming more evident.

e) [From an editorial in *The Globe and Mail*, 10 July 2010, commenting on the announced $925-million cost of the 2010 Winter Olympics in Vancouver.] Canada brought home a record number of gold medals . . . [held] a large international competition with few hitches, and . . . [enjoyed] a resurgence of national pride. How do you place a price on that?

f) Pakistan is at a crossroads in its history. It needs the support of Western countries now more than ever, because without them it cannot battle the Islamic extremists trying to destabilize the country from within. Abandoning a nuclear-armed Muslim nation would only bring catastrophic consequences.

g)* [From the web site of the US Food and Drug Administration Center for Devices and Radiological Health, www.fda.gov, (accessed 5 January 2003)] FDA and other organizations of the US Public Health Service (USPHS) continue to investigate the safety of amalgams used in dental restorations (fillings). However, no valid scientific evidence has ever shown that amalgams cause harm to patients with dental restorations, except in the rare case of allergy.

The safety of dental amalgams has been reviewed extensively over the past ten years, both nationally and internationally. In 1994, an international conference of health officials concluded there is no scientific evidence that dental amalgam presents a significant health hazard to the general population, although a small number of patients had mild, temporary allergic reactions. The World Health Organization (WHO), in March 1997, reached a similar conclusion. They wrote: "Dental amalgam restorations are considered safe, but components of amalgam and other dental restorative materials may, in rare instances, cause local side effects or allergic reactions. The small amount of mercury released from amalgam restorations, especially during placement and removal, has not been shown to cause any other adverse health effects." Similar conclusions were reached by the USPHS, the European Commission, the National Board of Health and Welfare in Sweden, the New Zealand Ministry of Health, Health Canada, and the province of Quebec.

h) [From St Augustine's *Confessions*, Book vii, paragraph 10] I turned my attention to the case of twins, who are generally born within a short time of each other. Whatever significance in the natural order the astrologers may attribute to this interval of time, it is too short to be appreciated by human observation and no allowance can be made for it in the charts which an astrologer has to consult in order to cast a true horoscope. His predictions, then, will not be true because he would have consulted the same charts for both Esau and Jacob and would have made the same predictions for each of them, whereas it is a fact that the same things did not happen to them both. Therefore, either he would have been wrong in his predictions or, if his forecast was correct, he would not have predicted the same future for each. And yet he would have consulted the same chart in each case. This proves that if he had foretold the truth, it would have been by luck, not by skill.

i) [The Guerrilla Girls are an American group of women who aim to fight discrimination with facts and humour. One of their campaigns is in support of women film directors, who are judged to be under-represented when it comes to recognition through awards. The following announcement accompanied a billboard depicting a female Kong dressed in a designer gown. The poster and text can be found on the web site www.guerrillagirls.com/posters/unchained. shtml, (accessed 26 February 2007)]

The 500-pound gorilla in Hollywood isn't King Kong—it's discrimination against women directors!

THE GUERRILLA GIRLS AND MOVIES BY WOMEN UNVEIL A NEW BILLBOARD AT SUNSET AND CAHUENGA IN HOLLYWOOD, FEB. 1– MARCH 5, 2006

We took Kong, gave him a sex change and a designer gown, and set her up in Hollywood, just a few blocks from where the Oscars will be awarded March 5, 2006.

Why? To reveal the sordid but True Hollywood Story about the lack of women and people of color behind the scenes in the film industry: Only 7% of 2005's 200 top-grossing films were directed by women.

Only 3 women have ever been nominated for an Oscar for Direction (Lina Wertmuller (1976), Jane Campion (1982), and Sofia Coppola (2003). None has won.

More embarrassing Hollywood statistics:

Of 2004's top-grossing films: 5% had female directors 2% had female writers 3% had female cinematographers

16% had female editors. Only 8 people of color have ever been nominated for an Oscar for Direction. None has won.

Hollywood guilds are 80 to 90% white.

Only 3% of the Oscars for acting have been won by people of color.

In the 21st century, low, low, low numbers like this HAVE to be the result of discrimination, unconscious, conscious or both. Hollywood likes to think of itself as cool, edgy and ahead of its time, but it actually lags way behind the rest of society in employing women and people of color in top positions.

There may be women heading studios these days, but what are they doing for women and people of color? Why do they keep the white male film director stereotype alive? Here's an easy way to change things: open up that boys' club and hire more women and people of color. It worked in medicine, business and law. It worked in the art world. Now it's Hollywood's turn. Rattle that cage, break those chains!

LET WOMEN DIRECT!

For more online exercises, review questions, and quizzes related to the material in this chapter, please go to www.oupcanada.com/GoodReasoning5e

HIDDEN ARGUMENT COMPONENTS

Communication frequently depends on an ability to understand what isn't said or what is said obliquely. To help understand and diagram arguments that employ communication of this sort, this chapter discusses:

- ▶ principles of communication
- ▶ abbreviated arguments
- ▶ hidden premises and conclusions
- ▶ verbal, non-verbal, and visual arguments.

The examples of argument we have examined so far are relatively straightforward combinations of premises and conclusions. Arguments are more difficult to analyze in cases that require more interpretation. This is especially the case with arguments that depend on claims or assumptions that are left unstated or obliquely indicated. In the latter case, a claim may be made by means of a picture or by pointing or by saying something that has hidden implications. Everyone is familiar with the classic example of a "loaded" question: "Have you stopped battering your wife?" One cannot answer "Yes" or "No" (as one is asked to do) without implicating oneself. We say the question is "loaded" with an implicit assumption: that you have battered your wife. The right way to answer the question is by exposing this assumption (by "unloading" it) and disposing of it.

In some ancient texts on argument, authors recommend that an arguer hide controversial components of his or her arguments so that they will not be readily apparent to an audience. In some cases, an important component of an argument is not stated because the arguer is clumsy and does not express his or her reasoning clearly. In other cases, a point may be more precisely made in other ways (by showing a photograph or video). We call the unstated components of arguments "hidden," not because they are purposely hidden in every case, but because they are not immediately apparent and you need to search for them when you are confronted with an argument. In this chapter, we introduce you to the principles and concepts that can make this search proceed more efficiently and effectively.

Speech Acts and the Principles of Communication

Attempts to communicate are called speech acts. The most obvious kind of speech act is the uttering of a statement, but such acts encompass any attempt to communicate, including attempts to do so that are not confined to spoken language. A remark in a conversation is a speech act, and so is a paragraph in a term paper, a "thumbs-up" gesture, a film, or a map that someone draws to show you where they live.

In trying to understand and interpret speech acts, it is helpful to note three principles of communication, which can guide us as we try to understand the meaning of a speech act:

Principle 1 (Intelligibility): Assume a speech act is intelligible.

Principle 2 (Context): Interpret a speech act in a way that fits the context in which it occurs.

Principle 3 (Components): Interpret a speech act in a way that is, as much as possible, in keeping with the meaning of its various elements (the words, gestures, music, etc., it explicitly contains).

Principle 1—the Principle of Intelligibility—directs us to approach speech acts with the assumption they are meaningful. This raises the question how a particular speech act should be interpreted. Principle 2—the principle of Context—directs us to interpret a speech act by considering the context in which it occurs. This context includes the other speech acts it is connected to and the broader social context in which it occurs. If a speech act is an answer to a question, then it must be understood in terms of this question. If someone approaches you in the middle of an election campaign with a button that says VOTE WRIGHT and begins telling you why Wright is remarkably well qualified to represent you in Ottawa or Washington, then it is reasonable to understand their comments as an argument for the conclusion that one should vote for Wright.

The third principle of communication—the principle of Components—tells us that we should, in interpreting a speech act, do so in a way that makes sense of its elements (the words, music, pictures and other carriers of meaning) and their relationship to each other. In the anti-smoking advertisement shown in Illustration 6.1, created by the California Department of Health Services, we can distinguish two key elements: (a) a beautiful image of a sunset—the kind of image we associate with advertisements for Marlboro cigarettes, and (b) a comment ("I miss my lung,") that alludes to the negative effects of smoking. When we interpret the image we need to resolve the tension between dissonant messages—that conveyed by Marlboro cowboy images, which promote smoking as an attractive, even beautiful, pastime; and that conveyed by the allusion to the negative effects of smoking (which may result in lung cancer). We can readily resolve this juxtaposition by understanding the advertisement as a rejection of the view of smoking inherent in Marlboro's advertising images. The message can be roughly summarized as the following argument: The attractive view of smoking presented in Marlboro advertisements should be rejected (*conclusion*), because smoking can have extremely serious health effects—such as lung cancer (*premise*).

Illustration 6.1 "I miss my lung, Bob."

Any attempt to interpret a speech act implicitly depends on our three principles of communication. When we try to understand arguments as they actually occur in our lives, the principles can be an aid as we interpret, diagram, and assess argumentative exchanges. We have already seen the role that the components of speech acts (e.g. inference indicators) and context play in determining what is an argument. The role that intelligibility plays can be illustrated by a Cox & Forkum commentary on one of the editorial cartoons featured on their website (www.coxandforkum.com, accessed 07 July 2012). In the case we are considering, the commentary explained a cartoon about Iran:

> **Iran says its nuclear drive is solely aimed at generating energy and that it does not aspire to nuclear weapons.**
> Yeah right. Here are some recent examples of Iran's "peacefulness.". . .
>
>> Iraqi insurgents are being trained in Iran to assemble weapons and Iranian-made weapons are still turning up in Iraq, the US military said Wednesday.
>> The statement comes two months after the United States said it had asked Tehran to stop the flow of weapons into Iraq.
>> Coalition forces found a cache of Iranian rockets and grenade launchers in Baghdad on Tuesday, spokesman US Maj. Gen. William Caldwell said Wednesday. . . .
>> He accused the Quds Force of supplying Iraqi insurgents with armor-piercing roadside bombs. . . .
>> He said Shiite extremists are being trained inside Iran. . . .
>
> Here is a list of articles indicating that Iran is not waging "peace" against the US in Iraq:
>
>> US troops attacked by Iranian military last year (*The Jerusalem Post*, 25 March 2007)
>> Iran's influence grows in Iraq, region (*Chicago Tribune*, 7 March 2007)
>> Iraqi extremists trained in Iran: US intelligence (AFP, 28 February 2007)
>> Military: more evidence of Iran-made explosives (*Seattle Times*, 27 February 2007)

Rumsfeld: Iraq bombs "clearly from Iran" (CNN, 10 August 2005)
       And finally MEMRI reminds us of the kind of government confronting us: "Thief's hand amputated in public in Iran; Official cleric calls for reinstating Islamic punishments."

This passage is obviously an argument—it forwards a series of reasons in defence of the conclusion that Iran is *not* a peaceful nation and aspires to nuclear weapons.

How do we know that this is the conclusion of the argument? The passage contains no logical indicators, and it begins not with the conclusion we suggest, but with a statement describing Iran's claims followed by the expression "Yeah right." How do we know to interpret these as a conclusion that Iran is not peaceful and does aspire to nuclear weapons? Because this is the only way to render the passage intelligible. It simply makes no sense to suppose that Cox & Forkum agree that Iran is only interested in the peaceful use of nuclear power in a passage where they go on to list a number of reasons for believing otherwise. In keeping with this, we interpret "Yeah right" as a sarcastic way of disagreeing with the statement that precedes it. It is this that gives us the conclusion we have noted.

THE PRINCIPLES OF COMMUNICATION

Principle 1 (Intelligibility): Assume that a speech act is intelligible.
       Principle 2 (Context): Interpret a speech act in a way that fits the context in which it occurs.
Principle 3 (Components): Interpret a speech act in a way that is in keeping with the meaning of its explicit components.

EXERCISE 6A

1. Take two of the arguments you analyzed in Exercise 3M. Explain how the principles of communication were implicitly applied in your analysis of the argument.

2. Suppose you are writing a term paper on the ancient sophist Protagoras and on his claim that "Humans are the measure of all things." According to the principles of communication, how should you go about trying to understand his claim?

3. In the 2011 Canadian federal election campaign, many people were confused by the daily reporting of opinion polls that seemed to provide conflicting and often contradictory results. Writing in *The Globe and Mail*, a columnist argued in favour of the practice of polling. Part of his argument is given in the following. Analyze this and explain how your interpretation depends on intelligibility, context, and explicit elements.

    [P]olling is regularly criticized for turning the election into nothing more than a horse race—and a confusing one at that. But survey the role of public-opinion research more closely and a greater good may emerge from the backstretch dust: Thanks to the largely unmediated power of statistics, a small sampling of the population gives the entire body politic a collective voice, in both campaigns and in government.

In the messiness of democracy, electoral polling offers a semblance of order, a numerical corrective that lets the thoughts of the people rise above the cries and whispers of party politics. "Good public-opinion research plays a grounding function in a campaign," says pollster Nik Nanos of Nanos Research. "It reveals how Canadians feel about public-policy issues and that prevents the parties from making claims that aren't founded in reality."

4. In 2007, the *National Post* reported on the gender gap in Canadian universities, suggesting that a larger proportion of females to males was not a problem. The report elicited several letters in response. The following is part of one of them (*National Post*, 5 December 2007). Analyze this argument and explain how your interpretation depends on intelligibility, context, and explicit elements.

I have always been opposed to preferential treatment. . . . I would be the first in line to applaud the university administrators who balk at implementing affirmative action for men, except for two things. . . .

So far, no one has promised to dismantle the existing institutions of preferential treatment for women that are rampant at Canadian universities, including female-only scholarships, women's centres (with no analogous men's centres), preferential hiring for female faculty and set-asides for research grants for women.

Second, if universities are not inclined to make any special efforts to attract men, the least they could do is end the things that repel them. The typical Canadian university is a hostile environment for men, who are constantly exposed to the most venomous and ill-informed nonsense emanating from women's studies departments, and who are disproportionately targeted by ever more draconian speech and behaviour codes by "equity commissars" run amok.

Hidden Conclusions

"Abbreviated" arguments are arguments that depend on hidden premises and/or conclusions that are not explicitly stated. In the process of analyzing arguments and constructing diagrams, we need to identify these hidden components so that their role in the argument can be recognized and assessed.

The principles of communication suggest that we identify an argument's hidden premises and conclusions by considering the context in which the argument occurs and by looking for clues in its explicit components. In doing so, you will want to identify all the hidden components relevant to the argument: you need to recognize the whole argument. But you must at the same time make sure that you do not add too many components and in this way misrepresent the argument. In identifying hidden components, you should work like an archaeologist rather than an architect: you do not want to build up an argument but to discover what is already there, even though it is there implicitly.

An argument is said to have a hidden conclusion when its premises propose a conclusion that is left unstated. Often, the argument contains some indication that the arguer is offering reasons for accepting the conclusion. Consider the following comment on seatbelts:

I think there is enough evidence to justify a reasonable conclusion. In the vast majority of cases that have been examined, wearing seatbelts has prevented injuries that would have resulted from automobile accidents. And these cases appear to vastly outnumber the relatively few cases in which people have avoided injury because they were not wearing seatbelts and were thrown clear of a vehicle.

The first sentence in these remarks suggests that a conclusion follows from the evidence that is given. No conclusion is explicitly stated, but the rest of the passage makes it clear that the hidden conclusion is the claim that wearing seatbelts is a good way to avoid injuries in automobile accidents. We can recognize the hidden conclusion in this abbreviated argument by diagramming the argument as follows:

P1 = In the vast majority of cases that have been examined, wearing seatbelts has prevented injuries that would have resulted from automobile accidents.

P2 = Cases where seatbelts have prevented injuries appear to vastly outnumber the relatively few cases in which people have avoided injury because they have been thrown clear of a vehicle.

HC = It is reasonable to believe that wearing a seatbelt is a good way to avoid injuries in automobile accidents.

Within legends and diagrams, we indicate hidden components by prefixing "H" to the symbols that we use to represent them. In this case, our conclusion is represented as "HC."

In supplying the hidden conclusion in this example, we have tried to capture the tone and content of the author's explicit statements. It is significant that she emphasizes that some of the accidents investigated do not confirm her point, qualifies one of her statements with the word "appear," and says that the conclusion is "reasonable to believe" rather than certain. In the midst of such qualifications, we would overstate her intentions if we expressed the conclusion as "Wearing seat belts always prevents injury." The conclusion "The wearing of seat belts should be required by law" would be equally out of place, for it introduces a new issue the writer has not touched upon, namely that of legislation. For all we know, she may not believe in legislation (she may be a libertarian opposed to government regulation) and may only advocate the voluntary use of seat belts.

Consider a different kind of example. The *National Post* reported, in April 2010, on a case in which a dispute over table manners was being reviewed by a human rights tribunal. A comment in response to this ["Now table manners are a human right?" *National Post*, 26 April 2010] provided the following argument:

Human rights tribunals offer an incentive to pursue frivolous cases which should never be in the legal system in the first place. If matters are really serious enough to warrant litigation, let plaintiffs go through the regular court system, where they will have to pay their own lawyers, court fees, and the like. Perhaps that will encourage more people to settle minor matters privately, instead of making them into a public circus at taxpayers' expense.

The logic of the passage indicates that the argument can be summarized as follows:

> P1 = Human rights tribunals offer an incentive to pursue frivolous cases which should never be in the legal system in the first place.
>
> P2 = If matters are really serious enough to warrant litigation, let plaintiffs go through the regular court system, where they will have to pay their own lawyers, court fees, and the like.
>
> P3 = Perhaps that will encourage more people to settle minor matters privately, instead of making them into a public circus at taxpayers' expense.
>
> HC1 = This is not an issue that should be heard by a human rights tribunal.

We identify this as a hidden conclusion, because the writer is clearly offering reasons against the proposed hearing. But this is a case in which our analysis can go further, for there is another implicit conclusion that is implied by the premises. The author does not explicitly say so, but the author's comments suggest that this example supports the case for not having separate human rights tribunals (and that human rights cases should be heard in the regular courts). In a diagram we can represent the full argument as follows:

> HMC = This kind of case shows that human rights tribunals should be disbanded in favour of using the regular court system.

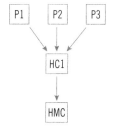

FINDING HIDDEN CONCLUSIONS

Ask yourself whether the remarks in question defend or invite some unstated conclusion. If the answer is "Yes," represent this claim as a hidden conclusion, "HC."

EXERCISE 6B

1. Each of the following comments is from a variety of sources debating the question whether Canada should increase immigration numbers. Each comment can be understood as an argument with a hidden conclusion. Diagram each argument.

a) A former Director of Federal–Provincial Relations at Immigration Canada has pointed to the fact that Canada's native labour force is declining and birth rates in most provinces are not expected to increase in the near future.

b) A recent study from the Fraser Institute suggests that immigration costs Canada up to $23.6 billion a year, since each immigrant received an average of $6051 more in benefits than they paid in taxes (according to data from the 2006 census).

2.* [From the back of a package of Novitra, a cream for treating cold sores] Clinically Proven. In a randomized double-blind, placebo-controlled study, NOVITRA is proven to shorten duration of cold sores, and goes to work immediately to reduce severity of symptoms.

3. [From an opinion piece criticizing a movement to ban incandescent light bulbs for environmental reasons (Andrew Potter, "Not the brightest bulbs in the pack," *Maclean's* magazine, 9 April 2007)] If a government believes it is entitled to micro-manage the preferences of its citizens with respect to electricity consumption, there is no reason to stop at light bulbs. Why not ban sales of 72-inch plasma screen tele-visions, or outlaw central air conditioning? Why not legislate limits on the number of hours a day I can spend surfing the Internet, or playing video games?

3 Hidden Premises

Hidden premises are unstated claims an argument depends on. Without assuming them, there is no way to move from the argument's explicit premises to the conclusion. Consider the following argument adapted from a letter to *Time* magazine, which responded to an article on reproductive technologies (surrogate motherhood, in vitro fertilization, cloning, etc.) used to help infertile couples have children of their own.

> We should stop aborting innocents, as that would eliminate the need for unnatural methods of making babies.

This is an interesting example because the argument is so condensed. Looking at the explicit claims the arguer makes, we can see that she is opposed to abortion, for she describes it as "aborting innocents," and, apparently, to technological methods of dealing with infertility, which she describes as "unnatural." We might diagram her argument as follows:

P1 = By stopping the abortion of innocent fetuses, we could eliminate the need for unnatural methods of making babies.

C = We should stop aborting fetuses.

You may sense that there is something right and something wrong with this diagram. This is the general structure of the reasoning, but there is something missing. There is a gap that must be bridged. Someone could accept P1 and not draw the proposed conclusion—because they might hold that unnatural ways of making babies are a legitimate way to satisfy some people's desire to have a baby. This tells us that our arguer must hold that unnatural methods of making babies are wrong and should, if possible, be avoided. It is this claim *together* with P1 that takes us to the conclusion.

Once we recognize the hidden premise in the argument, our diagram becomes:

P1 =   By stopping the abortion of innocent fetuses, we could eliminate the need for bizarre and unnatural methods of making babies.

HP2 = Unnatural methods of making babies are wrong and should, if possible, be avoided.

C =   We should stop aborting fetuses.

It is important to identify hidden premises when they are controversial claims. In the present case, we need to recognize HP2 because many people would argue that unnatural methods of making babies are not wrong. They might back their position by arguing that we all depend on unnatural methods of doing things (driving, flying, emailing, etc.) that are based on technological innovation. The last argument of the previous section (on human rights tribunals) also depended on a controversial claim that was assumed by the arguer. A full diagram of that argument would need to also include this assumption as a hidden premise:

HP =   A dispute over table manners is a frivolous case.

This assumption is controversial (and thus elevated to the status of hidden premise) because whether such a case is frivolous is one of the things the human rights tribunal should be deciding. At the very least, the arguer has the burden of proof to support this assumption. Including it as a hidden premise in the diagram ensures we focus on this problem when we come to analyze the argument.

In diagramming, then, our aim is to make explicit all aspects of the argument we will want to discuss when we assess the argument. This sometimes means that we identify as hidden premises assumptions that the arguer has taken for granted. We cannot treat every assumption as a hidden premise, for every argument presupposes an endless number of assumptions that are too numerous to be catalogued (in the abortion argument above, they include assumptions like "Science has made unnatural ways of making babies possible," "Making babies naturally is not wrong," and "The words used in this argument are meaningful English words").

Every argument makes many assumptions. There is no reason to enumerate them when they are not controversial assumptions, for they do not need to be discussed. They can be taken for granted because they reflect widespread agreement about the world, about language, and about what is right and wrong. In contrast, those assumptions that are speculative or debatable need to be represented as hidden premises in the diagramming of an argument, so that such assumptions can be recognized and discussed.

In some cases, the process of identifying hidden premises forces you to choose between different possibilities. In such cases, we encourage you to be cautious. Be charitable when you identify the hidden premises in an argument. Make sure any unstated claim you attribute to the arguer is both necessary to the argument and something the arguer would accept.

Consider the following response to a Canadian Senate committee's recommendation in the fall of 2002 that marijuana use be decriminalized. One supporter of the report wrote the following to *The Globe and Mail* (6 September 2002):

> Adults should have the right to decide whether or not to use it because no scientific study has ever shown marijuana to be even as harmful as alcohol.

The premise indicator "because" shows us that the second statement is intended as support for the first, and hence we have an argument. Initially, we might diagram it as:

P1 = No scientific study has ever shown marijuana to be even as harmful as alcohol.

C = Adults should have the right to decide whether or not to use marijuana.

It should be clear that there is something missing from this diagram. Indeed, the reasoning is somewhat peculiar, for why should the absence of a scientific study showing marijuana to be as harmful as alcohol count as a reason for adults having the right to use it? One possibility, which focuses on the references to a scientific study and harm, is that the arguer believes that adults have a right to decide for themselves in cases where a significant harm has not been scientifically proven. Adopting this interpretation, the hidden premise in the argument is:

HP2 = Adults have a right to decide for themselves in cases where a significant harm has not been scientifically proven.

The diagram becomes:

This interpretation is plausible, but it commits the arguer to a very general claim that may have applications beyond her or his intention. Because we are committed to as charitable an interpretation of the argument as possible, we prefer a different diagram that uncovers an assumption that commits the author to no more than he or she is likely to believe. Thus, we identify the hidden premise in the argument as:

HP2 = Adults have the right to decide whether or not to use alcohol or other substances that are less harmful.

This is a weaker claim than our first HP2. The new HP2 reports something that is debatable (one might argue that there are prescription drugs that are less harmful than alcohol, but that this does not mean that we have the right to decide whether to use them) but it is not as controversial. This HP also allows us to see how the expressed components of the argument are connected. In choosing this as our hidden premise, we are not saying that the argument is, in the final analysis, a good one—only that this hidden premise is sufficient to explain the inference it incorporates.

Our next example comes from the same dispute over the Canadian Senate report on the decriminalization of marijuana:

The criminalization of marijuana use cannot be justified. In spite of the eagerness of the police to devote many hours to the enforcement of pot legislation, the logical course of action would leave the police free to investigate crimes that actually hurt people.

If we wanted to diagram the expressed reasoning we might begin by establishing the following legend:

P1 = In spite of the eagerness of the police to devote many hours to the enforcement of pot legislation, the logical course of action would leave the police free to investigate crimes that actually hurt people.
C = The criminalization of marijuana use cannot be justified.

But this is a case in which the move from P1 to C depends on at least two assumptions that may be identified as hidden premises. The first is the assumption that the enforcement of pot legislation requiring many hours of police work is not logical. The second is the assumption that marijuana use does not hurt people. It is only by accepting these two (controversial) assumptions that one can move from P1 to the conclusion, so we need to include them as two hidden premises on which the reasoning depends.

FINDING HIDDEN PREMISES

Ask yourself whether the stated premises lead directly to the conclusion or depend on some unstated assumption. If the latter, and if this assumption needs to be assessed, present the unstated assumption as a hidden premise.

EXERCISE   6C

1. Each of the following passages can be read as a simple argument but with hidden components that should be made explicit. Diagram each argument:

    a)* God is all good. So God is benevolent.

    b) You can't rely on what that witness said. Two other witnesses contradict her.

    c) Politicians of today are no longer leaders. Democracy forces them to do whatever will get them elected.

    d) Let's go see *Harry Potter and the Deathly Hallows: Part 2*. The first Part was a fine example of filmmaking.

    e)* Sports are good for kids because they teach discipline.

    f) Father-only families are single-parent families. So we should make special efforts to help them.

    g) Strengthening the Endangered Species Act should be a legislative priority, because doing so will preserve genetic diversity on the planet.

    h) The Endangered Species Act needs to be watered down. In its current form, it severely damages the economy.

    i) Cheerleading should be a recognized sport because cheerleaders belong to squads (or teams), try out, train, compete, and hone specialized skills.

    j)* It's morally wrong to treat human beings as mere objects. So it is wrong to genetically engineer human beings.

    k) It is morally acceptable for humans to eat animal flesh. Humans have teeth designed for eating animal flesh.

    l) We have a duty to provide food for future generations. So we have a duty to develop genetically engineered crops.

    m) The environment is under enormous stress as a result of human activity, and we have the means to do something about this.

2. The following excerpts are from different Internet discussions of the question whether humans are naturally meat eaters or vegetarian. Each passage can be interpreted as an argument with hidden components. Diagram the argument in each case.

    a)* Our early ancestors from at least four million years ago were almost exclusively vegetarian.

    b) The animals most similar to us, the other primates, eat an almost exclusively vegan diet. Their main non-plant food often isn't meat, it's termites.

    c) Our closest relatives among the apes are the chimpanzees (i.e. anatomically, behaviorally, genetically, and evolutionarily), who frequently kill and eat other mammals (including other primates).

    d) Some who claim we are meat eaters point to our so-called "canine teeth," but they are "canine" in name only. Other plant-eaters (like gorillas, horses, and hippopotami) have "canines," and chimps, who are almost exclusively vegan, have massive canines compared to ours.

    e) As far back as it can be traced, clearly the archeological record indicates an omnivorous diet for humans that included meat. Our ancestry is among the hunters and gatherers from the beginning. As soon as we began domesticating food sources, they included both animals and plants.

3. Diagram the reasoning attributed to the Chinese in the following argument narrative on Chinese-American relations in the wake of "the bloody suppression of the Tiananmen Square democracy movement" [adapted from *Time* magazine, July 1995]:

Since the Tiananmen incidents, a series of disputes have arisen with the United States. The only logical conclusion the Chinese have been able to draw is that Washington is making a concerted and coordinated attack on the Chinese government.

4 Non-Verbal Elements in Argument: Flags and Demonstrations

In interpersonal argument, we frequently use gestures, facial expressions, and other non-verbal means of communication. Especially as information technology has made it easier to convey images and sounds, public arguments are often conveyed in ways that do not rely on words alone. Many of the arguments you encounter every day exploit images, music, and other non-verbal carriers of meaning. Visual arguments convey premises and conclusion with non-verbal visual images one finds in drawings, photographs, film, videos, sculpture, natural objects, and so on. In most cases, they combine visual and verbal cues in a manner that can be understood as argument.

In trying to understand and diagram some of these arguments, you must identify and interpret their non-verbal aspects. This is less difficult than it might at first appear, for these non-verbal speech acts can, like the verbal aspects of argument, be understood by applying the principles of communication we outlined at the beginning of this chapter. The intelligibility principle suggests that there is a "logic" to non-verbal attempts to communicate argumentative ideas, i.e. that these speech acts are in principle intelligible. Context and essential elements suggest that we must try to make sense of them by considering the contexts in which they occur and the explicit components (visual, musical, etc.) they employ.

In many cases, the non-verbal aspects of a speech act that constitutes an argument do not play a significant role in the reasoning it contains. The visual backdrop to an argument—the room or other surroundings in which it is presented—may not have any argumentative significance. In such cases, it is not a key component of the argument and need not be considered in argument analysis. In other cases, the background to an argument is more significant and needs to be discussed, for it has been consciously chosen specifically to facilitate the argument in one way or another.

In the simplest cases, an image or some other non-verbal aspect of a situation functions as an argument flag that draws attention to an argument. Flags play a significant role in ordinary argument because an argument cannot convince someone of its conclusion unless they take the time to consider it. Flags attract the attention that allows arguments to do their work. An arguer may, for example, announce their argument with a drum roll or piece of music, present it before a stunning natural landscape or while sitting in the high-backed chair of a judge, or convey it through an announcer with eye-catching good looks. Insofar as these non-verbal means are intended as attempts to attract our attention (and not as content in the actual argument), they are examples of argument flags.

We have already seen an example of an argument flag in the anti-Marlboro advertisement from the California Department of Health Services. It—and other advertisements like it (including Marlboro advertisements) typically use images (or on television or video, images and music) to grab our attention. In a world in which we are accosted by millions of advertisements every month—a situation that teaches us to ignore most advertisements—this is one of the things that makes artistic creativity so important to successful advertising. Once the advertiser captures our attention, they usually attempt to convince us of something, often in a manner that can be understood as argument.

A historical example of a visual flag is the 1920s illustration of a cricket we have reproduced below (Illustration 6.2). It was featured in an early advertising campaign for home insurance. This image is properly classified as a visual argument flag because it was used to attract the reader's attention to the argument that accompanied it. In doing so, it exploited the way a picture on a page may "jump out" at you. In this case, the image's ability to catch the viewer's eye was enhanced by the quality of the artwork and by the vivid colour in the original, which was published at a time when colour printing was rare and remarkable. In a case like this, the non-verbal cue that catches our eye is only a flag and not itself an element of argument, for the flag is not used to convey the argument and only functions as a means of directing us to the text that conveys the actual argument. Within that text, we are told that the painting is of a field cricket building a home, a theme that introduces the argument that we should purchase insurance, for we, like the cricket in the illustration, care about our homes.

Source: Traveler's Insurance. Used with permission.

Illustration 6.2   1920s ad campaign for home insurance

Visual and musical flags are a common element in argument, especially at a time when technology makes it easier and easier to present arguments with images, sound and multi-media. Arguers use these tools to attract our attention, especially in contexts in which there are many other arguments that vie for our attention. They take advantage of the fact that we are naturally drawn to a stunning photograph or piece of music. Some flags serve only to attract attention and are not themselves arguments or argument components. In interpreting arguments in which they function in this way, we should learn to recognize flags for what they are, but we treat them as noise rather than as an argument component. They might be compared with many headlines and striking verbal claims that are used to draw attention to an argument but cannot themselves be classified as a premise or conclusion.

Non-Verbal Demonstrations

The most basic way in which non-verbal elements function as argument components occurs when music, sounds, images, or even aromas provide evidence for some conclusion. This is one of the most primitive forms of argument, which we use when we try to prove something by literally presenting it (in a case of murder it might be a murder weapon, the body of the person who has been murdered, or visual evidence that allegedly records the murder). Demonstrations of this sort appeal to evidence in favour of a conclusion, not with words (or not only with words), but by using images, sounds and other non-verbal elements. In a situation in which one wishes to prove something about Victorian homes in San Francisco; the anatomical structure of a fly; van Gogh paintings; ancient fertility gods; the symptoms of a particular disease; urban blight in Calgary; or the rituals of a particular indigenous people, etc., images and sounds may be the most important element of your argument.

In some cases it is visual evidence which is the heart of an argument, as in the most discussed controversy in North American ornithology, which debates the question whether the Ivory-billed Woodpecker (the species which was the inspiration for that animated classic *Woody Woodpecker*) is extinct or not—a debate that revolves around a controversial video alleged to document a sighting in Louisiana. Our first example of visual evidence is the photograph of an eight-legged starfish found by a fisherman in the North Sea, reproduced in Illustration 6.3. Beside it is a normal starfish, which is smaller and has five legs. In this case, the image—and for those who have seen it, the actual specimen (now named "Stan") functions as a premise which shows that our ordinary assumptions about starfish—that they

Photo by Rex Features

Illustration 6.3   "Stan"

have five legs—are in some cases mistaken. The question how this should be accounted for—by seeing Stan as a genetic mutation or a different species—remains a matter of argument and debate.

Our second example of a visual demonstration arises in the context of the 1999 renovation of the Brantford Carnegie Library. It was an important heritage building and one of the issues raised by the renovation was whether it would be renovated in a manner that successfully preserved the look of the original. Of course, one could provide many different kinds of evidence to this effect (for example, the Heritage award that the renovation received from Brantford's heritage committee), but the most effective way to do so is by comparing photographs of the library in the early 1900s and after the renovation, as we have done with Illustration 6.4 and Illustration 6.5. To keep things simple, we have included only two photos (of the exterior, which is typically considered the most significant part of a building from a heritage point of view) but such a presentation could, of course include tens or hundreds of photographs or video evidence (as in a documentary that was done on this and other heritage buildings in Brantford). In a case such as this, we might diagram our own simple argument as follows:

P1 =   In 1999, the library looked as it does in our first photograph.
P2 =   In 1910, the library looked as it does in our second photograph.
C =   The 1999 renovation of the Brantford Carnegie Library successfully preserved the look of the original.

When we analyze a visual argument like this, we build a reference to the image into the premises or conclusion. In this way, the sentences in our legend do not replace the images the argument includes, but direct us to them and the evidence they provide.

Like any other argument, visual and other **non-verbal demonstrations** need to be evaluated by considering the acceptability of the premises and the question whether the conclusion follows. In many ways, such evidence can be misleading—images and sounds can be "doctored" (more easily all the time), can be misinterpreted, and may provide a very limited view of a circumstance or situation. One of the reasons to recognize a visual argument as an argument is precisely because that paves the way to an assessment of the reasoning proposed. In many cases, non-verbal evidence can convey shapes and features that would be difficult to describe in words. In many cases effective arguments combine non-verbal elements with words that discuss them. A sophisticated attempt to make our argument about the Carnegie library the basis of an extended argument for the conclusion that its renovation was an important project in heritage renewal would, for example, probably combine the visual demonstration available through photographs with a detailed account of the building's Beaux Arts style, the heritage significance of Andrew Carnegie libraries, and so on.

Brant Museum and Archives

Illustration 6.4 The Carnegie Library as the Brantford Public Library (circa 1910)

Leo Groarke

Illustration 6.5 The Brantford Carnegie Library renovations (2000)

Non-verbal demonstrations are common in science. The identification and classification of a species, for example, often depends on a visual identification which is

accomplished through photographs or video or a comparison with an actual item taken from a specimen collection. In other cases, microscopic or diagnostic imaging may provide images that are the heart of a conclusion. One sometimes finds more questionable uses of non-verbal demonstrations in advertising, where before-and-after photographs are used to promote a particular weight loss program, a trailer is used to advertise a new movie, and the scent sprayed from a sample bottle is used to promote a perfume. In such cases, non-verbal demonstrations are a means of supporting some conclusion the arguer hopes to convey to you—that you can lose *this* kind of weight, that this movie is *this* compelling, or that this perfume smells *this* good.

In the case of a movie, the aim is to convince you that you should see a particular film on the basis of the compelling nature of the sample presented in the trailer. We might diagram the general form of such arguments as follows:

P1 =   The trailer is compelling (funny, motion packed, poignant, etc.).
HC =   The movie is compelling (funny, motion packed, poignant, etc.).
HMC =   This is a movie you should go to see.

So construed, we can see that the main conclusion of the argument is founded on a prior inference that the trailer is an accurate sample of the movie. This is a generalization and needs, in view of this, to be evaluated according to the criteria for good generalizations we introduce in Chapter 9.

Traditionally, non-verbal demonstrations were highly regarded forms of argument, for they present evidence more directly than an argument expressed in mere words. A witness who tells you that she saw a person wearing a ring that was stolen from you may be lying, but not if she points to a person and you can identify the ring on his right hand. A photograph or video is one step removed from this kind of presentation, but it captures evidence in a relatively direct way. At a time when technology makes it relatively easy to record sounds and visual images, non-verbal demonstrations of this sort are increasingly prevalent and important. They are accompanied by challenges as well as benefits, for the technological advances that have made it easier to provide visual evidence also make it easier to manipulate it. It would be naïve to assume that they necessarily convey "things as they are."

These caveats being noted, non-verbal demonstrations are an especially compelling form of argument in many circumstances. The image in the advertisement for the province of Newfoundland and Labrador that we have reproduced in Illustration 6.6 is a case in point. Especially when you consider it together with the many other photographs posted on the website of the provincial tourism office www.newfoundlandlabrador.com), the image is a reasonable way to demonstrate some of the sights and experiences available on a trip to Newfoundland and Labrador. We might diagram the intended argument as:

P1 = If you visit Newfoundland and Labrador, you will be able to experience sights like this.

HP2 = Experiencing this is something you should pursue.

C = You should visit Newfoundland and Labrador.

Illustration 6.6 The glacier-carved freshwater fjord at Western Brooke Pond, Newfoundland and Labrador

Courtesy of Newfoundland and Labrador Tourism.

EXERCISE   6D

1. Analyze the visual demonstration in the following popular poster.

Illustration 6.7   Fast Food

2. Go to your university or college website. Go to the section for "Prospective Students." Analyze the images and statements (and music and sounds). Identify flags and demonstrations. What messages do they communicate? How do the non verbal aspects of the pages contribute to the overall attempt to attract students to your school?

3. The following photograph is a Robert Croft image of figures in a fresco on St Mary's Cathedral in Lincoln, Lincolnshire, England (available on Wikimedia). Like many medieval paintings and statues it functions as a visual argument that reinforces a key message of the church? What is the message? How might you diagram the argument the fresco proposes?

Illustration 6.8   Lincoln cathedral: sculptured relief of the sufferings of the damned on the western front

5 Symbols and Metaphors

Argument flags and non-verbal demonstrations are the most direct ways in which arguments may employ non-verbal elements. In such circumstances, these elements are understood in a straightforward, literal way. In other cases, such elements may be used in a more figurative way to convey a message that turns on the proper interpretation of the non-verbal elements.

A political cartoon that depicts a politician as a devil with horns employs non verbal elements, but it is not a demonstration. The artist is not claiming that this is how the politician actually looks. He is, rather, using his drawing as a way of saying that the politician is engaged in wrongdoing, which is the business of a devil. In this and similar cases, the non-verbal elements of arguments function as symbols that can replace words, represent some idea, or refer to someone or something. You use and interpret non-verbal symbols every day. You know that a crucifix represents Christ, that a skull represents death, that "The Star Spangled Banner" symbolizes the United

States of America, that a peace sign stands for peace, that a thumbs-up means "Okay!," and that a "swoosh" represents Nike sports equipment. Even if you don't follow the NHL, you probably recognize the blue maple leaf that stands for the Toronto Maple Leafs and the CH symbol for the Montreal Canadians.

In contexts of argument, visual symbols are often used either to state a position or to make a case for one. Consider the image below, posted on a website which asked visitors to give their "reasons why abortion rights must be protected." By now you should recognize this as a request for arguments that provide premises (reasons) for this conclusion. In response, one visitor posted the image below. The context in which this image appears makes it plausible to interpret the image as a visual argument, but what is the argument that the image forwards?

In answering this question, we can begin by recognizing that the context (in which the image functions as the answer to a question) makes the (hidden) conclusion in the argument relatively straightforward: it is the claim that we should protect a woman's right to an abortion. To understand the premises that have been conveyed in support of this conclusion, we need to interpret two elements of the image that function as visual symbols: the (red) circle with a diagonal line and the coat hanger. The first of these symbols is readily understood as a visual symbol of negation that is typically used as an injunction in signs that tell us: no smoking, no guns, no rights, no swimming, and so on. In this case, the no sign clearly qualifies the coat hanger, which has

become a symbol for "coat hanger abortions"—illegal abortions carried out by back street abortionists, often with coat hangers, when abortion was illegal. Such abortions were notorious because of their frequently disastrous consequences for the desperate women who sought them. Understanding this background, we can plausibly interpret the visual image as the following argument:

HP1 =   Coat hanger abortions have disastrous consequences for the desperate women who are forced to seek them.

C1 =   We must not allow coat hanger abortions.

HP3 =   If we do not protect a woman's right to an abortion, there will be coat hanger abortions.

HMC =   We should protect a woman's right to an abortion.

In diagramming the argument we have designated C1 as the only explicit argument component because it is what the image explicitly asserts. We have designated the other premises and the conclusion as hidden components because they are not asserted, visually or verbally. It is important to recognize HP2 as a hidden premise in the argument because it provides the unexpressed crucial link that that ties the explicit claim to the main conclusion.

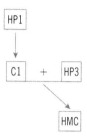

Metaphors

A fourth kind of non-verbal meaning is conveyed when arguments use non-verbal metaphors. A metaphor describes one thing as though it were another. "Jill is a block of ice" and "The world's a stage" are verbal metaphors. They make no sense if we try to understand them literally, for people are not made of ice and the world is not a theatre. We therefore understand them, in a figurative way, as claims that Jill is unfriendly and that our lives are like roles in a stage play.

Non-verbal metaphors operate in a similar way. Political cartoons are a form of political commentary that frequently uses visual metaphors to comment on matters of political significance. The Henry Payne cartoon in Illustration 6.9 (from www. henrypayne.com) is a comment on Mitt Romney in the midst of his 2011 campaign to become the Republican Presidential candidate for the 2012 American election. At the root of the message is a drawing of President Obama's health care plan ("Obama Care") as Frankenstein. This depiction, which Payne uses in a number of cartoons that address the plan, is a metaphorical way of saying that Obama Care, which has been severely criticized by Republicans, is monstrous and horrific (as was Frankenstein). In the cartoon, this visual metaphor is employed in a criticism of Romney, who played a key role instituting a similar health care program in Massachusetts while he was governor. This plan, which Payne dubs "Romney Care," is presented as a twin of Obama Care, and is depicted as another Frankenstein. The application of the same visual metaphor in both cases (and the look of surprise and uncertainty on the face of "Romney Care") suggests that Romney is denying the obvious when he claims that there is no relation between the two. We might summarize the argument the cartoon forwards as the claim that (*premise:*) Romney Care is, despite Romney's denials, similar to Obama Care; therefore (*conclusion:*) Romney is not a credible Presidential candidate for the Republican party.

Our second example of a visual metaphor is a cartoon commenting on the Canadian seal hunt by the Victoria artist, Adrian Raeside (Illustration 6.10). It shows a woman in a fur coat, which casts a shadow in which we see a crazed Atlantic fisherman

Illustration 6.9   "No. No relation"

with a wild grin who holds a bloody seal pup that he has clubbed to death. The cartoonist is not, of course, suggesting that this is the shadow that is really cast by a woman in a seal fur coat. Rather, he metaphorically suggests that the brutal killing of the seal pups used to create such a coat "casts a shadow" on the wearing of it. We can understand the cartoon as a simple argument which criticizes such fashion and those who wear such coats, who are represented by the unflattering image of the woman in the cartoon. We might summarize this argument as:

Illustration 6.10   "Seal Hunter's Shadow"

P =   Behind each seal coats lies the brutal killing of seal pups.
C =   Those who wear such coats are acting without conscience.

Our final example of a non-verbal metaphor employs sounds rather than images. It is taken from a series of radio advertisements that helped Durex Condoms become the largest condom manufacturer in the world (available on the Durex website, www. durex.com). One of the advertisements (which the company calls "Guitar") can be summarized as follows:

1.   [An enticing female voice:] "This is what sex is like with an ordinary condom."
2.   [One hears the sound of:] A pedestrian, slow march.
3.   [The female voice returns:] "This is what sex is like with a Durex Sheik condom."
4.   [One hears the sound of:] A rock and roll tune with a driving beat.
5.   [The female voice returns:] "Feel what you've been missing. Set yourself free with the condom designed for excitement. Durex Sheik condoms. For super sensitivity. So you can enjoy all of love's pleasures. Now safer sex doesn't have to feel like safe sex. Set yourself free with Durex Sheik condoms."

The crux of this advertisement is the difference between the two pieces of music it contains, the first representing ordinary condoms, the second representing Durex. In a context in which Durex is obviously promoting its condoms, we have no problem recognizing that the energy and the driving beat in the second clip, when contrasted with the boredom and lack of vigour conveyed in the first piece of music, suggests that sex with an ordinary condom is ho-hum in comparison to sex with a Durex condom and that Durex condoms can "set you free" so that you can "enjoy all of love's pleasures."

If we eliminate the repetition in the argument and isolate the reasons it provides for its conclusion, we can diagram it as follows:

P1 =   Durex Sheik condoms will provide a more exciting sex life than ordinary condoms (one that includes all of love's pleasures; one that doesn't feel like safe sex)
P2 =   Durex Sheik condoms are designed for super sensitivity.
C =   You should use Durex Sheik condoms.

When you recognize and diagram this as an argument, it you should see that it is weak. Durex is attempting to convince us that we should buy Durex Sheik condoms on the grounds that they will make our sex life more exciting. But there is no proof that they will do so. Indeed, this claim is inherently peculiar. For why should we think that a particular condom can turn a pedestrian sex life into one that we would associate with rock and roll? There are ways in which one might plausibly argue for Durex Sheik condoms (by comparing their properties to those of competing brands, by appealing to testimony, etc.), but the radio advertisement for Durex is a clear instance of a company deciding to try to sell their product by charming us with music and humour, not by engaging in a reasonable attempt at argument.

A Complex Example

Non-verbal means of communication have a strong emotional appeal. Images and music captivate us. They make us laugh and smile and can play upon our fears and frustrations, our likes and dislikes. At times, the emotional pull of non-verbal messages can be used legitimately in argument. For instance, in an attempt to convince you that you should help the homeless, photographs (or an actual tour) of a shelter may be the best way to convey to you the needs of homeless people.

But there are many circumstances in which arguments are couched in non-verbal terms because this encourages us to be emotional *rather* than critical when we relate to them. It is important to recognize the communicative role that non-verbal elements play in many arguments, because this will encourage us to properly recognize them as something that needs to be subjected to criticism and inquiry. The Durex radio advertisements are clever and witty, but we need to see them as something more than this, especially if we are considering buying condoms—i.e. if we are part of the audience to which the advertisements are directed. In that case, we should be concerned that this attempt to persuade us to buy Durex condoms rather than some other brand has little argumentative force because it fails to provide reasons.

Of course, many of the arguments we encounter are complex combinations of verbal and non-verbal elements. In cases such as this, we need to interpret the argument as a whole. Consider Mazda's popular "zoom, zoom" advertisements for the Mazda Tribute, its popular sport utility vehicle. These advertisements have been carefully crafted to include stirring music with an African beat, stunning visuals, and a verbal commentary that all lead to the inevitable conclusion that one should drive a Tribute. In diagramming and analyzing the argument, we need to recognize that these are all parts of a package and need to be interpreted together. We might begin by summarizing the advertisement for the Tribute, which unfolds as follows:

1. Music
2. [Male voice:] "What would happen if an SUV was raised by a family of sports cars?"
3. Pause with visuals (wheat blowing in the wind)
4. [A boy in a suit whispers:] "Zoom, zoom."
5. [Male voice:] "Introducing the 200-horsepower Mazda Tribute, the SUV with the soul of a sports car."
6. [One hears a driving African beat, scat singing with the sounds:] "zoom, zoom, zoom . . . heh . . . zoom, zoom, zoom . . . yah . . . zoom, zoom, zoom . . . ."

7. The music is accompanied by scenes on the open road, where a Mazda Tribute weaves its way through a pack of sports cars racing along a highway.

8. After the Tribute emerges at the front of the pack, it refuses to take a turn in the highway and races off the road into open country.

What is the message conveyed in this advertisement? Clearly, it is an attempt to sell the Mazda Tribute. But what are the reasons it offers for the conclusion that this is a car one would want to own? To understand these reasons, we need to understand both the verbal and the non-verbal elements of the advertisement. The non-verbal elements include instances of all the forms of non-verbal communication we have already noted. They might be summarized as follows:

- **Argument flags.** The vivid music and the visuals function as argument flags that capture our attention.
- **Non-verbal demonstrations.** The visuals demonstrate the principal message of the advertisement—that the Mazda Tribute combines the qualities of a sports car (the speed, the handling, etc.) with the SUV's ability to drive off-road. The qualities of the sports car are demonstrated as the Tribute weaves its way through a pack of sports cars. The off-road capability is demonstrated when it refuses to take a turn and drives off the highway into the outback.
- **Metaphor.** The "zoom, zoom" theme is Mazda's (highly successful) attempt to adopt a slogan that captures what it has called "the joy of motion." This is a theme enunciated in the words that accompany the advertisement and in the music, which is strong, fun, lively, energizing. The Tribute itself is alleged to embody all these traits.
- **Symbols.** The boy in the suit may initially seem perplexing. Why a boy? Boys don't drive automobiles. And why a boy in a suit? Boys don't wear suits. To understand this aspect of the advertisement, we need to consider the implicit symbolism. Men are the traditional market for automobile advertisements. And the professional men who can afford a Mazda Tribute wear suits. The boy in the advertisement is the boy who still exists inside the businessman—the boy who still enjoys the simple thrill of motion. It is this "inner child" who whispers the crucial "zoom, zoom" in the advertisement. He whispers because his comment is a thought inside the head of the man that he is speaking to— the man thinking about the Mazda Tribute.

When we combine these non-verbal elements with the statements made in the advertisement, we can see an argument that we can begin to diagram as follows:

P1 = The Mazda Tribute combines the driving qualities of a sports car (the speed, the handling, etc.) with the SUV's ability to handle off-road driving.

C1 = The 200-horsepower Mazda Tribute is an SUV with the soul of a sports car.

P2 = Driving the Mazda Tribute (like driving other Mazdas) is boyishly fun, thrilling, and energizing.

MC = You should purchase a Mazda Tribute.

We can develop this further by recognizing that the sub-argument from P2 to MC depends on two unstated premises that can be expressed as follows:

HP3 =   One should purchase an automobile that is fun, thrilling, and energizing.
HP4 =   The tribute is *more* fun, thrilling, and energizing than the competition.

HP3 is needed because the fun of driving a Tribute provides significant support for the conclusion that one should purchase the Tribute only if this is what really matters in an automobile (and not safety, economy, etc.). We can see why we must add HP4 to our diagram if we imagine that the Tribute is *not* more fun than its competitors, for in these circumstances, the assumption that one should buy a car that is fun and appeals to one's youthful sense of play (HP3) may lead to the conclusion not that one should purchase a Tribute but that one should purchase a competing vehicle. Our full diagram is:

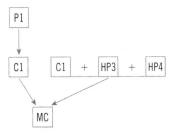

Once we have this diagram, a number of debatable aspects become apparent. Despite its emotional appeal (especially to the "boy inside the man" that Mazda is targeting), HP3 could easily be debated. HP4 is also open to debate, as is the staged visual presentation that is supposed to demonstrate the qualities claimed in P1.

But these and other concerns lie beyond the scope of our present discussion, where we want only to demonstrate that complex arguments employing non-verbal elements can be identified and diagrammed by recognizing the different forms of non-verbal meaning we have noted. Once we have identified and diagrammed the elements of such arguments, we can assess them the same ways we will assess other arguments, by asking whether their premises are plausible and their conclusions follow.

FOUR KINDS OF NON-VERBAL MEANING

There are four kinds of non-verbal elements that may function in an argument:

1. **Argument flags** draw our attention to an argument.
2. **Non-verbal demonstrations** provide some direct evidence for a conclusion.
3. **Symbolic references** make a non-verbal reference to some idea, person, or thing.
4. **Metaphors** figuratively ascribe some characteristic to the subject of the metaphor.

In some complex arguments, all four kinds of non-verbal meaning may be used. Sometimes the same non-verbal elements (e.g. a particular piece of music) may convey more than one kind of non-verbal meaning.

EXERCISE 6E

1. Visit the web site Ads of the World at http://adsoftheworld.com. Pick an advertisement that can be understood as an argument. Dress and analyze the arguments, and then explain how the principles of communication were applied in your treatments of the arguments. What kinds of non-verbal meaning were evident?

2. The following is an advertisement for the French newspaper, *Aufait*. What is the role of the visual image in the advertisement. Analyze its meaning in terms of the kinds of non-verbal meaning we have introduced.

Source: Au Fait

Illustration 6.11   "The Facts" from *Aufait* newspaper

3. What is the visual argument forwarded by the following illustration, labelled "The downward spiral of debt."

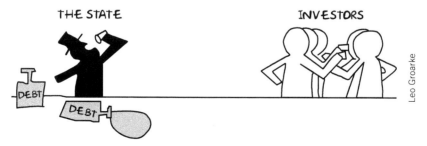

Leo Groarke

Illustration 6.12   The State and Investors

4. The lithograph reprinted in Illustration 6.13 was created by Adolfo Mexiac and turned into a political poster during the 1968 Mexico Olympics, when over 300 student protestors were killed in the Plaza de las Tres Culturas, in an incident known as the Tlatelolco Massacre. Explain the message in terms of our account of non-verbal meaning.

Illustration 6.13   "Libertad de Expresion: Mexico 68" by Adolfo Mexiac

A Note on Argument Construction

In many circumstances, we communicate in ways that are not entirely explicit. This is not a bad thing. If we could communicate only in ways that were explicit and used only words, communication would be cumbersome, difficult, and mundane. But there are circumstances where explicitness is a goal we should aim for. The attempt to identify and diagram an argument is one such case, for it is an attempt to reveal *all* the important parts of the argument. Identifying these parts prepares us for the inspection of them that will allow us to decide whether the argument is strong or weak.

In the process of dressing arguments, we can "fill in the blanks" and recognize their implicit aspects by applying the three basic principles of communication outlined at the beginning of this chapter. They suggest that the interpretation of any speech act should aim for a coherent meaning that is in keeping with its context and its explicit elements. In earlier chapters, we implicitly relied on the process of interpretation this suggests in deciding what is and is not an argument and in deciding how the components of ordinary arguments should be identified and diagrammed. In this chapter, we have explained how this process can be used in identifying hidden premises and conclusions and in understanding the non-verbal elements of many arguments.

In constructing arguments of your own, your goal should be arguments that do not depend on implicit elements in a way that makes them difficult to interpret or easy to misconstrue. The first step toward this goal is a commitment to use premise and conclusion indicators whenever you construct an argument. This is the only way to ensure that your arguments will be recognized as arguments.

In the body of your arguments, you can avoid confusion by using words and, if you decide to use them, non-verbal elements that clearly and precisely express what you want to say. Though no one can expect to avoid hidden premises in every circumstance (because our audiences will, in some cases, want to take issue with assumptions that seem to us obvious and unproblematic), you should try to explicitly express any important premise your argument depends on. In Chapter 1, we introduced the device of imagining an opponent for your argument to help you see what objections might be raised. You can use the same device to anticipate what statements will be controversial. If you can reasonably expect a premise to be controversial to such an opponent, then you should not hide it. Instead, you should create an extended argument that includes a sub-argument to support the premise in question.

In constructing arguments, especially in public contexts that are conducive to images, music, and other elements, it is not unreasonable to use non-verbal elements, so long as they are not exploited in order to promote poor reasoning or substitute purely emotional appeals for combinations of premises and conclusions that will stand up to scrutiny. It is a positive thing to be clever, witty, and creative, but not in a way that undermines the force of the arguments you construct.

EXERCISE 6F

Construct an extended argument for or against the death penalty (no more than three paragraphs long). Use non-verbal elements if you choose. After you have constructed the argument, discuss it from the point of view of clarity: How have you presented your argument and structured it so that it is clear what you are saying? What potential confusions did you need to avoid? How have you avoided them? What mistakes might occur in a poorly constructed version of your argument?

7 Summary

The focus of this chapter has been the implicit nature of much argumentative material. We have discussed ways in which both conclusions and premises may be hidden and left unstated. These need to be drawn out and made explicit. We have also explored the non verbal nature of some argumentative components, when images and sounds are used as evidence. We have also explored the more figurative ways to convey messages, through symbolic references and metaphors.

MAJOR EXERCISE 6M

1. For each of the following passages, say whether it contains an argument. If it contains an argument, dress it with a diagram, adding hidden premises and conclusions as necessary. (Don't assume that all passages are arguments or that all contain hidden components. Qualify your discussion of borderline cases.)

    a) Section 598b of the California Penal Code makes it illegal to eat domesticated animals like cats and dogs. But the only community in California that eats such animals is the Vietnamese community. So section 598b of the California Penal Code discriminates against the Vietnamese community.

    b)* [From an advertisement for "Arthur's Pom Plus Smoothie"] A healthy diet containing foods high in potassium and low in sodium may reduce the risk of high blood pressure, a risk factor for stroke and heart disease. Arthur's Pom Plus Smoothie is high in potassium and low in sodium.

    c) [The same advertisement continues]: A healthy diet rich in a variety of vegetables and fruit may help reduce the risk of some types of cancer. Arthur's Pom Plus contains 2½ servings of fruit per serving as per the Canada Food Guide.

    d) [Adapted from a column in the *Detroit Free Press*] Airlines are funny. They make sure you aren't carrying a weapon of destruction and then sell you all the booze you can drink.

    e) [An old-fashioned advertisement:] ARE YOU GULLIBLE? Then our product is for you. For years people believed there was no simple cure for this ailment. People who succumbed to its ravages were considered beyond help. They studied critical thinking, they worked hard to develop a critical attitude. All with little chance of success. Why work so hard? Now there's TINDALE'S CREDULITY FORMULA. $25 for the completely gullible. Smaller bottles, priced at only $10, are available for the slightly gullible.

f)   [The following is part of a response to the long-gun registry debate in Canada. It was published as a letter to the editors of *National Post*, 22 September 2010] The most frustrating part of the whole gun registry debate is hearing the phrase "if it saves even one life it's worth it." This is the argument of those who have no concrete evidence to support their position. We keep statistics on many things in Canada and we can identify pretty well those things which actually save lives.

g)* [From a discussion of Bill Moyers's PBS television series on poetry in *Time* magazine, 7 March 1995] Moyers makes virtually no attempt to place the poet in a larger social context—to view poetry as a profession (or, perhaps more to the point, to analyze what it means that ours is a culture where it's all but impossible to be a professional poet). Ezra Pound once pointed out that history without economics is bunk. To which one might add that poetry without economics—without some sense of the ebb and flow of the megamercantile society surrounding the poet—is bunk too.

h)* [From a discussion in a philosophy class] Abortion is not murder. The soul does not enter the body until the first breath is taken. Up to this point, the fetus is a biological entity only.

i)* [From a comment on an article that appeared in the *National Geographic*, November 1999, which declared the Archaeraptor Fossil to be "a true missing link in the complex chain that connects dinosaurs to birds"] How did the *National Geographic* come to publish the fraud with such fanfare? This was due to the fossil's origins being cloaked in mystery since it was discovered in China, and to there being insufficient time to have the article peer-reviewed [reviewed by experts in the field].

j)   [Odysseus in the *Odyssey*, Book 7, 215] For nothing in the world is so shamelessly demanding as a man's confounded stomach. However afflicted he may be and sick at heart, it calls for attention so loudly that he is bound to obey it.

k)   [Pierre Théberge, the organizer of an exhibit of automobiles at the Montreal Museum of Fine Arts in 1995] In design circles the automobile is still something of an "orphan" because it has been looked upon as essentially an outgrowth of technological development.

l)   [Gene Laczniak and Patrick Murphy, in *Ethical Marketing Decisions*, Boston: Allyn & Bacon, 1993, p. 263] A final argument that can be made for televised political advertising is that it motivates voters. TV advertising is thought to reach and vitalize individuals who otherwise might not participate in the election.

m)   [From *The Calgary Herald*, Opinion, "Lessons on obese kids,"2 November 2010, www.calgaryherald.com, p. A12] Parents, schools, teachers and society all have a role to play in getting kids off the couch and stopping children from becoming overweight. Overweight otherwise leads to obesity, which can soon turn into a lifelong sentence.

n) Cigarettes are the greatest public health problem we have, and the most flagrant example of drug pushing, since most tobacco is pushed on teenagers, who are led by advertising into thinking it's cool to smoke.

o)* [A sign on a public bench] You just proved Bench Advertising Works.

p) [From a radio advertisement for a Subaru four-wheel drive] Have you ever seen an agile dog on two legs? For better agility and handling, see your Subaru dealer today.

2. We have already seen that arguments tend to reflect the values of the times in which they are constructed. We have included two advertisements below. The first is an advertisement for "Motor Bus Lines of America" that appeared during the Second World War. The second is a contemporary advertisement promoting the use of Amorim natural cork stopper in wine bottles. Analyze and dress the arguments proposed in each case. How does each reflect the consciousness of the time in which it appeared?

Illustration 6.14   "To keep the flames of America burning . . ."

CORK oak forests offset over
10 million tonnes of carbon
every year.

CORK oak trees also provide
the bark that we harvest to make
natural cork stoppers for your
wine bottles. We never chop the
trees down, many live for as
long as **250 years.**

SO next time you buy a bottle
of wine, choose natural cork
and help put a cork in pollution.

JOIN the cause at savemiguel.com

Illustration 6.15   "Save Miguel"

3. The following is a controversial advertisement featuring Pamela Anderson, created by PETA (People for the Ethical Treatment of Animals). It created much controversy and was banned in Montreal, where the official in charge of issuing permits with the city's television and film office defended this decision, writing that "We, as public officials representing a municipal government, cannot endorse this image of Ms. Anderson. It is not so much controversial as it goes against all principles public organizations are fighting for in the everlasting battle of equality between men and women." In light of this controversy:

    a) Dress, diagram, and analyze the visual argument the advertisement presents (explain the elements of visual meaning).
    b) Dress, analyze and diagram the city's argument against it.
    c) Construct your own argument supporting one side of the debate or the other.
    d) Dress, analyze and diagram your own argument.

Illustration 6.16   "All animals have the same parts"

4. Pick a topic (on women's or men's health, government debt, the environment, human rights, poverty, etc. and construct an argument using visual images you create of find on the web, in a newspaper, on YouTube, etc.).

 For more online exercises, review questions, and quizzes related to the material in this chapter, please go to www.oupcanada.com/GoodReasoning5e

9

LOOKING FOR THE FACTS

In Chapter 3, we introduced the notion of argument schemes as tools in the construction and evaluation of arguments. In this and subsequent chapters, we explore some of the more popular schemes employed in different types of argumentation. Here, we introduce "empirical" schemes of argument that are used when arguers debate factual issues. In each case, we outline the basic structure and conditions of the scheme and sketch the conditions for a good "counter-argument" that can be used to combat reasoning of this sort. Our discussion focuses on three key ways of arguing that we employ when we "look for the facts" in such circumstances:

- ▶ generalizations
- ▶ polling
- ▶ causal reasoning.

In Chapter 8 we discussed the general criteria for strong arguments. Every strong argument must have premises that are relevant, acceptable, and sufficient to establish its conclusion. When we evaluate a particular argument, we always do so by applying these criteria to the case at hand.

In our preliminary review of argument schemes in Chapter 3, we described them as patterns of argument that commonly occur in arguments on the hoof. By identifying them, and by learning to recognize them in the arguments we analyze (our own as well as others' arguments), we can enhance our ability to assess reasoning. In identifying individual schemes we specify the conditions that must be satisfied to ensure that an instance of a scheme meets the standards of acceptability, relevance, and sufficiency required for a strong argument. In each case, these conditions allow us to identify a "counter-scheme" that may be used to contest conclusions based on the scheme in question. Counter-schemes reject a particular instance of a scheme by arguing that it fails to meet the conditions necessary for good instances of that scheme.

The schemes we introduce in this chapter apply to "empirical" or "factual" issues. We use them when we are looking to establish "facts" about the world: what causes certain things to happen, or how individuals or groups think or behave. In the next chapter we will take our discussion further by looking at other schemes and methods used to establish what the facts are. Because an exhaustive list of schemes used in empirical arguments is beyond the scope of this book (and arguably impossible to construct), there will be times when you must deal with arguments about the facts that do not fit any of the patterns that we will introduce. This is something to keep in mind as you work your way through empirical arguments on the hoof. But you should not think of it as a problem, for you are already equipped to deal with arguments of this sort. In such cases where you cannot rely on the definition of a specific scheme you can revert to the general criteria for strong arguments we discussed in Chapter 8 (i.e. our general account of acceptability, relevance, and sufficiency).

1 Generalizations

Generalization is the process of moving from specific observations about some individuals within a group to general claims about the members of the group. Occasionally, we make generalizations on the basis of a single incident. One painful experience may convince children not to place their tongues on a frozen lamp post, and one good experience may convince us that the Magic Carpet Cleaning Co. does a good job cleaning carpets. More frequently, generalizations are based on a series of observations or experiences. By recording a series of experiences or observations, researchers who conduct polls, surveys, and studies try to determine whether the majority of the population favours capital punishment, whether mandatory seatbelt legislation really reduces injuries in traffic accidents by 40 per cent, and so on.

Generalizations are, by definition, based on an incomplete survey of the evidence. In most cases, this is because a complete survey is, for practical reasons, impossible. Consider the following example: Suppose you operate a small business that assembles cell phones, and you have ordered a thousand microchips for them from a firm in Japan. The firm has agreed to produce them to your exact specifications. Upon their arrival, you open one of the 10 boxes at random, pull out five of the 100 chips it contains, and examine each one carefully to ensure that it meets your requirements. You find that all five do. At random, you open another box from the 10 and test five more chips, finding once again that they have been properly manufactured. You do the same with a third and a fourth box, with the same results. By this time you have carefully examined 20 of the 1000 chips and are fully satisfied. Twenty out of 1000 is a small ratio, but you conclude that "The computer chips meet our specifications."

As we shall see, this is a good inference, even though the premises, consisting of limited observations, do not guarantee the truth of your conclusion about the entire order. You could guarantee the truth of the conclusion if you examined all 1000 of the chips sent and found each and every one to meet your specifications. For practical reasons, we are rarely able to undertake such a complete review. Nor is it necessary, given that we have the basis for a reasonable generalization, even though it remains *possible* that a significant portion—indeed, most or even all the remaining chips—are not what you had ordered. You may, by accident, have happened to pick out the only good chips in the entire order. We must accept that this is possible, but the chance of it is very small, so we accept the reasoning and let the generalization stand.

Sometimes, the end result of such a generalization is a *universal* claim. A universal claim has the form "All Xs are Y." Appendix 1 discusses syllogistic arguments that involve such claims. For the present example, the universal conclusion would read, "All the microchips are good." In other cases, generalizations support *general* claims. A general claim has the form "Xs are, in general, Y," or "Xs are Y," or "Each X is probably Y." In the case at hand, you could express a general claim by concluding that "The microchips meet our specifications."

General claims are not as strong as their universal counterparts. The statement "The microchips meet our specifications" is not as strong a claim as "All the microchips meet our specifications." The general claim implies that the microchips are, on the whole, satisfactory. It leaves open the possibility that some chips may be defective. In contrast, the universal claim allows no exceptions. It is proved mistaken if we find one microchip that is defective. This is why such claims are deemed to be defeasible, that is, they are always open to revision. Defeasible reasoning comes in many forms. It is good reasoning in situations characterized by uncertainty, but it is reasoning that carries the proviso that its conclusions may always be revised if further relevant evidence comes to light.

General claims do not assert as much as universal claims, so they are easier to defend. When we say that "Salmon is good to eat," we may mean that it is usually palatable, and our claim is not refuted if we are served a piece of salmon of poor quality. It is wise to draw general rather than universal conclusions unless you are confident that there are no exceptions to your generalization. In the microchip case, this suggests that you should favour a general conclusion over a universal conclusion.

In some cases, generalizations lead to neither universal nor general claims but to *proportional* claims. Suppose that you had found a defective microchip among the first five you examined. In that case, you would probably have pulled out a few more—say, four more chips—from the same box and inspected them. Suppose you found them to be satisfactory. From one of the 10 boxes you have found one out of nine chips to be defective. Having found one defective chip, you may be more wary than you were. Suppose you open all 10 boxes and at random select a dozen chips from each. You examine them all and conclude that the proportion of defective chips is probably three out of every 120, or that 2.5 per cent of the chips fail to meet your specifications. More generally, you conclude that the vast majority of the chips meet your specifications but that some proportion of them is defective. In both cases, you are making a "proportional" claim.

We have seen that generalizations can lead to universal, general, or proportional claims. In all three cases, the key to a good generalization is a sample of the members of the group that is free from any errors in its selection. If such errors are avoided the sample will represent the group such that we can reasonably draw inferences from the one to the other such that what is true of the sample is true of the group.

Other considerations have to do with what is being sampled. In the case of microchips, which are manufactured using sophisticated technology capable of producing identical items on a production line, we can assume a high level of consistency and predictability. The situation changes if your business is selling fresh fruit rather than computers and the product you received is not microchips but perishable goods like strawberries or bananas. In this case, it is more difficult to assume the consistency of the product, for bananas are not "produced" identically in the way that microchips are, nor do they retain their quality over an extended period of time. Given that fruit will be affected by many factors that can cause imperfections, there is a greater chance that its quality will vary and good generalizations will require a more careful sampling.

In everyday life, we are inclined to make generalizations without a good sample. Often this is because our generalizations rely on "anecdotal evidence," which consists of informal reports of incidents that have not been subjected to careful scrutiny. Though anecdotes of this sort are rarely collected in a systematic way and are sometimes biased and unreliable, they are often used as a basis of generalizations about the unemployed, welfare recipients, professors, women drivers, the very rich, "deadbeat dads," particular ethnic groups, and so on. You should be wary of such generalizations, which are often based on a few instances that may have been embellished and slanted according to the prejudices of those who proffer them.

The "hasty generalizations" that frequently characterize ordinary reasoning have convinced some people that it is wrong to generalize. But bad generalizations do not rule out the possibility of good generalizations, and we can, if we are careful, use our critical faculties and our common sense to decide whether a generalization is based on a good sample. Two kinds of considerations must play a key role in this assessment.

Sample Size

The first thing you must consider in determining the suitability of a sample is its size. Samples that are too small are unreliable and more likely to be affected by pure chance. In the cell phone example, you examined 20 of 1000 microchips and concluded that they met your specifications. Assuming that you have confidence in the firm that manufactured the chips and the process by which they were produced, you have good reason to accept your conclusion, despite the small sample you examined. In contrast, a sample size of one or two or three chips chosen from one box is too susceptible to the luck of the draw. As more and more chips are examined, the chances that your results are mere coincidence diminish.

In the case of the proportional generalization, the discovery of a defective chip led you to enlarge your sample. Problems can occur on a production line. So to get a more accurate picture of the condition of the microchips, you examined more of them. If you had settled for your first five chips, you would have concluded that 20 per cent of the order was defective. As it turns out, a larger sample suggests that there are only problems with 2.5 per cent.

Sample Bias

A sample must be sufficiently large to give us confidence that its characteristics are not due to chance. A good sample must also avoid bias. Anecdotal evidence is problematic because it tends to be biased. Thus, individuals tend to accept and repeat anecdotes that conform to their own perspective in the process of eliminating counter cases.

In a sample used for generalizations, a bias is some way in which the individuals in the sample differ from other individuals in the larger group specified in the generalization. If the microchips in your order had been made in two distinct ways, "A" and "B," and your sample comprised only chips made by process A, then your sample would be biased. This is a serious bias, for each process is likely to have its own potential problems and you cannot expect to detect problems caused by process B if no process-B chips are included in your sample. In this case, a representative sample must include chips from process A and process B (ideally in equal portions, if the same number of chips were made in each way).

A common source of bias is a natural tendency to generalize from the situations with which we are familiar without asking whether these situations are representative. When social workers generalize on the basis of their experiences with single-parent families, they must keep in mind that they are working in a specific geographic area with particular social, ethnic, economic, and political characteristics. They must therefore ask themselves whether single mothers and fathers elsewhere share a similar situation. Otherwise, their generalizations cannot be extended beyond their sphere of experience.

Bias is particularly problematic when generalizations are made about groups of people. Problems easily arise because humans are not a homogeneous group and people are characterized by differences in religious commitment, political affiliation, ethnic background, income, gender, age, and so on. In Chapter 1, we saw how these factors may contribute to someone's belief system, which affects his or her opinions and attitudes about virtually anything we may wish to investigate. Consequently, any attempt to generalize about people and their behaviour must carefully avoid a sample that is imbalanced in any way, by taking account of relevant differences and variations in perspective.

Criteria for Good Generalizations

We can summarize our discussion of generalizations by defining good generalizations as strong arguments (i.e. with acceptable, relevant, and sufficient premises) that conform (implicitly or explicitly) to the following scheme:

> **Premise 1:** S is a sample of Xs.
> **Premise 2:** Proportion 1 of Xs in S are Y.
> **Conclusion:** Proportion 2 of Xs are Y.

In this scheme,

- **Xs** can be anything whatsoever—dogs, cats, worlds, dreams, cities, etc.
- **Y** is the property that Xs are said to have.
- **Sample (S)** is the group of Xs that has been considered—the particular microchips selected for examination, the bananas inspected in a shipment, the people questioned in a poll, etc.

- **Proportion 1** and **Proportion 2** refer to some proportion of the Xs—*all* Xs, *some* Xs, *most* Xs, Xs *in general*, etc., or some specified percentage, e.g. 2.5 per cent, 10 per cent, 70 per cent, and so on. Proportion 1 must be equal to or greater than Proportion 2.

An explicit instance of this scheme would be the following:

P1 = The group of microchips examined (Sample S) is a sample of the chips sent (Xs).

P2 = All (Proportion 1) of the microchips examined (i.e. in Sample S) are made to specification (Y).

C = All (Proportion 2) of the microchips sent (Xs) are made to specification (Y).

In this case, Proportion 1 and Proportion 2 are the same proportion "All," which is normally the case, though it is possible that they will be different. In this example, we could have let Proportion 2 = "Most" and made our conclusion the general (rather than the universal) claim that "Most of the microchips sent are made to specifications."

Our scheme for generalizations raises the question of how we can establish its first premise. This will be explored further in the section on polling. For now we will simply say that we expect a sample that is (a) large enough not to be overly influenced by chance and (b) free of bias. In considering whether a generalization is a strong generalization or not, we will, therefore, need to spend much of our time considering arguments like the following:

The researchers considered a reasonable number of Xs.
The group of Xs considered is not biased.
Therefore, the sample considered is a good sample.

In ordinary reasoning, you need to consider the kinds of things that are being sampled in order to decide whether a particular sample of them is reasonable and unbiased.

As you do exercises and consider other examples of ordinary reasoning, you will see that generalizations are often presented in implicit ways in ordinary argument. An arguer may not explicitly address the question of whether a sample is biased or reasonably sized. Sometimes they will not even recognize that they have based their general, universal, or proportional claim on a process of generalization that needs to be evaluated. In such contexts, it is up to you to recognize the issues that the implicit generalization raises. In this way, you can subject the argument to proper critical assessment.

Counter-arguments against Generalizations

A strong argument against a generalization must show that strong reasoning does not support the conclusion allegedly established by the generalization. This can be done in one of two ways: (1) by showing that the sample of Xs in question is not characterized by the property alleged (Y); or (2) by showing that the sample of Xs does not accurately reflect the group. In the latter case, we need to argue that the sample is too small or that it is biased in one way or another. In the process, we must, of course, clearly explain why we believe the sample to be inadequate.

GENERALIZATIONS

Generalization is the process of moving from specific observations about some individuals within a group to general claims about members of the group. Generalizations can be the basis for universal, general, or proportional claims. A strong generalization shows:

1. That the individuals in the sample have some property Y, and
2. That the sample is good—i.e. that it is (a) of reasonable size and (b) free of bias.

A good counter-argument to generalization shows that one or more of these criteria is not met.

EXERCISE 9A

1. For each of the following topics, state whether you are in a position to make a reasonable generalization, and why. In each case, discuss the issues this raises and the problems you may encounter in forming a generalization. Giving examples of possible generalizations, discuss how you could improve the sample in order to yield a more reliable generalization and/or modify your generalization to fit your sample more accurately.

    a) Students' work habits at your institution.
    b) The policies of a particular political party.
    c)* Bus service where you live.
    d) The exams of one of your instructors.
    e) Psychology courses.
    f)* The attitudes of Americans.
    g) The spending habits of tourists to California.
    h) The colour of squirrels.
    i) The price of automobiles.
    j) The reliability of your make of car.

2. Identify the generalizations contained in the following examples and assess their strength:

    a) [From "Women like practicality in cars, men go for the looks—study" DETROIT—Reuters, 11 April 2011] Men prefer their cars beefy or fast, while women go for lower price tags and better fuel economy, according to a new survey. TrueCar.com, which studied data from 8 million purchases in the United States last year, found BMW AG's Mini had the highest percentage of female buyers at 48 per cent, while 93 per cent of buyers for Fiat SpA's Ferrari were men.

        "The study shows that women car buyers are more cost-conscious and purchased fuel-efficient vehicles while male buyers were completely the opposite, purchasing vehicles that were either big and brawny, like a large truck, or chose a high-priced, high-performance vehicle," TrueCar analyst Jesse Toprak said in a statement.

Following Mini with the women were Kia Motors Corp (47 per cent) and Honda Motors Co Ltd (46 per cent) branded vehicles, according to the study. Last year, General Motors Co's Saturn and Kia tied at 45.2 per cent, followed by Mini at 45 per cent.

There were 15 brands with more than 40 per cent female buyers, TrueCar said.

Maserati (84 per cent), Porsche (80 per cent) and General Motors' GMC (74 per cent) followed Ferrari for the highest percentage of male buyers, according to the study.

The top-selling model for women, with a minimum of 1,000 retail sales, was Volkswagen AG's New Beetle at 61 per cent, while for men it was the Porsche 911 at 88 per cent, TrueCar said.

b)* "I've owned two Toyota's with no problems. My wife bought a Toyota that she is still driving seven years later with only minor repairs in the course of tune-ups. I'll never drive another vehicle."

c) [From *Redbook* magazine, 3 March 2011, p. 72] If your little one is anti broccoli, spinach, and veggies in general, it is okay to surrender and stop stressing, says New Jersey-based dietician Erin Palinski, R.C. A recent study at the University of Bristol in the United Kingdom followed more than 13,000 children from infancy to age 7 and found that picky eaters met the same calorie and nutrient quotas as veggie-loving kids. And there were no major differences in weight and height between the two groups.

d) [From the manifesto of the "Unabomber," widely available on the Internet] It is said that we live in a free society because we have a certain number of constitutionally guaranteed rights. But these are not as important as they seem. The degree of personal freedom that exists in a society is determined more by the economic and technological structure of the society than by its laws or its form of government. Most of the Indian nations of New England were monarchies, and many of the cities of the Italian Renaissance were controlled by dictators. But in reading about these societies one gets the impression that they allowed far more personal freedom than our society does.

 2   Polling

One context in which generalizations play an important role is polling. Media outlets regularly release the results of professionally conducted polls under headlines that make claims like "Most Americans believe the economy will improve in the next year," or "Over 90 per cent of people support increased health care spending," or even "Few people trust the results of polls." Beneath these headlines we read an array of details that supposedly justify them. They may tell us who was polled (how many), what was asked, how it was asked, who conducted the poll, and how reliable the results are deemed to be (the "margin of error"). Given the prevalence of conclusions inferred from polls, it is important to learn how to judge them—in order to distinguish strong conclusions from weak ones, to know what information to expect to be present, and to appreciate when a problem lies in the poll itself or in the way it is being reported.

In deciding whether a poll is a reasonable generalization, we need to begin by identifying three aspects of it:

1.   *The sample:* the group of people polled—who they are and how many of them there are.
2.   *The population sampled:* the larger group to which the sample belongs and is deemed to be representative of.
3.   *The property in question:* the opinion or characteristic studied in the poll about which a conclusion has been drawn.

These three concepts can be illustrated with the following example.

Under the headline "41% of US doctors would aid executions" (Andre Picard, *The Globe and Mail*, 20 November 2001, p. A9—available in the paper's archives under the headline), we read that 1000 practising physicians were asked whether they would carry out one or more of 10 acts related to lethal injection. In this example, the *sample* is 1000 practising American physicians, the *population* is all practising American physicians, and the *property* is "willingness to aid in executions." As the headline indicates, the researchers conducting the poll concluded that 41 per cent of practising American physicians have the property "would aid in executions." They based this conclusion on the fact that 41 per cent of their sample said they would, at least according to the news story.

Implicitly or explicitly, polling arguments are instances of the general scheme for generalizations. Good arguments from polling are strong arguments that have the form:

Premise 1:   S is a sample of Xs.
Premise 2:   Proportion 1 of Xs in S are Y.
Conclusion: Proportion 2 of Xs are Y.

where:

- **Xs** are the population—the group of people about whom the conclusion is drawn.
- **Y** is the property the people in the population are said to have.
- **Sample S** is the sample of people studied.
- **Proportion 1** and **Proportion 2** are the proportion of people in the sample and the population who are said to have property Y.

In most arguments from polling, Proportion 1 and Proportion 2 are identical, as with the 41 per cent assigned to both sample and population in the above example. In many arguments, premise 1 (the claim that the sample is of the population) is a hidden premise.

Because polls may study more than one property in a sample, many arguments from polling will specify not only the proportion of the sample and the population that has the principal property investigated but also the proportion that has other properties. In trying to determine the percentage of physicians who would act in executions, for example, a poll is likely to reach conclusions about the percentage opposed to such actions, the percentage who have no opinion, and so on. For this reason, the second premise in a polling argument often has the form "Proportion 1 of Xs in S are Y; Proportion 2 of Xs in S are Z; Proportion 3 of Xs in S are W. . . ." In such cases, the conclusion of the polling argument will be "Proportion 1 of Xs are Y; Proportion 2 of Xs are Z; Proportion 3 of Xs are W. . . ." This can be illustrated with respect to the above poll, by going to the newspaper's own source, the *Annals of Internal Medicine*. The information contained there varies from *The Globe and Mail*'s report in significant ways, and we will comment on this below. But using the newspaper's interpretation and information from the study we can produce the following argument:

P1 = The 1000 practising American physicians polled constitute a representative sample of practising American physicians.

P2 = Forty-one per cent of the physicians polled indicated that they would perform at least one action related to lethal injection disallowed by the American Medical Association; 25 per cent said they would perform five or more disallowed actions; only 3 per cent knew of any guidelines on the issue.

C = Forty-one per cent of practising American physicians would perform at least one action related to lethal injection disallowed by the American Medical Association; 25 per cent would perform five or more disallowed actions; only 3 per cent know of any guidelines on the issue.

In this case, the sample is the physicians polled, the population is practising American physicians, and the properties investigated are the three properties mentioned in premise 2.

Sampling Errors

In determining whether a polling argument is a strong argument, we need to assess the acceptability of the premises. There are two kinds of issues that can arise in this regard, which correspond to each of our two premises.

The first issue that polls raise is tied to premise 1. It concerns the sample used. In deciding whether it is representative, we need to ask questions like: *Is the sample reliable? Is its size sufficient? How was it selected? Does it include all relevant subgroups? Is the margin of error it allows within reasonable bounds?* If these kinds of questions cannot be answered satisfactorily, we say that the poll contains a *sampling error* and that the polling argument is a weak one. It can be compared to other kinds of generalizations with samples that are biased or too small.

In many cases, the reports we read of polling results will not give us the answers to all our questions. In considering what has been omitted, remember that sample size is important. As we have seen in our discussion of generalizations, too small a sample will not permit reliable conclusions. How much is enough? For most studies pollsters aim for samples of around 1000. That may seem small to you, given that the population in question involves a national membership. But as populations grow, the sample sizes required for reliable results increase by only small amounts. A number of 1000 is adequate for the kinds of national polls you are likely to find reported in the media. Where populations are smaller, such as the number of people in your year at your institution, much smaller samples can be used.

Even when a sample is large enough, there may be problems with the group chosen as a sample. When you judge a sample to determine whether there is a sampling error, consider how it was selected. Did people self-select, say, by voluntarily answering a mail survey or by logging on to a website? If so, you need to judge what kind of people are likely to do so and whether conclusions based on such results actually reflect the populations identified. A certain portion of the public does not use the Internet. Another portion will not answer surveys. These portions of the public will not be represented in a self-selected Internet poll. In such a case, we need to ask whether this creates a bias—whether it means that the sample does not accurately represent the population it is drawn from.

One of the most famous unrepresentative samples in the history of polling was used by *The Literary Digest* to predict the results of the 1936 US presidential election. It sent surveys to 10 million individuals, with 2.4 million responses. This should have given them statistically significant information. *The Literary Digest* predicted that the election would result in 370 electoral college votes for Landon and 161 for Roosevelt. History showed the pollsters to be drastically mistaken as Roosevelt won hands down. How could this be? How could such a large sample fail to be representative? The problem lay with polling techniques flawed in ways that biased the results. They surveyed their own readers—a group with incomes above the national average. And they used lists of automobile owners and telephone users. Again, in the Depression years of the 1930s, both of these groups had higher incomes than the national average. The sample represented an economic class that was overwhelmingly predisposed to Landon's Republican party. The error cost the magazine its life.

The preferred means of sample selection is one that is random. A sample is "random" if every member of the population has an equal chance of being selected. In the survey of American physicians, we are told that the participants were randomly selected. In this and other cases of random sampling, we need to determine whether relevant subgroups of the population have been included. Relevant subgroups can include men, women, and people of a particular age, education, geographical location, etc. As you can imagine, there are many possibilities. In any particular case, the possibilities that matter are those that are likely to affect the property in question. In the poll of American physicians, we would want to know how many of the 1000 doctors who participated in the survey practise in states that carry out executions and how many are from states that do not, because it is plausible to suppose that the possibility that one really will be asked to assist with an execution may influence a participant's response.

Because truly random samples are difficult to obtain, polls and surveys conducted by professional pollsters tend to use a method called "stratified random sampling." In stratified random sampling, a group of people polled is divided into categories relevant to the property in question, ensuring that a suitable number of individuals from each group is included in the sample. If 25 per cent of Americans have an income under $20,000, then a poll aiming to discover what percentage of Americans support their present government should attempt to have 25 per cent of its surveys answered by Americans with an income under $20,000. The sample should be selected in a way that ensures that all other significant subgroups are considered.

Most reports on polls include a margin of error that gives the confidence interval this size of sample allows. While this is a complex matter, it is sufficient for our purposes to understand how to read margins of error. As scientific as polling has become, the results are still approximations that tell us what is *probably* the case. To underscore this point, statisticians report results that fall within a margin of error that is expressed as a percentage ("plus or minus 3 per cent," or "± 3%") that indicates the likelihood that the data they have collected are dependable. The lower the margin of error, the more accurately the views of those surveyed match those of the entire population. Every margin of error has a "confidence level," which is usually 95 per cent. This means that if you asked a question from a particular poll 100 times, your results would be the same (within the margin of error) 95 times.

Margin of error is particularly important when it leaves room for very different possibilities, for this raises questions about the significance of the results. For example, if a poll tells us that in the next election 50 per cent of people will vote for party "A" while 45 per cent will vote for party "B" (the rest undecided or refusing to tell) and that there is a margin of error of ± 3 per cent, then we need to proceed with caution. For although it looks as if party A is ahead, the margin of error tells us that party A's support could be as low as 47 per cent (–3) or as high as 53 per cent (+3); party B's support lies between a low of 42 per cent and a high of 48 per cent. Who is ahead in the polls? In this situation, the overlap makes it too close to call.

Measurement Errors

Assuming that a poll does not contain a sampling error, we still need to ask whether it has attained its results in a manner that is biased or in some other way problematic. Otherwise, the results reported in premise 2 in our polling scheme may be unreliable. Here we need to ask: *How reliable is the information collected about the measured property? What kinds of questions were asked? How were the results of the immediate questions interpreted? Were the questions or answers affected by biases (of wording, timing, sponsors, etc.)?* If these kinds of questions cannot be answered satisfactorily, we say that the poll contains a *measurement error*. Here the problem may be that the results of the poll are biased because of the way in which the sample was studied. A current suspicion of polling during political election campaigns, fuelled in part by the very different results announced by different polling companies, reflects the possibility that measurement errors are at work in at least some of the published polls. In the 2011 Canadian federal election disparities between voter preferences reported by pollsters were as high as 15 percentage points (from John Allemang, "In the messiness of democracy, polling offers semblance of order," *The Globe and Mail*, 8 April 2011, p. A7). As Allemang notes, some of this is due to the obsolescence of traditional techniques. A generation ago, telephone samplings achieved 70 per cent response rates; now call-display features have lowered this to 20 per cent. All of which should encourage you to look carefully for possible measurement errors in published polls.

We know from Chapter 6 that statements can be vague or ambiguous. If survey respondents have been asked questions that lend themselves to different interpretations or are vague ("How do you feel about X?"), then we may question the reliability of the results. If a sample of university students is asked whether they "use condoms regularly," it matters whether the respondents are left to decide what should count as "regularly" or are given an indication of what the pollster means by the term.

It can also be important to ask how pollsters arrive at percentages from the types of questions asked. To learn that 70 per cent of health club members in a certain city are males seems unproblematic because we can imagine what kind of straightforward question was asked. People tend to know whether they are male or female, and it would be no problem for the pollsters to take the numbers of each and convert them into percentages. But when we are told that 70 per cent of adults are "largely dissatisfied" with the government's response to crime, then the matter seems not so straightforward. What questions have the pollsters asked to arrive at this percentage? People may not know their views in quite the same way as they know their sex, and so the clarity of the questions and any directions accompanying them become crucial.

There are other ways in which the questions, or the way they have been posed, may result in a measurement error. Psychologists tell us that people are more likely to answer truthfully when participating in face-to-face interviews. Interviews conducted over the phone are less reliable, as are the results of group interviews, where participants feel pressure to answer in certain ways. In judging polls, we need, therefore, to ask whether some factors may have influenced people to answer in ways that did not reflect their real behaviour or opinions.

In other cases, a poll may contain a measurement error in view of the time when it was conducted, who conducted it, or who commissioned it. We are usually told when a poll was conducted. At this point, we should ask ourselves whether there were things occurring at that time that may have influenced the responses. A poll assessing people's views on their country's involvement in a war just after a number of casualties have been incurred may elicit a different set of responses from those elicited by the same poll conducted at another time. In view of this, the poll may not reflect how people *generally* feel about the issue. Likewise, we may ask whether the group or agency that commissioned the poll released the results in a timely fashion or held on to them until a time that suited them. If they have waited, the results may no longer be reliable because intervening events could have altered the views given.

Finally, when dealing with polls reported in the media, be charitable. To properly assess a poll, you need a significant amount of information on the way it was conducted. When this information is omitted, ask yourself whether the problem lies with the poll itself or with the media outlet reporting it. Sometimes the report does not give the information we require to properly assess the poll. Our analysis of the reasoning should mention this, and we should refrain from making conclusions that the information we have does not justify. Also, be alert to the way that both editors and reporters (and those quoted in reports) themselves have interpreted the results of polls, as reflected in the headlines they choose and the statements they make. Sometimes such headlines and statements are not justified by the information provided, as an analysis of that material (according to the procedures we have explained) will tell you. Our opening headline—"41% of US doctors would aid executions"—is an eye-catching claim. But it also exploits the vagueness of the word "aid." The details provided in the report tell us that only 19 per cent of the doctors included in the survey said they would actually give the injection. So the reporter's lead statement that "More than 40 per cent of US physicians are willing to work as executioners" is misleading. More problematic, the actual study in the *Annals of Internal Medicine* indicates that the 1000 number important to the report was the number of surveys distributed. Only 413 responded—a serious omission in the newspaper report—and the sample of 41 per cent who were willing to do one or more of the actions involved in capital punishment is the percentage of *this* lower number. The authors of the study rightly worry that the number of nonresponses produced a biased result. So the report on the poll is quite misleading. As always with second-hand reports, we are vulnerable to the kinds of selection and distortion we discussed in Chapter 2. The lesson is that before we act on such information, we should investigate further.

Counter-arguments to Polls

Once we understand polls and the ways in which they can support good generalizations, we can also understand how to construct counter-arguments to contest the conclusions based on them. This requires that we show that the features of good arguments from polls are missing in the case at hand. In such cases, the poll (or media source) misreports the results of the polling or suffers from a sampling or a measurement error. In this way, the criteria for good arguments from polls can help us construct and assess arguments against a poll result.

POLLING

A poll is a kind of generalization that surveys a sample of a larger population in order to establish what proportion of this population has one or more properties. A strong generalization based on a poll shows:

1. That the individuals polled have the properties in question to the extent claimed; and
2. That the sample is (a) free of sampling errors and (b) free of measurement errors.

A good counter-argument to a generalization based on a poll shows that one or more of these criteria is not met.

EXERCISE 9B

For each of the polls reported here, identify the sample, population, and property, and set out the argument scheme. Then assess the reliability of the conclusion by means of the questions raised for dealing with polls. Where you identify problems, determine whether they lie with the poll itself or the way it has been reported.

a) [From Brian Lilley "Canadians still want to marry: Poll," *Toronto Sun*, 23 July 2011] With or without the statistics, most single Canadians say they want to marry, and the overwhelming majority of adults consider a successful marriage an important life goal, according to a new survey.

When asked—in a poll conducted for Sun News Network by Abacus Data—how important it was to have a successful marriage, 82% of those surveyed said it was either "the most important" or "very important but not the most." A successful marriage came second only to being a good parent on the list of life goals, which also included owning a home, being successful in a high-paying career and living a very religious life.

When single Canadians, representing 237 of those surveyed were asked whether they wanted to get married, 64% said yes while 36% said no. The online poll of 1,005 adult Canadians was conducted June 23 and 24 (2011)

b)* [From a report in the journal *Nature*, December 1997] Cheating remains wide-spread among students at US universities, according to a recent survey of 4,000 students at 31 institutions. The survey found that incidents of serious mal-practice have increased significantly over the past three decades and, although highest among students on vocational courses such as business studies and engineering, they are also significant in the natural sciences.

The survey report by Donald McCabe, professor of management at Rutgers University in New Jersey, appears in the current issue of the journal *Science and Engineering Ethics* (Vol. 4, No. 433–45, 1997). Based on the experience of the university departments, McCabe concludes that strict penalties are a more effec-tive deterrent than exhortations to behave morally. Cheating is more common at universities without an "honour code"—a binding code of conduct for students, with penalties for violation. More than half of science students at universities with no honour code admitted falsifying data in laboratory experiments.

More than two-thirds of all students polled said they had cheated in some way. Seventy-three per cent of science students from universities without an honour code admitted "serious cheating." The figure for those from universities with a code was 49 per cent. "Serious cheating" includes copying from someone during an examination and using crib notes.

c) [From an Angus Reid survey of British Columbia residents after the riots that followed the last game of the Stanley Cup. We have focused on one question asked: the actions of the Vancouver police force. *Angus Reid Public Opinion*, 20 June 2011, www.angus-reid.com/polls/43930/british-columbians-want-vancouver-rioters-and-looters-to-face-justice]

British Columbians Want Vancouver Rioters and Looters to Face Justice

Residents of British Columbia and Metro Vancouver are dismayed at the events that unfolded after the conclusion of the Stanley Cup Final, and call for those responsible for the rioting and looting that took place in Downtown Vancouver to be prosecuted to the full extent of the law, a new Angus Reid Public Opinion poll has found.

The online survey of a representative provincial sample of 906 adult British Columbians also shows support for new measures to deal with crowds, and opposition to the idea of banning street parties.

Two-thirds of British Columbians (66%) and Metro Vancouver residents (64%) are satisfied with the way the Vancouver Police Department (VPD) handled the events that took place after the conclusion of the Stanley Cup Final. In addition, practically all respondents (96% in BC, 95% in Metro Vancouver) want the people who took part in riots to be prosecuted to the full extent of the law. For the most part, British Columbians agree with some of the prevailing arguments that have emerged in the aftermath of the riots . . . that police officers handled the situation properly, and that those who broke the law must be brought to justice.

The level of satisfaction with the way the VPD handled the events is high.

Methodology: From June 16 to June 17, 2011, Angus Reid Public Opinion conducted an online survey among 906 randomly selected British Columbia adults, including 515 Metro Vancouver adults, who are Angus Reid Forum panelists. The margin of error—which measures sampling variability—is +/– 3.3% for the British Columbia sample and +/– 4.3% for the Metro Vancouver sample. The results have been statistically weighted according to the most current education, age, gender and region Census data to ensure a sample representative of the entire adult population of British Columbia. Discrepancies in or between totals are due to rounding.

 General Causal Reasoning

Often, generalizations are used to establish cause-and-effect relationships. When dieticians tell us that people with low-fat diets tend to be healthier overall, it suggests that it is the diet that causes the health effects. When a university tells you (or potential students) that graduates earn such-and-such an impressive average income, it is suggesting that a high income is, at least in part, a causal consequence of the stature of their institution and the quality of education it provides.

General causal arguments attempt to establish general or universal causal claims. We make general causal claims when we say that students from a particular school are better prepared for university, or that wearing seatbelts saves lives. Scientists use general causal reasoning to show that a chemical behaves in a specific way under certain conditions, that smoking causes lung cancer, or that car emissions and the burning of other fossil fuels are causing global warming.

Two kinds of causal conditions play a role in general causal reasoning. A constant condition is a causal factor that must be present if an event is to occur. For example, the presence of oxygen is a constant condition for combustion: without oxygen, there cannot be combustion. This gives oxygen an important causal role in combustion, but we would not, under normal circumstances, say that oxygen causes combustion. The event or condition we designate as the cause is the *variable condition*, i.e. the condition that brings about the effect. Since dry foliage is a constant condition for a forest fire and oxygen is a constant condition for combustion, we would normally designate the carelessly tossed match—the variable condition—as the cause of a particular fire.

We call the set of constant and/or variable conditions that produce some event its *composite cause*. A comprehensive account of the composite cause of some event is difficult to produce, for most events are the result of a complex web of causal relationships and a number of constant and/or variable conditions. Often, our interest in a composite cause is determined by our interest in actively affecting the outcomes in some situation. If we can establish that the (variable) condition in the cause of forest fires is the embers from campfires, we may be able to reduce this risk by educating campers. If we are concerned about spring flooding, we must accept that we cannot control the variable conditions that produce such floods (e.g. spring rains and runoff), but we may build dams and reservoirs that allow us to control the constant conditions that make these floods possible (e.g. the height of a river).

Our interest is in constructing and evaluating causal arguments in everyday reasoning, so we will keep our discussion as simple as possible. We will begin with arguments for general causal claims, i.e. claims of the form "X causes Y," where X is either a variable condition or a composite cause. In the next chapter, we will look at particular causal arguments.

A good general causal argument is a strong argument that establishes (implicitly or explicitly) three points in support of a general causal conclusion. We can summarize these points in the following scheme for general causal reasoning:

Premise 1: X is correlated with Y.
Premise 2: The correlation between X and Y is not due to chance.
Premise 3: The correlation between X and Y is not due to some mutual cause Z.
Premise 4: Y is not the cause of X.
Conclusion: X causes Y.

One key to a good argument for the general claim "X causes Y" is a demonstration that X and Y are regularly connected. This is captured in the first premise of our scheme, for in a case of such regularity we say that there is a correlation between X and Y. The claim that gum disease is caused by the build-up of plaque is ultimately based on the work of scientists who have established a correlation between the build-up of plaque and gum disease. That is, they have observed a regular connection between the two phenomena.

Every causal relationship implies the existence of a correlation between two events, X and Y, but the existence of a correlation does not in itself guarantee a causal relationship. The assumption that this is the case is the most common error made in causal reasoning. The problem is that an observed correlation may be attributable to other factors. Most notably, it may be the result of simple chance or of some third event, Z, which really causes Y or causes both X and Y and is referred to as a "second" cause. Our scheme guards against these two possibilities in its second and third premises.

Moreover, given an established correlation between X and Y, we must also have some reason to rule out a causal relationship whereby Y is actually the cause of X. Our fourth premise addresses this. In many instances, the context alone will suffice to support this premise: we can be confident, for example, that house fires do not cause careless smoking. In other cases, the relationship may not be so clear and can lead to the problem of confusing cause and effect. Does stress during exams cause errors, or do errors cause stress? The fourth premise requires us to consider carefully whether the causal relationship may be the reverse of what is being concluded.

In many cases, a good argument for the claim that X causes Y will be built on sub-arguments that establish the four premises in our scheme. In arguing that there is a correlation between X and Y, the results of a study or even casual observations may be cited. In arguing that this correlation is not due to chance, a sub-argument may explain why it is plausible to see X and Y as causally connected. In arguing that there is no mutual second cause, a sub-argument may try to eliminate the likely possibilities. And in arguing that Y does not cause X, a sub-argument will aim to show that this is implausible or unlikely.

Consider a case of causal investigation reported on the CBC radio program Dispatches (www.cbc.ca/dispatches/episode/2011/06/02/june-2-5-from---lima-peru---amsterdam---syria---rondonia-brazil---lomardi-italy), under the headline "Why Are Italian Soccer Stars Coming Down with Lou Gehrig's Disease?" This disease, also known as ALS, is a fatal muscle-wasting disease with no known cause. Apparently, over the last 30 years there has been a high incidence of ALS in Italian soccer players, nearly 50 out of 40,000. This means that Italian soccer players are 20 times more likely to contract the disease than the rest of the population. Why?

One hypothesis is that the cause is doping. Unfortunately, because of the timeline involved, it has been very difficult for investigators to test for toxicity in former players. But they did look at another sport—cycling, which is notorious for its doping scandals. And there are no incidences of ALS among professional cyclists. A second hypothesis is trauma. But when investigators looked at professional basketball, with a high incidence of trauma injuries, they again found no incidence of ALS among present or former players.

The issue is compounded by the fact that all the cases of ALS involve only four teams: AC Milan, Como, Fiorentina, and Torino. Investigators then turned their attention to the fields involved. While the Italian Soccer Federation has not cooperated in the studies, they have found heavy metal under the pitch at Como. But as an official of the Como ground points out, many players have played on that pitch without contracting the disease. So if it turns out something in the fields like heavy metal is the constant condition, investigators will still need to uncover a variable condition that brings about the effect in some players but not others. At the time we write this, no such condition has been uncovered.

It is possible to understand the scheme for good general causal reasoning as a variant of the scheme for good generalizations. This is because the correlation that is the heart of an argument for a general causal claim is a sample of the instances of the cause. If we claim that "Taking a vacation in February is one way to cure the winter blahs," on the basis of our own experience and the experience of our friends, then we have made a general claim on the basis of a sample of vacations in February (i.e. those taken by ourselves and our friends). In our reasoning, we have used the correlation between these vacations and the curing of the winter blahs as a basis for a causal generalization. In any general causal argument, the correlation between the cause and the observed effect in the sample studied is used to justify the broader claim that the cause always, or in general, leads to the effect. "X causes Y" is a general claim in which the property "causes Y" is assigned to X. As in any generalization, we must be sure that the sample offered is representative, that it is not biased in any way, and that its connection to the alleged effect is not due to coincidence. The second premise in our scheme discounts the first possibility; the third rules out bias as an explanation for the existence of Y in the correlation.

Given our account of general causal reasoning, good arguments *against* a general causal claim can be constructed by showing that the reasoning the claim depends on violates the conditions for good causal reasoning. In such cases, we will need to show:

1. That the claimed correlation does not exist;
2. That the correlation is due to chance;
3. That there is a second cause that accounts for the correlation between the alleged cause and effect; or
4. That it is more likely that the causal relation is the other way around.

Most problematic causal arguments are undermined by the third possibility.

Key features of general causal reasoning are evident in a study published in the journal *Pediatrics* (Lee et al., "Weight status in young girls and the onset of puberty," 5 March 2007) and widely discussed in the media. Researchers studied 354 girls from the National Institute of Child Health and from the Human Development Study of Early Child Care and Youth Development. The girls were measured and weighed at 36 and 54 months and grades 1, 4, 5, and 6 and with assessment of pubertal stage by physical examination and maternal report in grades 4 through 6. The researchers discovered a correlation between body mass index and early puberty such that the higher a girl's body mass index (or fat mass) by age three, the more likely she was to reach puberty by her ninth birthday. "Puberty" was determined by breast development and first menstruation.

Some media outlets saw this as "Obesity may cause early puberty" (CanWest News Service, 5 March 2007), a clear causal claim drawn from the correlation. But the researchers themselves were less definite in their conclusions. Lead author Dr Joyce Lee, an assistant professor in the division of pediatric endocrinology at the University of Michigan, stated, "By no means have we proven weight gain causes early onset of puberty." But the study's finding adds further evidence to the hypothesis that excess body fat is a potential cause of early sexual maturation in girls. Other studies have found that girls are entering puberty at younger ages compared with 30 years ago, and rates of childhood obesity have increased dramatically over the same period, supporting the hypothesis of a link between the two. The mechanism by which obesity might trigger puberty in girls is unclear. One theory is that the higher the body mass index, the more fat cells, and that those fat cells secrete hormones that kick-start puberty. But Lee pointed out that that is "all speculation." She also stated in an interview that it was unclear "if puberty is causing the weight gain, or the weight gain is causing puberty." But the study now favours the latter.

The study, then, has serious causal import. In terms of the questions we have raised, the tracking of the girls from 36 months through grade 6 found that increased body mass (or fat) and early puberty were "consistently and positively associated," thus presenting a strong correlation between the two variables. Nor, given the number of girls and time frames involved, does chance seem to be a factor in the correlation. That the causal relationship may be the other way around (with early puberty causing obesity), a possibility before this study, is also addressed by the systematic measurements taken at 36 and 54 months and grades 1, 4, 5, and 6. What had not been explicitly ruled out is the possibility of a third factor accounting for both the variables. But the study decreases this likelihood. In terms of the possible consequences, given the increases in obesity among North American children and the social and psychological problems associated with early puberty (higher rates of depression and anxiety, increased likelihood of drinking alcohol and having sex at an earlier age, increased risks of teenage pregnancy as well as obesity and breast cancer as adults), then prudence favours accepting the causal claim.

GENERAL CAUSAL REASONING

General causal reasoning attempts to establish general causal principles that govern causes and effects. A good general causal argument is an argument that establishes that X causes Y (where X is a variable condition or a composite cause) by showing:
1. That there is a correlation between X and Y;
2. That this correlation is not the result of mere coincidence;
3. That there is no second cause, Z, that is the cause of Y or of both X and Y; and
4. That Y is not the cause of X.

EXERCISE   9C

Discuss the following arguments from the point of view of the account of causal arguments we have provided. Diagram the arguments. Are the arguments made for or against causal claims plausible or implausible, weak or strong? What would be needed to strength the claim?

a)   [An advertisement in *Redbook*, 3 March 2011, p. 36. The line "brings fever down faster" is in red type in the advertisement]

> FACT:
> Children's Advil
> **brings fever down faster**
> than Children's Tylenol.
>
> Children's Advil also keeps your
> child's fever down longer.
>
> Nothing is proven better on fever.
> Not even Children's Motrin.
>
> Look for Children's Advil in
> the cough/cold aisle today.

b)   [Bjørn Lomborg, in *The Skeptical Environmentalist: Measuring the Real State of the World*, Cambridge University Press, 2001, p. 10] Recent research suggests that pesticides cause very little cancer. Moreover, scrapping pesticides would actually result in *more* cases of cancer because fruits and vegetables help to prevent cancer, and without pesticides fruits and vegetables would get more expensive, so that people would eat less of them.

c)*   Every time there's a test on a Friday morning after Thursday pub night, the class tends to do terribly. So if we move the test to Wednesday, results should improve.

d)   [From Mark Kingwell, 'Number-crunching satisfaction and desire,' *The Globe and Mail*, 23 June 2007, p. F6. Regarding a study from the US National Bureau of Economic Research] The paper argues that there is a significant correlation of low blood pressure and happiness. Countries with higher reported rates of happiness showed lower national levels of hypertension. "[I]n constructing new kinds of economic and social policies in the future, where well-being rather than real income is likely to be a prime concern," the authors say, "there are grounds for economists to study people's blood pressure."

But which came first, the calmness of the happiness—and why? Social policy is indeed important, but how exactly do we get there from blood pressure?

e)*   [From Michael Kesterton, "Social Studies: a daily miscellany of information," *The Globe and Mail*, 13 May 1997 p. A20] The murder rate in Britain would be at least triple what it is now if it weren't for improvements in medicine and the growing skills of surgeons and paramedics, experts believe. "The murder rate is artificially low now," says Professor Bernard Knight, a leading pathologist.

"People say there were far more murders in the old days, but the woundings that happen now would have been murders then," he told the *Independent* on Sunday. "If you look at the rise in [the] murder rate, it is very small, but look at the wounding figures and the graph goes up 45 degrees. If that number of woundings had occurred years ago the murder rate would have been massive."

Summary

In this chapter we have begun looking in detail at the most popular argument schemes. The ones here are schemes that tend to be employed in empirical reasoning, where people are trying to establish facts. To this end, we have looked at the schemes for generalization, and an extension of this in the reasoning used for polling. Then we have begun to explore causal reasoning by looking at the scheme for general causal arguments.

MAJOR EXERCISE 9M

1. This assignment is intended to test your understanding of argument schemes by using some of them in conjunction with specific issues.

   a) How might one construct arguments employing the following schemes (one for each argument) in support of the claim "Public ownership of assault rifles should be prohibited":
      i)   generalization
      ii) causal reasoning
      iii) polling.

   b) How might one employ the same schemes in support of the opposite claim, "Public ownership of assault rifles should be allowed."

   c) Using any of the argument schemes of this chapter, construct a short argument on one of the following issues:
      i)   industrial safety
      ii) nuclear testing
      iii) pollution.

2. Decide whether each of the following passages contains an argument. If it does, assess the reasoning. For any specific argument schemes dealt with in this chapter, explain whether the argument fulfills the conditions for good arguments of that scheme.

   a)* Walking in the bird sanctuary I again saw my neighbour with his dog, and as on previous occasions, the dog had a bird feather in his collar. My neighbour now tells me that when his dog wears a feather, he thinks he's a bird and thus doesn't chase other birds. I assume he's relying on the hidden premise that "birds don't chase birds." But that's not the case: birds do chase other birds.

   b)* [From "The Corrosion of the Death Penalty," www.globeandmail.com, 21 May 2002, p. A18] This month, the Governor of Maryland temporarily banned the death penalty in his state, over concerns that gross racial disparities exist in the way it is used. Illinois has had a moratorium on the death penalty for two years, after its governor said the risk of executing the innocent was unconscionably high. These states are opening their eyes to the obvious. Race matters in who is put to death. Between 1977 and 1995, 88 black men were executed for killing whites; just two white men were executed for killing blacks. Two years ago, a federal Justice Department study found that white defendants were almost twice as likely as black ones to be given a plea agreement by federal prosecutors that let them avoid the death penalty. Of the 13 on death row in Maryland, nine are black. Only one of the 13 was convicted of killing a non-white.

c) [From Steven Pinker, "A History of Violence," *The New Republic*, 19 March 2007, www.edge.org/3rd_culture/pinker07/pinker07_index.html] In the decade of Darfur and Iraq, and shortly after the century of Stalin, Hitler, and Mao, the claim that violence has been diminishing may seem somewhere between hallucinatory and obscene. Yet recent studies that seek to quantify the historical ebb and flow of violence point to exactly that conclusion.

Some of the evidence has been under our nose all along. Conventional history has long shown that, in many ways, we have been getting kinder and gentler. Cruelty as entertainment, human sacrifice to indulge superstition, slavery as a labor-saving device, conquest as the mission statement of government, genocide as a means of acquiring real estate, torture and mutilation as routine punishment, the death penalty for misdemeanors and differences of opinion, assassination as the mechanism of political succession, rape as the spoils of war, pogroms as outlets for frustration, homicide as the major form of conflict resolution—all were unexceptionable features of life for most of human history. But, today, they are rare to nonexistent in the West, far less common elsewhere than they used to be, concealed when they do occur, and widely condemned when they are brought to light. . . . Social histories of the West provide evidence of numerous barbaric practices that became obsolete in the last five centuries, such as slavery, amputation, blinding, branding, flaying, disembowelment, burning at the stake, breaking on the wheel, and so on. Meanwhile, for another kind of violence—homicide—the data are abundant and striking. The criminologist Manuel Eisner has assembled hundreds of homicide estimates from Western European localities that kept records at some point between 1200 and the mid-1990s. In every country he analyzed, murder rates declined steeply—for example, from 24 homicides per 100,000 Englishmen in the fourteenth century to 0.6 per 100,000 by the early 1960s.

d)* [From *The Globe and Mail*, 9 March 1987, from London (Reuters), p. A16] Farmer John Coombs claims his cow Primrose is curing his baldness—by licking his head. Mr Coombs, 56, who farms near Salisbury, in southwestern England, says he made the discovery after Primrose licked some cattle food dust off his pate as he was bending down.

A few weeks later hair was growing in an area that had been bald for years.

The farmer has the whole herd working on the problem now, The Daily Telegraph reported yesterday.

Mr Coombs encourages his cows to lick his head every day and believes he will soon have a full head of hair.

e)   [From a Letter to the Editor, *Omni* magazine, September 1983] I am surprised that a magazine of the scientific stature of *Omni* continues to perpetuate a myth. Bulls do not charge at a red cape because it is red. Bulls, like all bovines, are colour-blind. They see only in shades of black, white, and gray. The reason a bull charges at a red cape is because of the movement of the cape. By the time a matador faces a bull, the animal has been teased into a state of rage by the picadors. They run at it, shout, wave their arms, and prick it with sword points. Any old Kansas farm girl, like me, can attest to the fact that when a bull is enraged it will charge at anything that moves.

f)   [From "Gas prices up, auto deaths down," Associated Press, 11 July 2008] WASHINGTON—Today's high gas prices could cut auto deaths by nearly one-third as driving decreases, with the effect particularly dramatic among price-sensitive teenage drivers, the authors of a new study say.

Professors Michael Morrisey of the University of Alabama and David Grabowski of Harvard Medical School found that for every 10-per-cent increase in gas prices, there was a 2.3-per-cent decline in auto deaths. For drivers ages 15 to 17, the decline was 6 per cent and for ages 18 to 21 it was 3.2 per cent. The study looked at fatalities from 1985 to 2006, when gas prices reached about $2.50 a gallon (about 66 cents Canadian a litre). With gas now averaging over $4 a gallon ($1.07), Prof. Morrisey said he expects to see a drop of about 1,000 deaths a month.

With annual auto deaths typically ranging from about 38,000 to 40,000 a year, a drop of 12,000 deaths would cut the total by nearly one-third, Prof. Morrisey said.

"I think there is some silver lining here in higher gas taxes in that we will see a public-health gain," Prof. Grabowski said. He warned, however, that their estimate of a decline of 1,000 deaths a month could be offset somewhat by the shift under way to smaller, lighter, more fuel-efficient cars and the increase in motorcycle and scooter driving. Prof. Morrisey said the study also found the "same kind of symmetry" between gas prices and auto deaths when prices go down. "When that happens we drive more, we drive bigger cars, we drive faster and fatalities are higher," he said.

g)   [The following is from the report *Study Links Obesity to Protein in Infant Formula*, Nutra ingredients-USA.com, 20 April 2007, www.nutraingredients-usa.com/, accessed 4 May 2009] The results of the EU Childhood Obesity Programme indicate that low-protein content in infant formula may have metabolic, endocrinal and developmental benefits for babies—which may also have an impact on obesity at a later age. Subject to further follow-up, the findings add weight to the idea that a tendency towards obesity is set in earliest childhood. They come shortly after another study indicated that tendency towards obesity could be genetic. Professor Berthold Koletzko, project co-ordinator from the University of Munich, Germany, said the results *"emphasise the importance of promotion of and support for breastfeeding, together with the development of the right composition of infant formula, and support for the choice of appropriate complementary food."*

The study involved 990 infants and ran from October 2002 to July 2006, when the youngest participants reached the age of two. The researchers hypothesised the primary hypothesis that one possible causal factor for the difference in long-term obesity risk between breast and formula-fed infants is the much lower protein content of breast milk compared to infant formula. The infants were randomised to receive either a low-protein formula (1.8g/100kcal, then 2.25g/100kg in follow on formulas) or a high protein formula (3g/100kcal, then 4.5g/100kcal). The intervention lasted for 12 months from birth, and the infants were followed until they reached the age of two. A group of breast-fed children was also followed. In addition to a body growth rate similar to that of breast-fed babies, those in the low protein group were seen to have metabolic and endocrinal benefits too.

h) [Barbara Dority, "Feminist Moralism, 'Pornography,' and Censorship," in *The Humanist*, November/December 1989, p. 46] In many repressive countries—whether in Central America, Asia, Africa, eastern Europe, or the Middle East—there is practically no "pornography." But there is a great deal of sexism and violence against women. In the Netherlands and Scandinavia, where there are almost no restrictions on sexually explicit materials, the rate of sex-related crimes is much lower than in the United States. "Pornography" is virtually irrelevant to the existence of sexism and violence.

i) [From Xenophon, *On Hunting*, Book 12] Nobler, I say, are those who choose to toil.

And this has been proved conclusively by a notable example. If we look back to the men of old who sat at the feet of Cheiron—whose names I mentioned—we see that it was by dedicating the years of their youth to the chase that they learnt all their noble lore; and therefrom they attained to great renown, and are admired even to this day for their virtue—virtue who numbers all men as her lovers, as is very plain. Only because of the pains it costs to win her the greater number fall away; for the achievement of her is hid in obscurity; while the pains that cleave to her are manifest.

j) [The following is part of a response to claims members of the media were exaggerating the danger of a flu pandemic: "Flu pandemic not nonsense," *NRC Handelsblad*, 12 May 2009, http://vorige.nrc.nl/international/opinion/article2239709.ece] According to a report by the World Health Organisation, the mortality rate of the current H5N1 birds-to-humans infection is still 60 percent, again despite antibiotics and other modern treatments (Cumulative Number of Confirmed Human Cases of Avian Influenza A/(H5N1), 2009). This high mortality rate, it seems, is not the result of a bacterial superinfection (pneumonia) but rather of a "cytokine storm" (or hypercytokinemia), a strong reaction of the immune system to the new virus, which affects the entire body. The patients die because all their internal organs—lungs, heart, kidneys, liver, the blood-forming organs and the brain—fail simultaneously (multiorgan failure), and antibiotics are no help.

Eyewitness accounts of the 1918 Spanish influenza indicate a similar multio-rgan failure reaction. (See: John M. Barry: *The Great Influenza: The Epic Story of the Deadliest Plague in History*, New York: Penguin) Ekkelenkamp's claim that the high death toll in 1918 was so high because the world population was exhausted and underfed because of World War I has long been discredited. The mortality rate in the United States, where there was no food shortage, did not vary substantially from the one in Europe.

Of course, there is no certainty that a new subtype of human-to-human influenza with serious virulence will ever see the light of day. But influenza experts from all over the world think the risk is substantial. It is also uncertain whether the H5N1 bird-to-human infection will be as lethal if it should mutate to a human-to-human infection; influenza viruses often lose virulence when they mutate.

But history teaches us that the consequences of even a mildly virulent pandemic should not be taken lightly. Ten serious influenza pandemics have been documented in the past three centuries. The mortality of the Spanish influenza—which caused 50 to 100 million deaths—was comparable to that of the 1830–1832 pandemic, except that the world population was much smaller then.

If a virus with the same pathogenicity as the Spanish influenza should return today, it will probably kill 100 million people worldwide—despite all the anti-viral and anti-bacterial medication, the vaccines and the prevention system available to modern medicine. Given a world population of 6.7 billion, even a moderately virulent pandemic could kill millions of people (see: Jeffrey Taubenberger and David Morens "1918 influenza: the mother of all pandem-ics," Vol. 12, No. 1, 2006, Emerging Infectious Diseases, pp. 15–22) On top of that will come the economic effects of a disrupting pandemic with 1.6 billion sick people worldwide.

For more online exercises, review questions, and quizzes related to the material in this chapter, please go to www.oupcanada.com/GoodReasoning5e

10

MORE EMPIRICAL SCHEMES AND THE REASONS OF SCIENCE

The last chapter introduced several empirical schemes that use patterns of reasoning to arrive at conclusions about facts. Some of these schemes are clearly involved in scientific discovery and communication, as we saw with the discussions of generalization and general causes. In this chapter, we continue to explore schemes of this nature, and end our investigation of empirical schemes with a discussion of the principles behind scientific reasoning—principles that are traditionally said to provide a "**scientific method**." To that end, this chapter investigates:

▶ particular causal reasoning
▶ arguments from ignorance
▶ scientific reasoning.

Particular Causal Reasoning

We begin with what amounts to our continuation of causal reasoning introduced in the previous chapter. As we will see, particular claims about causes often assume general causal principles on which they implicitly depend. In Chapter 3, we distinguished between arguments and explanations. We saw that many of the indicator words we use in constructing arguments are also used in explanations. One kind of explanation that plays a particularly important role in lives gives the cause of some event or situation.

Consider the following statements:

- The fire was the result of smoking in bed.
- He died of a massive coronary.
- You brewed the coffee too long. That's why it's so bitter.
- The reason the car wouldn't start is that the battery was dead.
- Motivated by greed, the banker embezzled the money.

Though none of the above statements uses the word "cause," they all express causal relationships. And they all refer to some particular case that requires a causal explanation.

Note also that these statements are not arguments. They are explanations; they seek to explain an event by pointing to the cause.

The causal arguments we discussed in Chapter 8 are arguments for general claims that express general causal principles. When we make particular causal claims, we usually invoke these general principles, scientific claims, or some generally established theory as a basis for the particular claims. In the most straightforward cases, such reasoning takes the form

X causes Y.
Therefore, this y was caused by this x.

where "x" and "y" are instances of the general categories of X and Y. If "X causes Y" means "Carelessly tended campfires (can) cause forest fires," then "This y was caused by this x" means "This particular forest fire was caused by this (particular) carelessly tended campfire." In more complex cases, we may not have a unique general causal principle that we can apply to a particular causal claim. If someone says that "Sarah was depressed because she did not get an A on her exam," they are not, thereby, committed to the simple principle that "Failing to get an A on an exam causes depression." In such a case, we need to investigate a more complex set of causes and interaction (perhaps involving Sarah's attitude and upbringing, her rivalries with siblings, and so on) that precipitated the event or circumstance in question. In simple and complex cases, an argument for an explanation of a particular causal claim is dependent on general causal principles.

In view of this, the following scheme captures the essence of a good argument for a particular causal explanation:

Premise 1: X causes Y.
Premise 2: This is the best explanation of the y in question.
Conclusion: This x caused this y.

A strong particular causal argument establishes (implicitly or explicitly) these two premises and, in view of this, the conclusion.

In keeping with this scheme, a good argument *against* a particular causal explanation must show that it is inconsistent with general causal claims (that the general claim X causes Y is not defensible) or that there is a better causal explanation of the event or circumstance in question. In showing that the general causal claim that a particular causal explanation depends on is problematic, we must typically appeal to the conditions for good general causal reasoning and show that there is no strong argument for establishing the general claim in question.

A dubious example of particular causal reasoning arises in the following excerpt from an opinion piece in the *Detroit Free Press* (8 November 2010):

> When we fill up at the pump, we are pouring millions of dollars a day into the treasuries of hostile nations. Much of that money funnels into the coffers of those same terrorist groups our soldiers, sailors, airmen and Marines face every day. Enemy bullets and IEDs are bought with our dirty oil money and fired back

upon our own men and women—often imported or funded by countries like Iran. This cycle is unacceptable, dangerous, and must be stopped. Congress failed to pass energy and climate legislation this summer, but there is still much that can be done to solve this threat to national security.

By raising our fuel efficiency standards we can dramatically lower the amount of oil we require as a nation to go about our daily lives, thereby stemming the flow of money to enemy nations and diminishing the disastrous consequences of climate change.

Several issues seem to occupy this writer, including a concern with climate change. But what interests us are the causal claims around the security of troops. Asserted here is a causal relationship between the everyday act of filling up with gas, and the threats faced by troops in other parts of the world. Many advocates for social justice in other parts of the world will point to the impact that our everyday behaviour has on others elsewhere. Buying regular coffee, for example, is said to contribute to the exploitation of coffee workers in the world. The reasoning here is similar. Because there is no attempt to identify any general causal principles, the first premise of our scheme would be implicit. We will present the key argument according to our scheme for particular causal reasoning:

Premise 1:   X causes Y.
Premise 2:   This is the best explanation of the *y* in question.
Conclusion: This *x* caused this *y*.

Perhaps we could understand X = economic activity in the United States, and Y = providing money for hostile nations. Then, in this case, *x* would = filling up at the gas pump, and *y* = threats to military personnel. Setting it out in this way allows us to see the problematic intermediate step that the argument requires, since it is Y that causes *y* by virtue of the hostile nations using oil money to fund those attacking American military personnel. This is the crucial causal claim that needs support. Read a different way, we could track back from the effect, which is the threat to military personnel, to the series of causes that arrives at the everyday practice of buying gasoline.

Clearly, the argument depends on the speculative leap from Y to *y*. The burden of proof lies with the writer to support this link and give reasons to believe the causal chain involved. As we have noted, our everyday practices often do have consequences for people elsewhere in the world. The point here is to *show* that *this* practice has *this* consequence. As it stands, the reader has been given no reason to believe this. The reasoning fails to conform to the standards governing good particular causal reasoning. Without fulfilling this obligation, the author cannot expect the further argument (to address the alleged situation) to follow, and change practices so as to raise fuel efficiency standards. This is not to say there would not be good reasons to raise such standards, but only that the argument given does not provide such reasons.

PARTICULAR CAUSAL REASONING

Particular causal reasoning attempts to establish the cause of some specific state of affairs. A good instance of particular causal reasoning shows that a certain event or state of affairs, *y*, is caused by *x*, by showing:

1. That this is consistent with good causal principles; and
2. that this provides the most plausible explanation of the state of affairs in question.

EXERCISE   10A

For each of the following, identify the causal claim, then evaluate and discuss the reasoning:

a)* After his criminal record was disclosed, the local politician's standing dropped in the polls, and he lost the election to his opponent.

b) My client had the right of way when she obeyed the left-turn signal and turned. The other driver should not have been entering the intersection at that point and is thus entirely at fault for what transpired.

c) [From Tim Flannery, *The Weather Makers*, HarperCollins, 2005, p. 19] Greenhouse gases are a class of gases which can trap heat near Earth's surface. As they increase in the atmosphere, the extra heat they trap leads to global warming. This warming in turn places pressure on Earth's climate system and can lead to climate change.

d)* Whenever Bob plays poker, he wears his suspenders, because he has never lost at poker while wearing his suspenders.

e) [From a Letter to the Editor, *The Windsor Star*, 8 November 2007] Out of a job yet? You can thank the Liberals. How many have forgotten the trade missions to China by Mr. Chrétien and Mr. Martin?

Tainted dog food, lead paint on toys, and now humidifiers that can cause fires. How many Canadians who made goods of all types have been affected by this flood of one-way trade from China? Thank you Liberals.

f) [From "Sixteen Scandals" http://drdawgsblawg.ca/2011/03/sixteen-scandals. shtml, accessed 1 July 2011] It only got a small mention in Finance Minister Jim Flaherty's Budget Speech of February 27, 2008—a proposal to re-establish passenger rail service between Peterborough and Toronto on an existing rail line—but it caught federal bureaucrats off guard and caught the attention of national media. . . . Commentators immediately noticed that the rail line happened to pass through Flaherty's Whitby-Oshawa federal riding, the same provincial riding for which Flaherty's wife, Christine Elliott, is the Ontario MPP. The rail line would also pass through Peterborough, a city of about 80,000 held by federal Conservative Dean Del Mastro.

2   Arguments from Ignorance

The last empirical argument scheme we will consider applies to cases in which we have no specific evidence—scientific or otherwise—to use in supporting or rejecting a particular claim. These arguments "from ignorance" (often referred to by their Latin name as arguments *ad ignorantiam*) take our inability to establish a proposition as evidence for its improbability or, conversely, our inability to disprove it as evidence in favour of it. We construct an argument from ignorance when we argue that ghosts do not exist because no evidence has been given that proves that they do. Traditionally, such arguments have been regarded as fallacious, but there are instances where they constitute good reasoning.

Arguments from ignorance are prominent in legal proceedings, where an accused person is presumed innocent until proven guilty, and in scientific reasoning, where hypotheses may be rejected if no confirming evidence is found. The failure to find evidence of living dodos or of certain kinds of subatomic particles does contribute to the evidence against their (present) existence. Everyday examples of arguments from ignorance are found in remarks like: "I've looked for my car keys everywhere and can't find them, so someone must have taken them." Here, a failure to find evidence confirming that the keys are where we might have put them is used as evidence for the conclusion that they are no longer there.

The criteria for good arguments from ignorance are implicit in these examples. In essence, a good instance of the scheme demonstrates a responsible attempt to garner evidence that confirms or disconfirms the claim in question. Accordingly, we define the scheme for good arguments from ignorance as follows:

> **Premise 1:** We have found no evidence to disprove (or prove) Proposition P.
> **Premise 2:** There has been a responsible attempt to garner evidence.
> **Conclusion:** Proposition P is improbable (or probable).

It is important to recognize that we can construct a strong argument from ignorance *only* after a careful search for evidence to disprove or prove the proposition that appears in our conclusion. It would not be convincing to argue that our car keys have been taken on the basis of our failure to see them unless we have made some effort to locate them. It is the responsible attempt to establish a claim that makes an appeal to ignorance plausible.

The first premise in an argument from ignorance is usually indisputable: if someone tells you they have found no evidence for a particular event or circumstance, this should probably be accepted. This means that when we are arguing against an argument from ignorance, we will normally need to show that the argument we are criticizing is not founded on a thorough enough investigation of the issue in question.

Consider the following extract from a letter to *The Globe and Mail* (15 July 2011), responding to an earlier correspondent who had claimed that South Africa's apartheid policy had been based on Canada's Indian Act.

This is a discomforting idea, one commonly deployed by Canadian academics and activists alike to highlight not only the injustices of Canada's policies toward its aboriginal peoples, but also the moral shortcomings of Canada's relationship with South Africa in the era of white settler domination.

Unfortunately, the idea is arguably no more than a bold assertion, lacking historical evidence from South Africa, and based on only the most doubtful evidence from Canada. Numerous historians (including myself) have searched diligently for hard evidence to support the idea, but none has been uncovered.

Quite independently of Canada, the settler colonies that became South Africa developed "native reserves" and elaborate segregation laws of their own in the 19th century, making it largely unnecessary to look elsewhere for models in the 20th.

We can show this to be a good argument from ignorance as follows:

Premise 1:   We have found no evidence that South Africa's apartheid policy was based on Canada's Indian Act.

Premise 2:   Numerous historians (including myself) have searched diligently for hard evidence to support the idea, but none has been uncovered.

Conclusion: It is improbable that South Africa's apartheid policy was based on Canada's Indian Act.

This is an argument from ignorance because the author uses the *lack* of supporting evidence of the Canadian association with apartheid South Africa as evidence against that association. And we can judge his argument a strong example because it indicates a serious attempt to investigate the matter on the part of historians (the relevant kind of investigators in such a case). Moreover, the last paragraph suggests an alternative reason that can account for the phenomenon in question (apartheid South Africa).

As this example indicates, strong arguments from ignorance can teach us the importance of supporting our rejection of a claim with some indication of a responsible attempt to find evidence for it. Here of course, our evaluation is dependent on someone's testimony that they carried out the right kind of investigation. But the writer is a historian from the University of Western Ontario, and thus the right kind of authority for judging historical questions. We look at the argument scheme associated with authority claims in Chapter 12. A good critical thinker is willing to admit that they are not in a position to know much about certain issues. Above all, they will recognize that they should not yield to an all-too-human tendency to hold tenaciously to prejudices and assumptions.

ARGUMENTS FROM IGNORANCE

Arguments from ignorance attempt to prove or disprove some claim *x* by appealing to the *lack* of evidence for or against it. A good appeal to ignorance claims that *x* is probable (or improbable) after the failure of a *responsible* attempt to find evidence for its improbability (or probability).

EXERCISE 10B

1. Describe specific circumstances in which you would or would not be in a position to construct a good argument from ignorance about each of the following topics:

   a)* ghosts

   b) the alleged racism of a provincial or state ombudsman

   c) the hypothesis that there is a tenth planet

   d) the question of whether someone is guilty of murder

   e) ESP

   f) the irradiation of food.

2. Dress each of the following in the scheme for appeals to ignorance and then decide whether they are strong instances of the scheme.

   a) [The following excerpt criticizes comments on "snuff films" made by the American lawyer Catherine MacKinnon in a speech on pornography, *The Globe and Mail*, 24 March 1987] I wonder if Ms MacKinnon has ever seen a snuff film, especially since no one else seems to have. In the absence of a genuine example, I continue to believe that snuff films are a fabrication of censorship crusaders, the purpose of which is obfuscation.

   b)* [Periodically, newspapers publish obscure photographs alleged to show Bigfoot. Such occurred in *The Globe and Mail*, 21 April 2005 eliciting the following response] The Loch Ness monster, UFOs and other such "mysteries" have one thing in common—the shadowy, grainy photo. Considering how many hunters are combing North America every year, it seems highly unlikely that one of them wouldn't have shot a Bigfoot by now.

   c) [From "The Myth of Voter Fraud," an Opinion in the *New York Times*, 13 May 2008] There is no evidence that voting by noncitizens is a significant problem. Illegal immigrants do their best to remain in the shadows, to avoid attracting government attention and risking deportation. It is hard to imagine that many would walk into a polling place, in the presence of challengers and police, and try to cast a ballot. There is, however, ample evidence that a requirement of proof of citizenship will keep many eligible voters from voting. Many people do not have birth certificates or other acceptable proof of citizenship, and for some people, that proof is not available.

3   Scientific Reasoning

Though one of the aims of "science" is precision, our use of the word is vague. Today, we might describe science as a set of disciplines (math, physics, biochemistry, geomorphology, etc. and disciplines like psychology and economics if we include the "social sciences") that study and attempt to understand different aspects of the world. The word "science" comes from the Latin word *scientia*, which means "knowledge." Though we often talk as though all science is based on one approach to understanding, it encompasses many different methods and approaches. Computer modelling, epidemiological studies (studies of patterns of health and illness in a population), and archaeological debates about the way of life that characterized early peoples assume, for example, distinct criteria for judging what should and should not be counted as scientific fact.

What we can say is that science is a rigorous attempt to generate evidence that allows us to draw conclusions about the subjects of scientific study. In this way, science is a key component of many of the arguments which play a key role in our debates, not only about the nature of the world, but also about public policy, the nature of knowledge, religious and metaphysical beliefs, and moral and political issues, which are predicated on assumptions about the way the world works. In considering such arguments, it would be naive to think that science and scientific conclusions are immune from controversy. The question whether science itself resists the development of new and better ways of understanding the world is itself a matter of dispute. Certainly it can be said that many of the views science now takes for granted—the Copernican view of the Earth's relationship to the sun, plate tectonics, the rejection of phlogiston theory, etc.—were once rejected out of hand.

However one views science, there can be no doubt that it is a major force in our attempt to understand that world. In some ways it is the engine that has driven the social and economic developments that characterize the modern (and postmodern) world. In view of this, an account of it must play a key role in our attempt to understand, analyze and assess many of the arguments we contend with. It is with this in mind that this chapter ends with a look at the method of inquiry which is the backbone of scientific inquiry.

The Scientific Method

Considering science from a general point of view, we might distinguish two types of scientific reasoning. On the one hand, there is the reasoning that scientists engage in as they go about their tasks of discovery and explanation. On the other, there is the reasoning that scientists use to communicate their conclusions to others, be they other scientists, members of the general public, or a funding agency. We expect scientists to communicate their ideas to other scientists in a different way than they do to the general public, but a scientist (or someone reporting on scientific findings) must in both cases communicate in a way that reflects the basic principles of scientific research. In elaborating these principles, we will outline a sequence of steps which much scientific reasoning uses to generate the evidence for its conclusions—a sequence of steps commonly referred to as "the scientific method."

At the core of the scientific method one finds hypotheses. They are tentative—and sometimes imaginative and ingenious—solutions to a problem or explanations for some strange and unexpected phenomenon. They are designed to be verified or falsified by some subsequent observation or experiment. It is the testing of hypotheses that is the crux of the arguments founded on the scientific method. In the course of confirming and rejecting hypotheses, many different kinds of evidence may be employed. The three schemes of argument we discussed in the previous chapter—generalizations, polling, and causal reasoning—and the particular causal arguments and appeals to ignorance of this chapter, are, for example, all common modes of reasoning in this context.

We can describe the general process that constitutes the scientific method as follows.

i) Understanding the Issue

The use of the scientific method begins with a problem or issue that arises from the examination of some data or phenomena. The issue may be generated by industry or by government, or it may arise in the speculative atmosphere of the laboratory, but we want to emphasize that the scientific method is a very general method that can be used to answer questions and solve problems. To this end, we will illustrate the method with three simple situations that pose issues that can be (or have been) tackled using the scientific method.

Example 1: Phlogiston Theory

Our first example is from the early history of chemistry. In the 1600s, chemists and alchemists saw combustion (fire, burning) as the most important chemical reaction, recognizing that it included phenomena like corrosion in metals and respiration in living things. A German physician, Johann Joachim (J.J.) Becher, suggested a hypothetical substance, which he called "inflammable earth," which every flammable substance contains. Georg Stahl called this mysterious substance "phlogiston" (pronounced "flow-giss-ton"), understanding combustion as the process that occurred when the phlogiston in a substance was given off into the air. The issue in this case was a basic one for chemistry: *what is combustion?*

Example 2: The Stradivarius Violin

Everyone knows the name Stradivarius. A "Stradivarius" is a violin made by the Stradavari family, the most notable luthier in the family being Antoni Stradavari (1644–1737). Violins made by the latter are highly prized musical instruments that may sell for more than a million dollars (in comparison with a well constructed contemporary violin, which might sell for $10,000). Owning and playing a Stradivarius is a mark of great distinction in the world of classical music. The issue we might pose in this case is: *What makes a Stradivarius so special? What makes it more valuable than other violins?*

Example 3: "Earthing"

A recent trend in "health and spirituality" promotes the notion that direct contact with the earth encourages better sleep and health. Walking in bare feet, sleeping on the ground, and other practices that accomplish this have, on these grounds (so to speak), been recommended by those who promote such "Earthing." The traditional teachings of Native American elders are said to support such practices. Here we may put the issue as the question: *should we believe that earthing promotes better sleep and health?*

ii) Formulating a Hypothesis

Once we understand the problem or issue we want to investigate, the next step in the scientific method is the formulation of a hypothesis. There may be a number of competing hypotheses, each offering a solution to or explanation of the problem. Observation is important, along with imagination and creativity. We might, for example, compare the problem we are considering to past phenomena in the hope of detecting common traits, which would suggest an appropriate hypothesis. In other cases, we might strive to think of possible solutions or explanations that are novel and challenge our way of looking at the world. In view of the other steps in the scientific method, we want a testable hypothesis: a hypothesis that it will be practical to test in one way or another. We can approach the three examples we have identified in the following way.

Example 1: Phlogiston Theory

In the case of phlogiston, the initial hypothesis is simply the hypothesis that combustion is a process of giving off phlogiston. This is a theory that derives from an earlier theory that sulfur was the ingredient that caused combustion. Evidence for this included the observations that it burned completely and was given off when wood burned. But it was clear that combustion did not yield ordinary sulfur in other cases. Such considerations were the basis of Becher's hypothetical substance, and the corresponding hypothesis that *combustion is a process that occurs when phlogiston leaves a substance and flows into the air.* This is the explanation of the problem that we began with (what is combustion?) that is the core of phlogiston theory.

Example 2: The Stradivarius Violin

In the case of the Stradivarius violin, its fame has precipitated scientific speculation on the reasons why it is a superior instrument. To this end, investigators have hypothesized that the wood used to build a Stradivarius had different properties than contemporary wood, that the use of pozzolana volcanic ash (Roman hydraulic cement) as a treatment for the wood imbued it with special properties, and that there is something special about the varnishes used by the Stradivari family and other Cremonese violin makers. But all of these hypotheses (and the scientific studies based on them) assume a more basic hypothesis that we will focus on: i.e. the hypothesis that *Stradivarius violins have a superior sound quality that makes them better to listen to* (typically put as the claim that they have better "sonority"—resonance—than other violins). Obviously, this hypothesis is one way to explain the extraordinary high value of Stradivarius violins.

Example 3: "Earthing"

The notion of Earthing as it is popularized today is founded on the thinking and personal experience of Clint Ober, whose views were the result of his experience with insomnia and his curiosity when he measured and thought about the electromagnetic fields in the house in which he lived. Having recorded different voltages in different parts of his house, and an extremely very high voltage in his bedroom, he grounded his bed to eliminate the correspondent electromagnetic fields and immediately slept better. This led him to the hypothesis that *grounding—an electrical connection to the earth—is a key ingredient of good sleep and health.* This gives rise to Earthing theory, which might be described as an attempt to explain the (alleged) health benefits of a direct connection to the earth that can be maintained by walking with bare feet, sitting on the ground, and so forth.

iii) Identifying the Implications of the Hypothesis

Having established a hypothesis, the next step in the scientific method is determining what observable consequences must follow if the hypothesis is correct. Such inferences use argument schemes founded on the premise that:

"If h is the case, then x would have to occur,"
where h is the hypothesis and x is the observable consequence.

These schemes are discussed in the appendices to this book. In our present context, we will simply note that this kind of statement is called a *conditional*. It is made up of two constituent claims, one that occurs after the "if" and before the "then," and one which occurs after the "then." The first ("h is the case") is called the antecedent of the conditional, the second ("x would have to occur") is called its consequent. In identifying the consequences of a hypothesis we need to identify the consequent in the above conditional. In our three examples, we can do so as follows.

Example 1: Phlogiston Theory

The testing of phlogiston theory is an important event in the birth of chemistry because those scientists who put the theory to the test did so by carefully weighing the effects of combustion (and in this way illustrated the importance of the careful measurement of physical properties in chemistry). They reasoned that *if it is true that combustion is a process that occurs when phlogiston leaves a substance and flows into the air, then the weight of what remains after combustion should be less than the weight before.*

Example 2: The Stradivarius Violin

We invite you to stop for a moment and think about the way that you would identify testable implications of the Stradivarius hypothesis we have already noted. It is not improbable that you will come up with the same conditional as those who have put this hypothesis to the test: i.e. *if Stradivarius violins have a superior sound quality that makes them better to listen to, then this should be evident in tests where listeners compare works performed on a Stradivarius and on other violins.*

Example 3: "Earthing"

In the case of Earthing we will follow the reasoning of Clint Ober, who identified consequences of his hypothesis by reasoning that: *if grounding is a key ingredient of good sleep and health, then grounding should help those who suffer from insomnia and sleep problems.*

iv) Testing the Hypothesis

Once we have identified the implications of our proposed hypothesis, the next step in the scientific method is an attempt to devise and conduct tests to determine whether the consequences do follow. Ideally, the tests will be designed to confirm or refute the hypothesis with observable consequences. If a hypothesis is not testable in practice, it should at least be testable in principle. Scientists have, for example, identified the implications of a nuclear winter that would follow a large-scale nuclear war. There is no experimental way to test these implications (fortunately so), but something approximating a test can be carried out using computer models. In our three examples, the hypotheses and implications we have identified have been tested as follows.

Example 1: Phlogiston Theory

A Russian chemist, Mikhail Lomonsov tested the phlogiston hypothesis by weighing a sealed bottle containing magnesium before and after it was burnt. Since phlogiston (like heat) was supposed to pass through glass, the theory implied that the sealed bottle should have weighed less after burning. Lomonsov discovered that the bottle weighed the same, contradicting phlogiston theory,

Example 2: The Stradivarius Violin

The hypothesis that a Stradivarius violin is a superior violin from a listening point of view has been tested many times. In the early 1900s, a series of rigourous tests were carried out under very careful conditions. They had listeners listen to a Stradivarius and other violins in blind and double blind tests where the listeners (and in the latter case the players) did not know which violins were being played. The tests showed that even accomplished listeners and players could not distinguish between violins and could not uniquely identify the Stradivarius. Other tests since that time have produced similar results. In a test in 2009, reported in *Science Daily* (14 September 2009), the British violinist Matthew Trusler played his 1711 Stradivarius and four modern violins made by the Swiss violin-maker Michael Rhonheimer to an audience of experts. One of Rhonheimer's violins, made with wood that a researcher had treated with fungi, received 90 of 180 votes for the best tone. The Stradivarius came second with just 39 votes, and the majority (113) of the listeners misidentified the winning violin as the Stradivarius.

Example 3: "Earthing"

Clint Ober, the founder of the Earthing movement, tested his hypothesis with the help of students at a university sleep clinic. He assembled 60 volunteers from spas (38 women and 22 men) who complained of sleep problems and joint and muscle pain. He split them into two groups. Thirty slept on beds that were grounded, thirty slept on beds that were not. There was no way for the volunteers to know whether the platform they slept on was one of the ones that was grounded. The subjects who slept on grounded beds reported very significantly improved sleep and relief from the symptoms they had suffered. One hundred per cent of those sleeping on grounded beds reported less muscles stiffness and pain, for example, while one hundred per cent of those who slept on beds that were not grounded reported that there was no change in their health from this point of view. Ober published the results in the *ESD Journal* (the journal of the Electrostatic Discharge Association: the paper is available at www. esdjournal.com/articles/cober/ground.htm). In this case, the results of the test provide confirming evidence for the hypothesis.

Re-evaluating the Hypothesis

In a case like the latter one, it is important to note that the confirmation of the implications of a hypothesis does not guarantee that it is correct. In Appendix 2, we shall see that the argument:

> If h, then x.
> x.
> Therefore, h.

is an instance of the argument scheme **affirming the consequent**, which is not a valid argument. The Austrian philosopher Karl Popper, therefore, argued that scientific theories are inevitably conjectural and more decisively disproved than confirmed (for the argument "If h, then x; not-x; therefore not-h" is always valid). In the present context it is enough to say that the implications of a hypothesis h may not show that it is true, because there may be other ways to explain them. If there are, then these implications will confirm these alternative hypotheses as much as they confirm h. For our purposes, it suffices to say that the confirmation of the implications of a theory does provide strong evidence for it if there are no clear counter-hypotheses.

Considering counter-hypotheses is one aspect of the final step of the scientific method, which is the re-evaluation of the proposed hypothesis in light of the evidence produced in testing. One might, in light of these results, reject the hypothesis, revise it in some way that the evidence suggests is appropriate, or consider it confirmed and adopt it as the best current solution to the problem or explanation of the phenomenon. The latter is an important rider, for our knowledge and understanding of the situation in question is inevitably incomplete and it is likely that new evidence and arguments may make us want to refine or revise a confirmed hypothesis in the future. To this extent, there is no "final" step in the scientific method, but rather a perpetual consideration and re-evaluation of new hypotheses on the basis of previous and new evidence. This "forward progress" is one of the hallmarks of science that has made it such a powerful tool in our attempts to understand the world. The consequences of the re-evaluation of the three hypotheses we have noted show how things tend to progress in practice.

Example 1: Phlogiston Theory

The discussion and testing of phlogiston theory led, not only to the conclusion that the theory was mistaken, but eventually to a new theory of combustion developed by Antoine Lavoisier. It held that combustion is not a process which gives off phlogiston, but one that occurs when it combines with another element (oxygen). The discussion and testing of this new theory set the stage for another, caloric, theory of combustion. The phlogiston debate became a significant one in the history of chemistry because it demonstrated the importance of the quantitative measuring of the physical properties, something that has been a central aspect of chemistry ever since.

Example 2: The Stradivarius Violin

The extensive evidence against the hypothesis that a Stradivarius is a superior violin from a listening point of view makes it difficult to uphold this hypothesis. In a context in which this has not inhibited the fame of Stradivari violins or their market value, this raises the question as to why? We cannot pursue a detailed exploration of this question here, but will refer you to an article by R.L. Barclay in *Skeptic* magazine in 2011 ("Stradivarius pseudoscience: The myth of the miraculous musical instrument"), which suggests that it is bad science that has maintained its prestige.

Example 3: "Earthing"

In the wake of the experiment we have described, Clint Ober and others have pursued systematic testing and theorizing about Earthing and its effects. This has included the investigation of a number of hypotheses beyond the one we have mentioned. They include the hypothesis that grounding reduces electromagnetic fields on the body; that grounding effects circadian rhythms; and, more specifically, that they affect the circadian secretion of cortisol (a steroid hormone which is related to stress). At this point, mainstream science and medicine has paid little attention, and it will take many studies to establish whether Earthing will be accepted as a theory.

Beyond the Scientific Method

In looking at scientific reasoning and arguments about science, it is important to note that they are not limited to what is incorporated in the scientific method. Scientists will, for example, use models or analogies to draw conclusions about something unknown based on some similar phenomena that is better known or understood. Early attempts to describe the structure of atoms included an analogy with the solar system, since it was reasoned that an atom resembled a very small solar system. Like the solar system with its sun, an atom has its positive charge at the centre, and just as the planets move in orbits around the sun, so electrons carry a negative charge around the atom's centre. Such analogies highlight the role that reasoning from analogy may play in our attempt to understand the physical world. Scientists examining the meteorite ALH84001, collected in Antarctica and recognized as originating from Mars, argued for the existence of past life on Mars based on its similarities to life in rock formations on Earth. While our next chapter does not focus on scientific reasoning, the discussion will include argument by analogy as a scheme of argument that is used in empirical as well as moral reasoning.

The scientific method as we have discussed it emphasizes observable experimental results. In contrast, some scientific arguments depend on mathematical models rather than empirical observation and some branches of science cannot provide immediate observations or experiments that support their conclusions. Stephen Jay Gould gave an example of this kind of scientific reasoning in a discussion of science in *Discover* magazine in 1987:

> Since we can't see the past directly or manipulate its events, we must use the different tactic of meeting history's richness head on. . . . Thus plate tectonics can explain magnetic strips on the sea floor, the rise and later erosion of the Appalachians, the earthquakes of Lisbon and San Francisco . . . the presence of large flightless birds only on continents once united as Gondwanaland, and the discovery of fossil coal in Antarctica.

No matter how scientific reasoning varies in its procedures, you might note that some hypothesis-forming is always present, whether it be the hypothesis that the solar system is a suitable model for explaining the structure of the atom or that plate tectonics can account for the diverse phenomena identified by Gould. Looked at from this point of view, hypothesizing lies at the heart of scientific reasoning.

THE SCIENTIFIC METHOD

As a general procedure, the scientific method involves five steps for proposing and testing a hypothesis:
1. *Understanding the problem* that requires a solution or explanation.
2. *Formulating a hypothesis* to address the problem.
3. *Deducing consequences* to follow if the hypothesis is correct.
4. *Testing the hypothesis* for those consequences.
5. *Re-evaluating the hypothesis* after testing.

EXERCISE 10C

1. Consider the following account of "How Gertie the chicken mysteriously switched genders," adapted from an April 2011 report by Alasair Wilkins at io9 (available at http://IO9.COM). How might you investigate what is happening using the five steps of the scientific method (note that the key question is what hypotheses you might investigate)? On the completion of your investigation, what further investigations might be warranted as your theory of sex change develops?

Gertie is one of two hens kept by Jim and Jeanette Howard in Cambridgeshire in England. Both their hens produced fewer eggs last winter, when Gertie then stopped laying eggs completely, and began losing her feathers. She emerged from the molting with more feathers and a stronger physique. She then developed the neck wattle of a rooster, and her comb grew. She began behaving like a rooster, and began to crow. "I'm not really sure whether Gertie has actually changed sex, but to all intents and purposes she's now a cockerel," said Jim. A veterinarian has suggested that something in her feed had acted as a synthetic hormone, causing her to suddenly develop male characteristics. But recent research shows that a chicken's cells are either inherently male or female, regardless of their hormones. So how did Gertie's "inherently female" cells allow her to look and act like a male? "We're not sure."

2. Find an account of scientific research in a recent magazine (read a scientific magazine or journal if you need to) or on a science website on the Internet. Explain the research in terms of the account of the scientific method introduced in this chapter.

3. Analyze the following account of the scientific process of discovery in terms of the five steps of the scientific method:

[Alfred Wallace, in *My Life: A Record of Events and Opinions*, Vol. 1, New York, 1905, pp. 360–2] It was while waiting at Ternate in order to get ready for my next journey, and to decide where I should go, that the idea already referred to occurred to me. It has been shown how, for the preceding eight or nine years, the great problem of the origin of the species had been continually pondered over. . . .

But the exact process of the change [of one species into another] and the cause that led to it were absolutely unknown and appeared almost inconceivable. The great difficulty was to understand how, if one species was gradually changed into another, there continued to be so many quite distinct species, so many that differed from their nearest allies by slight yet perfectly definite and constant characters. . . . The problem then was, not only how and why do species change, but how and why do they change into new and well-defined species, distinguished from each other in so many ways. . . .

One day something brought to my attention Malthus's "Principles of Population," which I had read twelve years before. I thought of his clear exposition of "the positive checks to increase"—disease, accidents, war, and famine—which keep down the population of . . . people. It then occurred to me that these causes or their equivalents are continually acting in the case of animals also; and as animals usually breed much more rapidly than does mankind, the destruction every year from these causes must be enormous in order to keep down the number of each species. . . .

Why do some die and some live? And the answer was clearly, that on the whole the best fitted lived. From the effects of disease the most healthy escaped; from enemies, the strongest, the swiftest, or the most cunning; from famine, the best hunters or those with the best digestion; and so on. Then it suddenly flashed upon me that this self-acting process would necessarily *improve the race*, because in every generation the inferior would inevitably be killed off and the superior would remain—that is, *the fittest would survive*.

Summary

In this chapter we have continued our examination of empirical schemes by examining first Particular Causal arguments and then Arguments from Ignorance. In each case we have approached the topic by understanding the schemes involved. Then we have turned to the primary place in which empirical schemes might be expected to be found—scientific reasoning. Traditionally, the reasoning in scientific discovery has been understood in terms of a five-stage method. We have detailed and illustrated that method, while also noting other aspects that can go into scientific reasoning.

MAJOR EXERCISE 10M

1. This assignment is intended to test your understanding of argument schemes by using some of them in conjunction with specific normative issues.

    a) Construct short arguments employing the following schemes (one for each argument) in support of the claim "technology has improved the lives of average citizens":

    i)* particular causal argument

    ii) appeal to ignorance.

    b) Employ the same schemes in support of the opposite claim, "Technology has not improved the lives of average citizens."

    c) Using any of the argument schemes of this chapter, construct a short argument on one of the following issues:

    i)   global warming

    ii)* the use of placebos in studies

    iii) built-in obsolescence of common household appliances.

2. Decide whether each of the following passages contains an argument. If it does, assess the reasoning. For any specific argument schemes dealt with in this chapter, explain whether the argument fulfills the conditions for good arguments of that scheme. Note that examples may involve more than one argument scheme and may also include applications of the scientific method.

    a)* It would be basically illogical to state that miracles cannot occur. This is because in order to state this, a person would have to have logical proof that miracles cannot occur. And no such proof is available.

    b) [From a Letter to the Editor, *The Globe and Mail*, 15 March 1997] So the Liberals have not come close to making the point that restrictions on tobacco advertising will lead to a reduction in the incidence of smoking among young people (Speaking Freely about Smoking—editorial, March 5). The following Statscan figures are provided with your March 8 front-page article: one in five deaths in Canada are attributed to smoking; in Quebec, the number is one in four. The average age of becoming a "regular smoker" in Canada is 15; in Quebec, it is 14. Fifty per cent of all sponsorship dollars provided by tobacco companies are spent in Quebec. Coincidence?

    c)* [From a report in *The Canadian Press*, 27 September 2007, titled "Teens with part-time jobs more likely to smoke: study"] High school students who take part-time jobs for pocket money may be more likely to start smoking than teens who don't join the after-school and weekend work force, a study suggests.

The study of Grade 10 and 11 students in Baltimore shows that those who took jobs, often in retail outlets and fast-food or other restaurants, had a greater propensity to begin lighting up—and that trend was strongest among teens who worked the most hours per week. "Of those who didn't smoke at Grade 10, kids who (began working) were at least three times more likely to start smoking than kids who didn't start working," lead author Rajeev Ramchand, a psychiatric epidemiologist, said Thursday from Arlington, Va. "What we found was the kids who worked more than 10 hours a week on average had an earlier age of initiation. So they started to smoke ahead of their peers," said Mr. Ramchand, who conducted the study with colleagues while a graduate student at the Johns Hopkins School of Medicine in Baltimore, Md. He now works for the Rand Corp.

The researchers posit a number of reasons for the change in smoking status: For one, teens may be exposed on the job to older youth or to adults who are more likely to smoke and where smoking is more common and acceptable, said Mr. Ramchand.

"Second is that they can now buy cigarettes, as before they may have not had the means, the money, to buy cigarettes," he said. Taking a part-time job also changes a teen's relationship with family members, and that can strongly affect behaviour. "When kids start working, we know from previous research, their bonds with their parents tend to weaken. So whereas in the past some have proposed that your bonds to your parents actually prevent you from drug-using behaviours like tobacco smoking, when you work, a parent kind of releases those bonds and . . . that freedom may increase the likelihood to smoke."

Stress may also be another factor, Mr. Ramchand offered. "Kids don't report that their jobs themselves are very stressful, but what they will report is that managing their time and their responsibilities—getting all their homework done, sports if that's part of their lives, as well as their work responsibilities—the combination of those things creates stress."

"And they may turn to cigarettes as a kind of self-medication to relieve that stress."

The research, published Friday in the *American Journal of Public Health*, is part of a larger, ongoing study of almost 800 Baltimore children, who were enrolled in Grade 1.

d)* [From *The Windsor Star*, 24 October 1995] Seven out of 10 women wear the wrong size bra, according to surveys by Playtex, a bra manufacturer . . . this statistic was based on women who came to Playtex bra-fitting clinics.

e) David M. Unwin concludes in *Nature* (May 1987) that the winged reptiles, pterosaurs, spent most of their lives hanging upside down from cliffs and trees because, while they may have been agile in the air, they could do no more than waddle clumsily on the ground.

This conclusion was drawn in part from recent discoveries in Germany and Australia of two relatively uncrushed pterosaur pelvises. In these pelvises, the acetabulum, a socket into which the tip of the femur bone fits, is oriented outward and upward, and this suggests that the pterosaurs' legs were splayed out, giving them a clumsy gait. Had the acetabulum pointed out and down instead, the pelvises would have supported another theory, held since the 1970s, that pterosaurs stood erect with their hind limbs beneath their bodies and were agile on the ground.

f)   [The following comes from a report on the Air France disaster in May 2009, "The riddle of flight AF447," *The Independent* newspaper, 10 June 2009] Airline disasters are meat and drink to conspiracy theorists. Several alternative explanations still exist for the Concorde disaster in Paris in 2000 and the terrorist bombing of a Pan Am jumbo over Lockerbie in 1988. The confusion and misinformation surrounding Flight AF447 will inevitably lead to similarly fevered speculation.

g)*   [The following comes from a BBC News report on a study on obesity, published in full in the *International Journal of Obesity*, "Obesity 'link to same-sex parent'" 12 July 2009, http://news.bbc.co.uk] There is a strong link in obesity between mothers and daughters and fathers and sons, but not across the gender divide, research suggests. A study of 226 families by Plymouth's Peninsula Medical School found obese mothers were 10 times more likely to have obese daughters. For fathers and sons, there was a six-fold rise. But in both cases children of the opposite sex were not affected. The researchers believe the link is behavioural rather than genetic. They say the findings mean policy on obesity should be re-thought.

Researchers said it was "highly unlikely" that genetics was playing a role in the findings as it would be unusual for them to influence children along gender lines. Instead, they said it was probably because of some form of "behavioural sympathy" where daughters copied the lifestyles of their mothers and sons their fathers. It is because of this conclusion that experts believe government policy on tackling obesity should be re-thought. . . .

Study leader Professor Terry Wilkin said: "It is the reverse of what we have thought and this has fundamental implications for policy. We should be targeting the parents and that is not something we have really done to date." His team took weight and height measurements for children and parents over a three-year period. They found that 41 per cent of the eight-year-old daughters of obese mothers were obese, compared to 4 per cent of girls with normal-weight mothers. There was no difference in the proportion for boys. For boys, 18 per cent of the group with obese fathers were also obese, compared to just 3 per cent for those with normal-weight fathers. Again, there was no difference in the proportion for girls.

h)   [From a cosmetics advertisement] Research among dermatologists reveals a lot of skepticism regarding anti-aging claims. Research also shows that 95% of the doctors surveyed recommended Overnight Success's active ingredient for the relief of dry to clinically dry skin.

The Overnight Success night strength formula dramatically helps diminish fine, dry lines and their aging appearance. . . . And after just 3 nights' use, 98% of women tested showed measurable improvements.

Discover Overnight Success tonight. Wake up to softer, smoother, younger looking skin tomorrow.

i) [From a Letter to the Editor, *Saturday Night* magazine, 15 July 2000] According to an article published in the *New England Journal of Medicine*, marking territory with urine may prevent incontinence in old age. The *Journal* looked at two patients' reports of using their urine to keep cats and dogs out of their garden. The male, clad in sandals and kilt, walked around the garden's edge, urinating a small amount every few steps. This constant use of the pubococcygeal muscles keeps the bladder and rectal sphincter strong, and is what scientists believed prevented incontinence among our ancestors.

j) [From a Letter to the Editor, *Kitchener-Waterloo Record*, 1 December 1984] I would like to respond to the news stories that have warned of possible increases in the taxes of cigarettes and liquor in the next government budget. As a smoker I am very upset. Does the government not realize that if people cannot afford to buy tobacco and stop smoking, many people will be out of work? By raising the price of tobacco, people will have to stop smoking because they cannot afford to buy cigarettes. So the cigarette companies and tobacco farmers will have to lay people off. The government exists to create jobs not to lose them, and if the government raises cigarette prices any more, the unemployment and welfare lines are going to get a lot longer.

k)* [The following is from *The Darwinian Paradigm: Essays on its History, Philosophy and Religious Implication*, Michael Ruse, Routledge, 1989, p. 38. Ruse is discussing Darwin's *Origin of the Species* (1859)]

Coming to selection itself, we find the same emphasis on the individual. For instance, to illustrate how natural selection might work Darwin gave the imaginary example of a group of wolves, hard-pressed for food (1859, p. 90). He suggested that the swiftest and slimmest would be selected, because it will be they alone who will catch the prey. Hence, there will be evolution towards and maintenance of fast, lean wolves. Obviously, the crux of this explanation is that some wolves survive and reproduce whereas others do not. There is no question here of selection working for a group; rather it is all a matter of individual against individual.

l) [Tim Radford, "Genes say boys will be boys and girls will be sensitive," in the *Guardian*, 22 June 1997, p. 14] The sensitive sex was born that way. And boys are oafish because they can't help it. Blame nature, not nurture. The gene machine switches on feminine intuition long before birth, British scientists reported last week. The same mechanism switches off in boy babies after conception, leaving them to grow up awkward, gauche and insensitive. The irony is that a girl's talent for tact, social deftness and womanly intuition comes from father, not mother.

"What we might call feminine intuition—the ability to suss out a social situation by observing nuances of expression in voice and so on—is a set of skills of genetic origin that has nothing at all to do with hormones, as far as we know," said David Skuse of the Institute of Child Health in London. Prof. Skuse and colleagues from the Wessex Regional Genetics Laboratory in Salisbury were actually studying Turner's syndrome, a rare condition that affects one female in 2,500.

"A high proportion of girls had serious social adjustment problems, which started around the time they entered school and continued right through to adolescence," he said. Intelligence was normal, but the girls were often short, and in adult life infertile. As children they were less aware of people's feelings, interrupted conversations, made demands of other people's time, and could not "read" body language.

Girls have two X chromosomes, boys an X and a Y. But girls with Turner's syndrome have only one. Some inherited their one X from the mother, some from the father. The ones with the mother's X had the more severe problems. So, the researchers reason, there would be a gene or set of genes switched on or off in the egg, according to the parent from whom they are inherited. Girls normally get the switched on version from fathers, and boys inherit a single X chromosome from their mothers, with the genes switched off. "Others might feel that men are somehow doomed. Well, we can learn social skills," Prof. Skuse said. "Women will pick them up intuitively."

This raised an evolutionary puzzle. "Why would it be advantageous for males to be socially insensitive? If you wanted to recruit boys into an army, a hunting party or a football team, it is an advantage to have those boys socially unskilled so the dominant male in that group can impose a set of social mores," he said.

m) [The following is excerpted from "Cinema fiction vs. physics reality: Ghosts, vampires, and zombies," by Costas J. Efthimiou and Sohang Gandhi, *Skeptical Inquirer*, Vol. 31.4, July/August 2007] Anyone who has seen John Carpenter's *Vampires*, or the movies *Dracula* or *Blade*, or any other vampire film is already quite familiar with the vampire legend. The vampire needs to feed on human blood. After one has stuck his fangs into your neck and sucked you dry, you turn into a vampire yourself and carry on the blood-sucking legacy. The fact of the matter is, if vampires truly feed with even a tiny fraction of the frequency that they are depicted as doing in the movies and folklore, then humanity would have been wiped out quite quickly after the first vampire appeared.

Let us assume that a vampire need feed only once a month. This is certainly a highly conservative assumption, given any Hollywood vampire film. Now, two things happen when a vampire feeds. The human population decreases by one and the vampire population increases by one. Let us suppose that the first vampire appeared in 1600 CE. It doesn't really matter what date we choose for the first vampire to appear; it has little bearing on our argument. We list a government website in the references (US Census) that provides an estimate of the world population for any given date. For 1 January 1600, we will accept that the global population was 536,870,911. In our argument, we had at the same time one vampire.

We will ignore the human mortality and birth rate for the time being and only concentrate on the effects of vampire feeding. On 1 February 1600, one human will have died and a new vampire will have been born. This gives two vampires and 536,870,911−1 humans. The next month, there are two vampires feeding, thus two humans die and two new vampires are born. This gives four vampires and 536,870,911−3 humans. Now on 1 April 1600, there are four vampires feeding and thus we have four human deaths and four new vampires being born. This gives us eight vampires and 536,870,911 − 7 humans.

By now, the reader has probably caught on to the progression. Each month, the number of vampires doubles, so that, after n months have passed, there are

$$\underbrace{2 \times 2 \times \ldots \times 2}_{n \text{ times}} = 2^n$$

vampires. This sort of progression is known in mathematics as a geometric progression—more specifically, it is a geometric progression with ratio two, since we multiply by two at each step. A geometric progression increases at a tremendous rate, a fact that will become clear shortly. Now, all but one of these vampires were once human, so that the human population is its original population minus the number of vampires excluding the original one. So after n months have passed, there are 536,870,911 − 2n + 1 humans. The vampire population increases geometrically and the human population decreases geometrically. We conclude that if the first vampire appeared on 1 January 1600, humanity would have been wiped out by June of 1602, two and a half years later.

We conclude that vampires cannot exist, since their existence would contradict the existence of human beings.

n) [Chandra Wickramasinghe, Milton Wainwright, and Jayant Narlikar, in "SARS— A clue to its origin?," Letter to the Editor, *The Lancet*, Vol. 361, No. 9371, 24 May 2003] Sir—We detected large quantities of viable microorganisms in samples of stratospheric air at an altitude of 41 km.[1,2] We collected the samples in specially designed sterile cryosamplers carried aboard a balloon launched from the Indian Space Research Organisation/Tata Institute Balloon Facility in Hyderabad, India, on Jan. 21, 2001. Although the recovered biomaterial contained many microorganisms, as assessed with standard microbiological tests, we were able to culture only two types; both similar to known terrestrial species.[2] Our findings lend support to the view that microbial material falling from space is, in a Darwinian sense, highly evolved, with an evolutionary history closely related to life that exists on Earth.

We estimate that a tonne of bacterial material falls to Earth from space daily, which translates into some 10^{19} bacteria, or 20,000 bacteria per square metre of the Earth's surface. Most of this material simply adds to the unculturable or uncultured microbial flora present on Earth.

[1] Harris M.J., Wickramasinghe N.C., Lloyd D., et al. The detection of living cells in stratospheric samples. *Proc. SPIE Conference* 2002; 4495: 192–198. [PubMed].

[2] Wainwright M, Wickramasinghe N.C., Narlikar J.V., Rajaratnam P. Microorganisms cultured from stratospheric air samples obtained at 41 km. *FEMS Microbiol Lett* 2003; 218: 161–165. [CrossRef] [PubMed].

The injection from space of evolved microorganisms that have well-attested terrestrial affinities raises the possibility that pathogenic bacteria and viruses might also be introduced. The annals of medical history detail many examples of plagues and pestilences that can be attributed to space-incident microbes in this way. New epidemic diseases have a record of abrupt entrances from time to time, and equally abrupt retreats. The patterns of spread of these diseases, as charted by historians, are often difficult to explain simply on the basis of endemic infective agents. Historical epidemics such as the plague of Athens and the plague of Justinian come to mind.

In more recent times the influenza pandemic of 1917–19 bears all the hallmarks of a space-incident component: "The influenza pandemic of 1918 occurred in three waves. The first appeared in the winter and spring of 1917–1918. . . . The lethal second wave . . . involved almost the entire world over a very short time. . . . Its epidemiologic behaviour was most unusual. Although person-to-person spread occurred in local areas, the disease appeared on the same day in widely separated parts of the world on the one hand, but, on the other, took days to weeks to spread relatively short distances."[3]

Also well documented is that, in the winter of 1918, the disease appeared suddenly in the frozen wastes of Alaska, in villages that had been isolated for several months. Mathematical modelling of epidemics such as the one described invariably involves the ad hoc introduction of many unproven hypotheses—for example, that of the superspreader. In situations where proven infectivity is limited only to close contacts, a superspreader is someone who can, on occasion, simultaneously infect a large number of susceptible individuals, thus causing the sporadic emergence of new clusters of disease. The recognition of a possible vertical input of external origin is conspicuously missing in such explanations.[4,5]

With respect to the SARS outbreak, a prima facie case for a possible space incidence can already be made. First, the virus is unexpectedly novel, and appeared without warning in mainland China. A small amount of the culprit virus introduced into the stratosphere could make a first tentative fallout east of the great mountain range of the Himalayas, where the stratosphere is thinnest, followed by sporadic deposits in neighbouring areas. If the virus is only minimally infective, as it seems to be, the subsequent course of its global progress will depend on stratospheric transport and mixing, leading to a fallout continuing seasonally over a few years. Although all reasonable attempts to contain the infective spread of SARS should be continued, we should remain vigilant for the appearance of new foci (unconnected with infective contacts or with China) almost anywhere on the planet. New cases might continue to appear until the stratospheric supply of the causative agent becomes exhausted.

[3] Weinstein L. Influenza: 1918, a revisit? *N Engl J Med* 1976; 6: 1058–1060. [PubMed].

[4] Hoyle F, Wickramasinghe N.C. *Diseases from Space*. London: JM Dent, 1979.

[5] Wickramasinghe N.C. *Cosmic Dragons: Life and Death on Our Planet*. London: Souvenir Press, 2001.

o) [From C.D.B. Bryan, *Close Encounters of the Fourth Kind: Alien Abduction, UFOs, and the conference at M.I.T.*, Knopf, 1995, p. 230] During the days immediately following the conference, I am struck by how my perception of the abduction phenomenon has changed: I no longer think it is a joke. This is not to say I now believe UFOs and alien abduction are *real*—"real" in the sense of a reality subject to the physical laws of the universe as we know them—but rather that I feel something very mysterious is going on. And based as much on what has been presented at the conference as on the intelligence, dedication, and sanity of the majority of the presenters, I cannot reject out-of-hand the *possibility* that what is taking place isn't exactly what the abductees are saying is happening to them. And if that is so, the fact that no one has been able to pick up a tailpipe from a UFO does not mean UFOs do not exist. It means only that UFOs might not have tailpipes. As Boston astronomer Michael Papagiannis insisted, "The absence of evidence is not evidence of absence."

p)* [Carl Sagan, in *The Dragons of Eden: Speculations on the Evolution of Human Intelligence*, Random House, 1977, pp. 92–3] So far as I know, childbirth is generally painful in only one of the millions of species on Earth: human beings. This must be a consequence of the recent and continuing increase in cranial volume. Modern men and women have braincases twice the volume of Homo habilis's. Childbirth is painful because the evolution of the human skull has been spectacularly fast and recent. The American anatomist C. Judson Herrick described the development of the neocortex in the following terms: "Its explosive growth late in phylogeny is one of the most dramatic cases of evolutionary transformation known to comparative anatomy." The incomplete closure of the skull at birth, the fontanelle, is very likely an imperfect accommodation to this recent brain evolution.

 For more online exercises, review questions, and quizzes related to the material in this chapter, please go to www.oupcanada.com/GoodReasoning5e

GLOSSARY OF KEY TERMS

abbreviated argument · an argument that contains hidden premises or conclusions.

acceptable premises, acceptability · premises that should (at least provisionally) be accepted by the audience to whom an argument is directed.

ad hominem **argument** · an argument that dismisses what someone says because of some feature of that person's character that shows them to be unknowledgeable, untrustworthy, or illegitimately biased.

ad populum **argument** · an argument that attempts to establish some conclusion on the basis of its popular appeal: a counter to *pro hominem* reasoning.

affirming the antecedent (AA) · the propositional logic argumentation scheme $X \rightarrow Y$, X, *therefore Y*, traditionally called "*modus ponens*."

affirming the consequent (AC) · the fallacious argumentation scheme $X \rightarrow Y$, *Y, therefore X*, which has instances that are not deductively valid.

ambiguous · An ambiguous word or phrase has more than one specifiable meaning in the context in which it is used. (See AMPHIBOLE, SYNTACTIC AMBIGUITY, and SEMANTIC AMBIGUITY.)

amphibole · an ambiguity that results from a confusing grammatical construction (also called a "syntactic ambiguity"), as when someone says, "Last night I shot a burglar in my pyjamas," which could mean "Last night I shot a burglar who was in my pajamas," or "Last night I shot a burglar while I was in my pajamas."

analogue · one of two or more things being compared in an analogy.

antecedent · the "if" proposition in a conditional, i.e. X is the antecedent in the conditional "If X, then Y."

appeal to authority · an argument that draws part or all of its support from the say-so of an expert or authoritative source.

appeal to eyewitness testimony . an argument scheme that draws evidence from someone's observation of an event or object. For the argument to be strong, the person must be in a good position to make the observation, be free from bias, and ideally have recorded the observation.

appeal to ignorance · (See ARGUMENT FROM IGNORANCE.)

appeal to precedent · an argument that uses analogical reasoning to show that some action will set a precedent whereby other relevantly similar actions will have to be permitted or not; or that a precedent has already been set such that a further action should be allowed (or disallowed) because it is relevantly similar to what has already been allowed (or disallowed).

argument · a set of reasons ("premises") offered in support of a claim (a "conclusion"). (See EXTENDED ARGUMENT and SIMPLE ARGUMENT.)

argument against authority · an argument against an appeal to authority. A good argument against authority will point out that one of the five requirements of a good appeal to authority has not been met.

argument by analogy · an argument that draws a conclusion that one analogue has a particular feature on the basis of other analogues to which it is relevantly similar having that feature.

argument by disanalogy · a counter-argument against analogy which attempts to show that two purported analogues are not analogous. A good argument by disanalogy does so by showing that the purported analogues do not share necessary similarities or that there are relevant differences that distinguish them.

argumentative essay · the form our writing takes when we are setting down the arguments for a position we hold, engaging in original research on a controversial issue, or conducting an inquiry to arrive at a position we will then hold.

argument diagram · a drawing that clarifies the structure of an argument by isolating its premises and conclusions (defined in a legend) and connecting them with + signs to indicate "linked" premises and arrows to indicate the lines of support that are proposed between the premises and conclusions. (See also SUPPLEMENTED DIAGRAM.)

argument flag · an image or some other non-verbal speech act used to draw attention to an argument.

argument from ignorance/appeal to ignorance · an argument that draws a conclusion that something is (or is not) a certain way on the basis of the absence of evidence disconfirming (or affirming) it.

argument narrative · a report of someone's argument that conveys their premises and conclusion without citing their actual words (or images or any other key components of their argument). A narrative can be the basis of an assessment of the argument but it is important to keep in mind that the person who narrates the argument may not present it accurately.

argument scheme · a pattern of argument that can be isolated and treated as a standard for judging and constructing arguments. (See also COUNTER-SCHEME.)

audience · an individual or group to whom an argument is directed.

begging the question · a type of circularity whereby a premise assumes the truth of a conclusion that it is supposed to be supporting, thereby making the premise unacceptable as a reason for that conclusion.

belief system · the basic set of beliefs and values held by an individual or audience.

bias · an inclination or prejudice for or against some view; an illegitimate bias is a bias that illegitimately influences the ways in which we argue in support of the claims that we defend, or interferes with our ability to listen to the reasons that others advance for their own points of view. (See also CONFLICT OF INTEREST and VESTED INTEREST.)

biconditional · a conditional in which the antecedent implies the consequent and the consequent implies the antecedent. In propositional logic, a biconditional is represented as $(X \rightarrow Y)$ & $(Y \rightarrow X)$.

burden of proof · in an argumentative situation, an obligation to argue for one's point of view.

categorical statement · a statement that expresses a relationship of inclusion or exclusion between two classes of things. "All textbook authors are wealthy" is a categorical statement.

categorical syllogism · an argument composed of three categorical statements that express relationships between three classes of things. A conclusion is drawn about the relationship between two classes based on their independent relationships to the third class in the premises.

causal argument (general), causal reasoning · an argument that attempts to establish a general or universal causal claim of the type "*X causes Y.*" (See also PARTICULAR CAUSAL REASONING.)

common knowledge · knowledge we expect to be held in common by an audience by virtue of its members sharing an intellectual environment of specific ideas.

complex proposition · in propositional logic, a proposition that is formed by combining simple propositions with a connective such as "not," "if . . . then," "and," or "or."

conclusion · the claim supported by the premises of an argument.

conclusion indicator · an expression that indicates that some statement or set of statements is the conclusion of an argument.

conditional · a statement that asserts that some statement (its "consequent") is true if some other statement (its "antecedent") is true. In propositional logic, a conditional is represented as $X \rightarrow Y$.

conditional proof ($\rightarrow$P) · the propositional logic argumentation scheme $X (S/\rightarrow P), \ldots Y, therefore$ $X \rightarrow Y$. In constructing a conditional proof, the lines of the sub-proof cannot be used elsewhere in a proof.

conditional series (CS) · the propositional logic argumentation scheme $X \rightarrow Y$, $Y \rightarrow Z$ *therefore* $X \rightarrow Z$.

confirmation bias · our tendency to favour certain things suggests that we favour arguments that confirm the biases and beliefs we already have, ignoring or dismissing evidence that contradicts them.

conflict of interest · a potential source of bias that occurs when someone, usually in a professional situation, is in a position to make a decision that might unfairly provide them with important benefits. (See also BIAS and VESTED INTEREST.)

conjunction · a statement that asserts that two or more propositions (its "conjuncts') are true. In propositional logic, a conjunction is represented as X & Y.

conjunction elimination (&E) · the propositional logic argument scheme X & Y, *therefore* X (or Y).

conjunction introduction (&I) · the propositional logic argument scheme *X, Y, therefore X & Y*.

consequent · the "then" statement in a conditional, i.e. Y is the consequent in the conditional "If X, then Y."

constant condition · a causal factor that must be present if an event is to occur.

contextual relevance · the relevance an argument must have to the context (of debate, or issues) in which it arises.

contradiction · a relationship between two statements whereby they cannot both be true or both false: one must be true and the other false.

contraposition · an immediate inference between categorical statements that allows us to reduce the terms of a syllogism to three.

contrary · a relation between two statements whereby they cannot both be true but they could both be false.

convergent premises · in an argument, premises that are separate and distinct and offer independent evidence for a conclusion (as opposed to "linked" premises).

conversion · an immediate inference between categorical statements that allows us to reduce the terms of a syllogism to three.

correlation · a relation between two or more variables, such that when one is modified, so is the other (or others).

counter-scheme · a type of scheme that is used to criticise arguments of a particular type by showing that the premises in question are unacceptable, or that the argument is not valid. (See also ARGUMENT SCHEME.)

deductively valid argument · an argument in which the conclusion necessarily follows from the premises in the sense that it is impossible for the premises to be true and the conclusion false.

DeMorgan's laws · the propositional logic argumentation schemes DeMV (which recognizes that ~(X V Y) is equivalent to ~X & ~Y) and DeM& (which recognizes that ~(X & Y) is equivalent to ~X V ~Y).

denying the antecedent (DA) · the fallacious propositional logic argumentation scheme X→Y, ~X, therefore ~Y, which has instances that are not deductively valid.

denying the consequent (DC) · the propositional logic argumentation scheme X→Y, ~Y, therefore ~X, traditionally known as "*modus tollens*."

diagram · see ARGUMENT DIAGRAM.

dilemma (D) · the propositional logic argumentation scheme X V Y, X→Z, Y→Z, therefore Z.

dilemma to disjunction (DV) · the propositional logic argumentation scheme X V Y, X→Z, Y→W, therefore Z V W.

disanalogy · an argument that shows two or more analogues to be relevantly dissimilar and thus not analogous.

disjunction · a statement that asserts that one or more of a number of propositions (its "disjuncts") are true. In propositional logic, a disjunction is represented as $X \lor Y$.

disjunction elimination (VE) · the propositional logic argument scheme *X V Y* (or *Y V X*), *~X, therefore Y*.

diagram · see "argument diagram."

double negation · a negation of a negation, in propositional logic ~~X, which is equivalent to X.

emotional language · language that consists of words or phrases infused with an emotional charge.

equivocation · a fallacy that occurs when an arguer conflates two or more meanings of a term or phrase.

escaping between the horns of a dilemma · showing that the disjunction a dilemma relies on is a false dilemma. (See also TAKING A DILEMMA BY THE HORNS.)

ethotic argument · one of a variety of arguments that is based in some way on issues of character.

euphemism · an expression used to substitute a mild and indirect way of speaking for words that might seem blunt and harsh (e.g. the expression "passed away" used instead of "died").

evaluative critique · an argumentative response to an argument that incorporates both the features of our evaluation and our own insights

exclusive disjunction · a disjunction that states (or assumes) that it is not possible for both disjuncts to be true, represented as *(X V Y) & ~(X & Y)* in propositional logic.

extended argument · an argument that has a main conclusion supported by premises, some of which are conclusions of subsidiary arguments.

extensional definition · a definition that clarifies a term by identifying members of the class of things it names.

fallacy · a mistaken argument. In terms of this text, a fallacy is an argument that fails either to meet the conditions that govern the good scheme of argument or to abide by the principles of good reasoning in some other regular way.

false dilemma · a disjunction that is false because its disjuncts fail to exhaust all alternatives (and some other potential disjunct may be true); also called a "false dichotomy."

generalization · the process of moving from specific observations about some individuals within a group to general claims about the members of the group.

guilt (and honour) by association · an argument that attributes "guilt" (or honour) to a person or group on the basis of some association that is known or thought to exist between that person or group and some other person or group of dubious (or strong) beliefs or behaviour. A conclusion is drawn on the basis of the alleged guilt or honour.

hidden conclusion · an implicit (unstated) conclusion in an argument.

hidden premise · an implicit (unstated) premise that an argument depends on.

immediate inference · one of the relations between the four pure forms of categorical statement. They are called "immediate" because there are no "mediate" inferences involved.

inclusive disjunction · a disjunction that states (or assumes) that it is possible for both disjuncts to be true, represented as $X \vee Y$ in propositional logic.

inconsistent premises · premises that cannot both (or all) be correct if they are contained within the same premise set for a specific conclusion.

inductively valid argument · an argument that is not deductively valid, which has premises that make the conclusion likely.

inference indicators · words or phrases that indicate that particular statements are premises or conclusions.

intensional definition · a definition that clarifies the meaning of a term by identifying the essential qualities that make something a member of the class of things it names, i.e. by referring to its meaning or "intension."

internal relevance · the relationship of relevance (see RELEVANCE) between the premises of an argument and the conclusions that they are intended to support.

invalid argument · an argument that is not valid. (See also VALID ARGUMENT.)

linked premises · in an argument, premises that work as a unit, i.e. that support a conclusion only when they are conjoined. (Compare CONVERGENT PREMISES).

logical consequence · a claim that follows from a specified set of claims (i.e. that is acceptable if the claims it follows from are acceptable). The conclusion of a good argument is a logical consequence of its premises.

macro-diagram · a diagram showing the support between sub-arguments within an extended argument. (Compare MICRO-DIAGRAM.)

metaphor · a description that describes one thing as though it were another (as in "Jill is a block of ice"); in non-verbal argument, a non-verbal element that operates in this way (e.g. the pig in a cartoon that represents a politician as a pig, in order to suggest that they have been greedy).

micro-diagram · a diagram showing the detailed support for each sub-conclusion within an argument. (Compare MACRO-DIAGRAM.)

modus ponens · see AFFIRMING THE ANTECEDENT.

modus tollens · see DENYING THE CONSEQUENT.

negation · a statement that denies another statement. In propositional logic, a negation is represented as $\sim X$, where X is the proposition that is negated.

non-verbal demonstration · an argument in which non-verbal elements (music, sounds, images, aromas, etc.) are used to directly present evidence in favour of a conclusion.

non-verbal metaphor · see METAPHOR.

obversion · an immediate inference between categorical statements that allows us to reduce the terms of a syllogism to three.

opponents · in the case of any argument, those individuals who hold an opposing point of view.

particular affirmative (PA) · a pure form of categorical statement that affirms a relationship between some members of one class and another class: Some S are P.

particular causal reasoning · a type of reasoning involving particular causal claims. They usually invoke general principles, scientific claims, or some generally established theory as a basis for the particular claims. (See also CAUSAL ARGUMENT.)

particular negative (PN) · a pure form of categorical statement that negates a relationship between some members of one class and all members of another class: Some S are not P.

poll · a specific kind of generalization that draws a conclusion about some population on the basis of a sample of that population.

premise · a reason offered in support of a conclusion.

premise indicators · expressions that indicate that particular statements are the premises of an argument.

principles of communication · basic principles of interpretation that make communication possible. We use the principles of communication when we interpret arguments and other "speech acts." The principles are (1) "Assume that a speech act is intelligible," (2) "Interpret a speech act in a way that fits the context in which it occurs," and (3) "Interpret a speech act in a way that is in keeping with the meaning of its explicit elements (the words, gestures, music, etc., it explicitly contains)."

principle of proportionality · the principle that the response to a wrong that someone commits must not be out of proportion with the wrong in question. The principle implies that one must not overreact to a wrong that is committed.

pro homine **reasoning** · reasoning that appeals to someone's good character (often the counter to *ad hominem* argument).

propaganda · information, especially of a biased or misleading nature, used to promote a political cause or point of view.

propositional logic · an account of deductively valid inferences that depend on the relationships between propositions that are expressed by the propositional connectives "if," "then," "and," "or," and "not."

pure form · one of the four distinct types of categorical statement: UA, UN, PA, or PN.

questionable premise · a premise for which we lack the information to determine whether it is acceptable or unacceptable. In such cases, the arguer assumes the burden of proof to supply such information.

random sample · a sample of some group chosen in a way that gives every member of the group an equal chance of being selected to be a member of it.

red herring · an irrelevant diversion in a chain of reasoning, whereby attention is shifted to another issue and not returned to the original issue.

reductio ad absurdum (RAA) · the propositional logic argumentation scheme X (S/RAA), . . . Y & ~Y, *therefore* ~X. In constructing an RAA proof the lines of the sub-proof cannot be used elsewhere in a proof.

relevance · a measure of the relationship between an argument's premises and its conclusions. The premises of an argument are *positively* relevant to a conclusion when they make it more likely and *negatively* relevant when they make it less likely. (See also INTERNAL RELEVANCE.)

representative sample · the sample examined during the course of a generalization.

rhetorical question · a question used (for stylistic reasons) to make a statement. The question in the argument "Our Phonics Package will ensure your child does not fail grade school. Do you want your child to fail grade school? Order our Phonics Package today!" is used as a way of making the statement that "You do not want your child to fail grade school."

rules for good definitions · four rules for constructing good definitions. *The rule of equivalence* stipulates that the defining phrase should include neither more nor less than the term being defined. *The rule of essential characteristics* stipulates that the defining phrase must specify the essential features of the thing defined, i.e. the traits that are indispensable to its being what it is, rather than accidental features. *The rule of clarity* stipulates that the defining phrase must clarify the meaning of the term defined by using words that make it readily understood by the intended audience. *The rule of neutrality* stipulates that the defining phrase must avoid terms heavily charged with emotion.

scientific method · method used to establish claims in scientific reasoning, which involves the formation and testing of hypotheses.

scope · the boundaries that govern the construction of an argument: what will be covered and how. The scope establishes some of the arguer's obligations in the argument.

semantic ambiguity · ambiguity that arises because a word or phrase has more than one possible meaning.

simple argument · an argument that has (only) one conclusion supported by one or more premises.

simple statement · a statement that expresses a proposition that is not a negation, conjunction, disjunction, or conditional. In propositional logic, simple propositions are represented as lower-case letters of the alphabet.

slanting · techniques used to distort reports and arguments. One slants *by omission* when one leaves out facts and details that are not in keeping with the impression one wishes to create. One slants *by distortion* when one uses words and descriptions that exaggerate or colour the facts that one is reporting in a manner that enhances an impression one wishes to create.

slippery-slope argument · an argument that purports to show that some action, if performed (or not performed), will set of a causal chain leading to an undesirable (or desirable) consequence.

speech act · an act of communication, which may be verbal (using words) or non-verbal, or a mix of both. A remark, the writing of a sentence, a wave to a friend, a "thumbs up" gesture, the drawing of a map, etc. all count as speech acts.

straw man · an argument that deliberately or accidentally misrepresents or exaggerates a position that it then proceeds to attack.

strong argument · as opposed to a "weak argument," an argument that provides premises that are acceptable and a conclusion that follows from them.

sufficiency · the degree to which there is enough evidence in the premises of an argument to support its conclusion. Premises in an argument are sufficient when they establish that a conclusion is more likely than not.

supplemented diagram · a diagram of an argument to which has been added information about the arguer, the audience to which the argument is directed, or those who oppose this point of view. A *fully supplemented diagram* contains information on all three. (See also ARGUMENT DIAGRAM.)

symbol, symbolic reference · in a non-verbal argument, a non-verbal symbol used to refer to some idea or claim or principle (as when a cross is used to represent Christ or Christianity).

syntactic ambiguity · see AMPHIBOLE.

taking a dilemma by the horns · refuting a dilemma by showing that one (or both) of the conditionals it relies on is not acceptable. (See also ESCAPING BETWEEN THE HORNS OF A DILEMMA.)

testimony · a statement or statements drawn from the personal experience of an individual.

two-wrongs argument/two-wrongs reasoning · an argument that something that would normally be judged (or is normally judged) a wrong should be permitted because it cancels or alleviates some unfairness or injustice.

two-wrongs by analogy · a two-wrongs argument that is based on an analogous relationship between two wrongs and that appeals to a principle of fairness in treating both in the same way.

universal audience · an audience made up of reasonable people, used as a tool in judging the acceptability of premises.

universal affirmative (UA) · a pure form of categorical statement that affirms a relationship between all members of one class and another class: All S are P.

universal negative (UN) · a pure form of categorical statement that negates a relationship between all members of two classes: No S are P.

vague · A vague word or phrase has no clearly specifiable meaning.

valid argument · see DEDUCTIVELY VALID ARGUMENT and INDUCTIVELY VALID ARGUMENT.

variable condition · in the case of a cause and effect, the variable condition is the change that brings about the effect.

Venn diagram · a tool for testing the validity of categorical syllogisms.

verbal dispute · a dispute in which the disputants do not really disagree but appear to because they assign different meanings to some key term or phrase.

vested interest · a potential cause of bias that exists when an arguer will benefit in some significant way if they and other arguers see issues in a particular way. (See also BIAS and CONFLICT OF INTEREST.)

visual arguments · are arguments that convey premises and conclusions with non-verbal images one finds in drawings, photographs, films, videos, sculpture, natural objects, and so on. In most cases they combine visual and verbal cues that can be understood as argument.

weak argument · as opposed to a "strong argument," an argument that fails to provide premises that are acceptable and/or a conclusion that follows from them.

CREDITS

INDEX

absurdity, reduction to, 432–5, 454
acceptability, premise, 55–6, 58, 197–9, 222, 375, 450; conditions of, 200–4
ad hominem arguments ("against the person"), 308, 318–20, 322, 330, 342, 450; abusive, 320
ad populum argument ("appeals to popularity"), 310–11, 450
advertisements, 144, 148
affirming the antecedent (AA), 414, 417, 429, 450
affirming the consequent, 264, 450
al-Ghazali, 23, 68
ambiguity, 171–2, 174, 180, 190, 342, 450; avoiding with brackets, 405; semantic, 454, 172; syntactic, 171
amphibole, 171–2, 450
analogies, 265–6, 280
analogues, 281, 450
analogy, arguments from (by), 178, 280–6, 450; counter-arguments to, 284–6
anecdotal evidence, 229–30
antecedent, 262, 402, 406, 450
antonyms, 186
"Arab Spring", 276, 291, 292
argumentation: in argumentative essays, 351; study of, 2, 5
argumentative essay, 340, 348–52, 450; addressing points of opponents, 351–2; argumentation, 351; clarity in, 349–50; objectivity, 351–2; scope, 348; structure, 350; summary of components of, 352
Argument Clinic (Monty Python skit), 1, 7, 173
argument narratives, 97–8, 451
argument, sample student paper, 353–62
arguments, 1, 2–3; abbreviated, 135, 450; assessing, 120, 351; balancing, 44–5; borderline cases, 89–91; circular, 206; criticism of, 58–9; defining, 7–9, 84, 450; definition through, 181; ethotic, 12, 307, 452; "from design", 282–4; distinguishing from non-arguments, 84–5, 92–4; drafts of, 174; dressed, 81, 94, 107, 161; evaluating

("assessing"), 52; ; without explanations, 94–6; explicitness of, 161; extended, 82, 107, 108, 110–14, 125, 209–10, 452; flaws in, 220–1; fully supplemented, 120–2; general causal, 241–5, 451; hidden components, 131, 351; on the hoof, 81, 84, 226; invalid, 453; principal, 82; revising, 220–2; simple, 7, 81, 82, 108–10, 454; steps in preparing, 127; strong, 52, 55–9, 196, 214, 222, 226, 455; sub-, 82, 107, 125, 202–3; uses of, 10; valid, 75; visual, 143, 455; weak, 11–12, 20, 52, 57, 58, 220–1, 455
Aristotle, 23, 307, 322, 323
arrows, 109, 111, 219
assent, condition of, 202
assumptions, 11, 139–40, 161
audiences, 14–20, 451; of argumentative essay, 348; different kinds of, 19–20; historical examples of, 14–19; hostile, 19, 20, 348; open, 19; specific, 19, 20; sympathetic, 19; universal, 20, 197, 200, 455
authorities, 314, 315; see also experts
authority: appeals to, 74, 75, 204, 312, 450; arguments against, 75, 322–4, 450; arguments from, 312–18; arguments given by person in position of, 313

balanced argument, 215–16
begging the question, 206–7, 451
belief systems, 10–12, 19, 20, 230, 451
bias(es), 3–5, 28–31, 451; cognitive, 28; confirmation, 4, 28, 451; conflict of interest, 34–5; detecting illegitimate, 35–41; difficult cases of illegitimate, 41–5; halo effect, 4; illegitimate, 28–30; lack of self-awareness, 4; looking for balance, 40–1; overconfidence effect, 3–4; sample, 229–30; survey opposing views, 40, 41; vested interests, 31–3, 41, 45, 122, 455
biconditionals, 406, 417–18, 451
brackets, 405
Brantford Carnegie Library, 146, 147
burden of proof, 52–4, 55, 197, 451